'Afterwards, you might feel like chaining your teenage offspring to the kitchen table.' *Sun*

'Clear, unsentimental, strongly reminiscent in tone of the shrewd, sharp ginswilling London children interviewed by Mayhew more than a hundred years ago.' *Observer*

'Riveting' *Sunday Times*

'If you fail to buy it as a parent you are neglecting your duty. It is as simple as that.' *Bedfordshire Times*

'H'
Autobiography of a Child Prostitute and Heroin Addict

Christiane F.

Translated by Susanne Flatauer

CORGI BOOKS
A DIVISION OF TRANSWORLD PUBLISHERS LTD

H: AUTOBIOGRAPHY OF A CHILD PROSTITUTE AND HEROIN ADDICT

A CORGI BOOK 0 552 11899 0

Originally published in Great Britain by
Arlington Books Ltd.

PRINTING HISTORY
Arlington edition published 1980
Corgi edition published 1981
Corgi edition reprinted 1981
Corgi edition reissued 1981

This book is set in 10/11 Souvenir

Corgi Books are published by
Transworld Publishers Ltd.,
Century House, 61–63 Uxbridge Road,
Ealing, London, W5 5SA

Printed and bound in Great Britain by
Cox and Wyman Ltd, Reading

The translator would like to thank Nick Dolezal of the Fortune Green Play Centre, Cathy Kohn and John Witton of the Institute for the Study of Drug Dependence, Dr. Maria Bamberg of West Berlin, and Frau Eva Bornemann of Scharten, for help with the vocabulary of this book, and her son for reading the manuscript and making helpful suggestions.

Foreword

Kai Hermann and Horst Rieck, two journalists for the West German news magazine, *Stern*, met Christiane F., then aged 15, at the beginning of 1978 in Berlin where she was a witness in a court case. They then arranged to meet her in connection with an interview which was intended to complete research concerning the situation of young people involved with the heroin scene. The interview was planned to take two hours — but these two hours became two long months of intensive work, during which their role changed from that of the interviewer to the concerned listener. From the tape recordings of these conversations emerged this book.

H, the harrowing story of Christiane, will shock many of its readers. However, it tells us more about the horrifying plight of a very large number of young people than any carefully researched report.

Christiane, herself, was anxious that this book should be published because, like almost every fixer, she wished to break the embarrassed silence concerning the drug addiction of adolescents and draw attention to the desperate needs of young people. All those of her fixer crowd who have survived, as well as their parents, have supported the project. They were ready to contribute towards the documentary character of this book with their photos, which appear on the back jacket, and their names. To preserve the anonymity of the various families, however, only Christian names have been given in full. Statements by Christiane's mother and other people in authority with whom she was in contact are intended to offer different points of view and attitudes, and also to contribute towards an analysis of the terrifying problem of heroin addiction.

THE INDICTMENT

Extracts from the prosecutor's indictment at the Berlin Criminal Court, 27th July, 1977.

The schoolgirl Christiane Vera F., a minor *mit Verantwortungsreife* (responsible in law), is accused of having, after 20th May, 1976, continuously and deliberately acquired substances or preparations which are subject to the provisions of the Narcotics Act, without the required permission of the Federal Health Ministry.

The accused has been using heroin since February 1976. She has injected — to begin with intermittently, later daily — approximately a 'scene quarter' (about a quarter of a gramme). She has been *strafrechtlich verantwortlich* (criminally responsible) since 20th May, 1976.

On the occasion of two separate checks, on 1st and 13th March, 1977, the accused was apprehended in the station hall of Zoo Station as well as at Kurfürstendamm tube station, and searched. She had upon her person 18 mg and 140.7 mg respectively of a substance containing heroin.

In addition, on 12th May, 1977, a tinfoil packet, similarly containing 62.4 mg of a substance containing heroin, was found among the personal property of the accused. Utensils for fixing were also found on her. Laboratory tests showed heroin-containing substances adhering in part to the fixing utensils. The urine test also showed morphine content.

On 12th May, Frau U.F., the mother of the accused, found among the personal property of her daughter 62.4 mg of a substance containing heroin, which she sent to the Criminal Investigation Department. In her defence the accused stated that she had been a heroin consumer since February 1976. Moreover, during the winter of 1976 she had worked as a prostitute in order to acquire the money to purchase heroin.

It must be assumed that the accused continues to consume heroin.

THE VERDICT

Extracts from the verdict of Neumünster Amtsgericht (County Court) of 14th June, 1978. Verdict in the name of the people.

In the criminal case against the schoolgirl Christiane Vera F. for offences against the Narcotics Act.

The accused is guilty of continuous purchase of narcotic drugs in coincidence with continuous tax evasion. Sentence for detention was suspended and the accused placed on probation.

Grounds: Up to her 13th year the development of the accused was normal. She is of above-average intelligence and fully aware of the fact that the purchase of heroin represents a punishable offence. Although there is sufficient evidence that as early as 20th May, 1976, the accused was addicted to drugs (prior to attaining *Strafmündigkeit* [the age of criminal liability]), this precludes neither her *strafrechtliche Verantwortlichkeit* (criminal responsibility) nor her *Schuldfähigkeit* (ability to be guilty). Meanwhile, the accused has fully realised her situation and has herself endeavoured withdrawal. She was, therefore, definitely in a position to realise the illegality of her conduct and to act according to this realisation.

At any rate, at the present time the prognosis for her future is favourable, although it cannot be said that a relapse of the accused might not be possible. The further progress of the accused will have to be carefully monitored, at least during the next few months.

1

It was really great. For days my mother was packing trunks and cases. I realised that a new life was starting for us.

I was six, and once we'd moved I was to go to school*. While my mother was packing nonstop and getting more and more nervous, I spent almost the whole day at Farmer Völkel's. I waited for the cows to come in for milking. I fed the pigs and the chickens and romped in the hay with the others. Or I carried the kittens around. It was a great summer, the first I experienced consciously.

I knew that soon we would go far away to a big city called Berlin. My mother went ahead by herself. She wanted to get the flat ready. My little sister, myself and my father followed a few weeks later. For us children it was the first time we'd flown. Everything was really exciting.

My parents had told us fantastic stories about this enormous flat with its six large rooms where we were to live from now on. And they were going to make a lot of money. My mother said we'd have a large room all to ourselves. They were going to buy great furniture. At the time she described exactly what our room would look like. I still remember it, because all the time I was a child I never stopped imagining this room. In my imagination it kept growing more and more beautiful the older I grew.

I'll never forget what the flat actually looked like when we got there. Probably because at first I was scared stiff. It was so big and empty that I was afraid I'd lose my way. If

* German children start school at the age of six, not five, as in Britain.

11

you talked loudly there was a weird echo.

Actually, there were a few sticks of furniture in only three of the rooms. In the nursery there were two beds and an old kitchen cupboard with our toys. In the second room there was a bed for my parents, and in the largest room an old settee and a few chairs.

After a few days I plucked up enough courage to take my bike out into the street all by myself. I was scared because the children playing there were a little older than me. In our village the older ones had always played with the little ones and kept an eye on them. The children outside our flat said immediately: 'What's she want here?' Then they grabbed my bike. By the time I got it back, it had a flat tyre and one of the mudguards was bent. My father belted me because the bike was broken. After that I only cycled round our six rooms upstairs.

Actually, three of the rooms were supposed to be an office. My parents wanted to start a marriage bureau. But the desks and armchairs they talked about never arrived. The kitchen cupboard stayed in the nursery.

One day the settee, the beds and the kitchen cupboard were loaded onto a lorry and taken to a high-rise block in Gropiusstadt. There we had two small rooms and a box room on the eleventh floor. And there was no room in our minute nursery for all the lovely things my mother had talked about, anyway.

Gropiusstadt, that's high-rise blocks for 45,000 people, with lawns and shopping centres in between. From a long way off it all looked new and very well-kept. But when you stood between the high-rise blocks, it stank everywhere of piss and shit. That was because in Gropiusstadt there were lots of dogs and children. The stench was worst on the stairs.

My parents grumbled about the slum kids who made a mess on the stairs. But mostly the slum kids couldn't help it. I found that out when I played outside for the first time and needed to go urgently. By the time the lift came and I had got to the eleventh floor, I'd wet my knickers. After a few

12

times of not getting upstairs in time and a few hidings, I did like the others and squatted somewhere. Since from the high-rise block you can see into practically every corner, the stairs were the safest place.

In Gropiusstadt I was the silly twit from the country again. I didn't have the same toys as the others. Not even a water pistol. I wore different clothes. I talked differently. And I didn't know the games they played. I didn't like them either.

In our village we had often taken our bikes into the woods, where there was a stream with a bridge over it. We built dams and water castles there. Sometimes all together, sometimes everyone for himself. And afterwards when we knocked them down, we all said it was okay and we'd all enjoyed it together. We never had a gang leader in our village. Everybody could suggest a game. Then everybody shouted their heads off until one suggestion won. It didn't matter if sometimes the older kids gave in to the little ones. It was a real kids' democracy.

In our block in Gropiusstadt one boy was the boss. He was the strongest and owned the best water pistol. We often played cops and robbers. The boy was the robbers' leader, of course. And the most important rule was that we had to do whatever he said.

Other times we played more against than with each other. Actually, it was always about how one could best annoy somebody else. Like taking away a kid's new toy and breaking it. The whole game was all about hurting someone and gaining advantages for oneself, about getting power and showing it.

The weakest copped most of the hidings. My little sister was a bit timid and not very strong. She was always being beaten up and I couldn't help her.

I went to school. I'd been looking forward to school. My parents had told me that at school I must behave and do what the teacher told me. I thought that quite natural. In the village we children had respected all the grown-ups. And I think I was pleased that at this school there would be a teacher all the other children would have to obey, too.

13

But it wasn't at all like that in this school. After only a couple of days, some children were running around the classroom during lessons playing tag. We had a woman teacher and she was completely helpless. She kept shouting 'sit down'. But the more she shouted, the worse they got, and the others just laughed.

I've always loved animals, even when I was quite small. In our family everybody was crazy about animals. That's why I was proud of our family. I never knew another family that was as crazy about animals as ours. And I felt sorry for children whose parents didn't like animals, and who were never given any animals either.

In time, our tiny flat came to be a small zoo. I had four mice, two cats, two rabbits, a budgie and Ajax, our brown mastiff, whom we had brought along when we moved to Berlin.

Ajax always slept by my bed. As I went to sleep I dangled my arm down the side of the bed so that I could feel him there.

I met other children who had dogs. And I got on quite well with them. I discovered that in a place called Rudow, away from Gropiusstadt, there were real bits of nature left. That's where we took our dogs. In Rudow we played on the old rubbish tips that had been covered over with soil. Our dogs always joined in the games. 'Trackerdog' was our favourite game. Someone would hide while we held on to his dog. Then the dog had to find him. My Ajax had the best nose of all.

Occasionally I took the other animals to play in the sandbox, or even to school. Our teacher used them as visual aids during biology lessons. Some of the teachers even allowed Ajax to stay with me during lessons. He never made a noise. Until the bell went for break he would lie next to my seat and never move.

I should have been quite happy with my animals if things with my father hadn't gone from bad to worse. While my mother was at work, he stayed at home. The marriage bureau had been a flop. Now my father was waiting for

14

another job to come along that he liked. He sat on our shabby sofa, waiting. And more and more often he would have these insane fits of temper.

My mother used to supervise my homework when she returned from work. For a time I couldn't tell the letters H and K apart. One evening my mother was explaining it all to me with fantastic patience, but I couldn't pay attention because I noticed my father getting more and more furious. I already knew what was going to happen: he fetched the long-handled brush from the kitchen and walloped me. And then he asked me to tell him the difference between H and K. Of course, I no longer knew whether I was coming or going, so I got another walloping and was sent to bed.

That was his way of helping me with my homework. He wanted me to be good at things and better myself. After all, his grandfather had been loaded. He'd owned, among other things, a printing works and a newspaper in Eastern Germany. After the war, all of it had been expropriated by the GDR. And now my father went mad when he thought I couldn't quite make it at school.

There are evenings I can remember in the tiniest detail. Once I was supposed to draw houses in my arithmetic book. They were to be six squares wide and four squares high. I'd finished one house and knew exactly what I was doing when suddenly my father sat down next to me. He asked from where to where I would have to draw the next house. I was so scared, I stopped counting the squares and started guessing. Every time I pointed at a wrong square he gave me a slap round the face. And when I just sat there bawling and couldn't answer him, he went over to the rubber plant. I knew very well what that meant. He pulled the bamboo stick supporting the rubber plant out of the flower-pot, and then used it to tan my backside literally until the skin came off.

I was even scared at meal-times. If I made a mess on the table-cloth, I would get a hiding. Whenever I knocked something over he belted me. I was afraid to touch my glass of milk. And because I was in such a funk, something

15

terrible happened to me at almost every meal. At night I would ask my father quite sweetly if he were going out. He went out quite a lot, and then we three women would heave sighs of relief. Those evenings were really peaceful. True, when he came home late at night, there might well be trouble again. He'd usually been drinking, and as a result would go berserk at the least little thing. Like toys or clothes lying around. My father always said that tidiness was the most important thing in life. And if he saw any untidiness in the flat, he'd drag me out of bed in the middle of the night and belt me. Afterwards my sister would get a walloping too. Then my father would throw our things on the floor and demand that everything be tidied away in five minutes flat. Generally we couldn't do it in the time, and he'd belt us again.

My mother usually stood in the doorway, crying. She didn't very often dare to defend us because then he would hit her, too. Only my dog Ajax would jump in to intervene. He gave a sort of high whimper and looked sad whenever someone in the family got a hiding. It was the dog that was most likely to bring my father to his senses for, like all of us, he loved dogs. Once he yelled at Ajax, but he never hit him.

In spite of everything I somehow loved and respected my father. I thought him far superior to other fathers. But, above all, I was afraid of him. At the same time I considered it quite normal that he lashed out so often. It was the same in the homes of many other children in Gropiusstadt. Sometimes they even had really nasty black eyes — their mothers, too. There were fathers who lay drunk in the streets or in the playground. My father was never as drunk as that. In our street pieces of furniture came flying out of windows and women screamed for help. Then the police would come. So things weren't really all that bad in our flat, considering.

My father was always getting at my mother for spending too much money. When it was she who earned the money. Sometimes she'd tell him that most of it went on his binges, his women and his car. And then they'd have a real fight.

His car — a Porsche — was probably the thing my father

loved best of all. He'd give it a shine almost every day unless it happened to be in the workshop. I doubt if there was another Porsche in Gropiusstadt. At any rate, there wasn't another out-of-work man owning a Porsche.

Of course, in those days I hadn't a clue as to what was the matter with my father, and why he went absolutely berserk all the time. It only dawned on me later when I talked more often about my father to my mother. Gradually I understood him: he simply couldn't quite make it. He always aimed too high and fell flat on his face. Because of that his own father despised him. Even before they got married, Gramps had warned my mother that his son was a good-for-nothing. The trouble was that Gramps had always had such plans for my father. The family was to be returned to its former glory, as it had been before the GDR expropriated everything they'd possessed.

If he hadn't met my mother, he might have become a land agent and bred his own dogs. He was training to be a land agent when they met. But she became pregnant with me, so he broke off his apprenticeship and married her. At some time it must have struck him that the mess he was in was the fault of my mother and I. All that was left of his dreams was his Porsche and a few flash friends.

My father didn't just hate his family, he rejected it completely. Even to the extent that he didn't want any of his friends to know he was married and had children. Whenever we met any of his friends or they came to call for him, I had to address him as 'Uncle Richard'. He had beaten it into me, and I never made a mistake. As soon as other people came, he was my uncle.

It was the same for my mother. In front of his friends she was not allowed to say that she was his wife and, most important, she mustn't behave like his wife. I believe he always said she was his sister.

My father's friends were younger than him. They had their whole lives ahead of them, at least I think that's what they thought. My father wanted to be one of them. One for whom everything was just beginning. And not someone who had lumbered himself with a family he couldn't even support. That's about the long and the short of it with my father.

Of course, between the ages of six and eight, I didn't have much of a clue. All my father had done for me was to confirm a rule of life I learnt in the streets and in school: beat or be beaten. My mother who, God knows, had had enough beatings in her life, had arrived at the same conclusion. Again and again, she'd din into me: 'Don't ever start anything. But if anyone hits you, hit back. As hard and as long as you can.' She wasn't able any longer to hit back herself, poor thing.

I was slow to master the game: sit on others or be sat upon. I started in school with the weakest teacher. I was constantly shouting during lessons. The others would laugh at me. When I did it with teachers who were much stricter I discovered that my fellow pupils really accepted me.

I had learnt how to get yourself accepted in Berlin: always shoot your mouth off. The bigger the better. Then you can play boss. Once I had proved myself so successful with my big mouth, I dared to try out my muscles. Actually I was not very strong. But I had a temper. And in a temper I could knock down even kids stronger than myself. I got to the point where I was almost glad when someone at school tried to rile me and I then ran across him outside the school. Most of the time I didn't need to rough them up. The kids simply respected me.

By now I was eight. My dearest wish was to grow up as quickly as possible, to become an adult like my father, to have real power over others. Meanwhile I tested what power I did possess.

At some time or other my father got a job. It wasn't one that made him happy, but it earned him the money for his drinking sessions and his Porsche. This meant that during the afternoons I was alone with my sister, who was a year younger*. I also had a friend who was a couple of years

---

* German children do not go to school in the afternoon.

older than me. I was proud to have an older friend, and when I was with her I felt even stronger. Almost every day, together with my little sister, we played a game we had learnt. When we came out of school we looked for fag-ends in ashtrays and dustbins. We smoothed them out, stuck them between our lips and puffed away. If my sister asked for a fag, we smacked her. We ordered her to do the house-work, like washing-up, dusting, and whatever else our parents told us to do. Then we got out our dolls' prams, locked the door to the flat and went for a walk. We locked my sister in until she had finished the work.

During this time, when I was about eight or nine, someone started a riding stable in Rudow. At first we were a bit pissed off, because almost the only bit of open ground where we could play with our dogs was fenced in and the trees cut down for this stable. But soon I got to be on good terms with the people running the stable, and helped with mucking-out and looking after the horses. In return for my work, I had a few free, fifteen-minutes rides every week. Of course, I thought this was great.

I loved the horses and the donkey they had. But there was something else that fascinated me: when I was riding I could again prove that I had strength and power. The horse I rode was stronger than I. And yet I could force it to my will. When I fell off, I had to climb back on again and refuse to give in until the horse obeyed me.

There wasn't always mucking-out for me to do. Occasionally, therefore, I had to find the money to pay for a fifteen-minute ride. We didn't get much pocket money, so I started to do a bit of cheating. I would go and redeem my mother's book of trading stamps and return my father's beer bottles to collect the deposit.

I was about ten when I started to nick things. I did my nicking in the supermarkets. Things which normally we didn't have. Especially sweets. Almost all the other children were allowed to eat sweets, but my father said sweets were bad for your teeth.

19

In Gropiusstadt you learnt automatically to do what was forbidden. It was forbidden, for example, to play at anything that was fun. Basically, absolutely everything was forbidden. At every corner in Gropiusstadt there is a board. The so-called 'grounds' between the high-rise blocks are full of boards. And most of the boards forbid children to do something or other. Later I copied for my diary what was written on these boards. The first one was at our entrance door. Strictly speaking, on the stairs and around the block children were supposed to creep about on tiptoe. Playing, romping, rollerskating, cycling were all forbidden. Then there was the lawn and at each corner a board saying: 'Keep off the grass'. Wherever there was a bit of green, there were these boards, too. We weren't even allowed to sit on the grass with our dolls. Then there was a tatty old rosebed and yet another board: 'Protected public park'. Under this notice they had quoted from some regulations, according to which you were fined if you came too close to their fucking roses.

So the only place we were allowed to use was the playground. There was a playground for every few high-class blocks. It consisted of piss-soaked sand and some broken climbing frames, and, of course, a huge board. The board was behind glass in a metal box. And in front of the glass were bars to stop us from smashing it. Written on the board were the words: 'Playground regulations' and under it words to the effect that children were to use this playground for their 'enjoyment and recreation.' We were, however, not allowed to 'recreate' whenever we fancied. For what came next was underlined three times: ' . . . between 8 and 1, and 3 and 7.' In other words, when we came out of school, recreation was forbidden. According to the rules my sister and I ought not to have used the playground at all, because it said on the board that one was allowed to play there only 'with permission and under the supervision of a parent or guardian'. And even then only very quietly: 'It is requested that special consideration and respect is shown for the need for rest of fellow tenants.' All one might do, at a pinch, was to play sedately with a rubber ball. For

'Ball games of a competitive nature are not permitted.' No football, no handball. This was particularly tough on the boys. They vented their superfluous energy on playground equipment and benches and, naturally, also on the boards themselves. It must have cost them a bomb to keep renewing the smashed-up boards.

There were caretakers to see that these rules were observed. It didn't take very long for our caretaker to get absolutely pissed off with me. After our move to Gropiusstadt this playground, all concrete and sand and a measly little tin slide, absolutely bored the pants off me. But I found something else interesting — the concrete rainwater gullies. At that time one could take off the grating over the drain. Later they fixed it so that it couldn't be removed. So I lifted up the grating, and then my sister and I would throw all sorts of rubbish down the gully. Then the caretaker arrived, grabbed us and dragged us to the manager's office. There the two of us, aged five and six, had to give our personal data, as best we could. My parents were informed, and my father had a good reason for thrashing me. I did not quite understand why it was so terrible to bung up the drain. By the stream in our village we had done all sorts of things without any of the grown-ups ever griping about it. But I did cotton on vaguely that in this Gropiusstadt you were allowed to play only with what the grown-ups had provided. Namely, sliding down the slide and digging in the sand. And that it was dangerous to have ideas of your own about playing.

My next encounter with the caretaker, as I remember it, was more serious. It happened like this: I was taking my dog Ajax for a walk, when it suddenly occurred to me to pick some flowers for my mother. As I had done in the old days in our village almost every time I had gone for a walk. However, there were between the high-rise blocks only those tatty old roses. I made my fingers bleed in an attempt to break a few flowers off the rose bushes. Either I couldn't yet read the 'protected public park' board or I didn't understand it anyway.

21

However, I understood at once when I saw the caretaker run across the forbidden lawn, screaming and waving his arms about. I was panic-stricken and called out: 'Ajax, mind out!'

Of course, my Ajax pricked up his ears immediately, and the fur on his neck stood up. He froze and gave the fellow a really mean look. The guy at once retreated, walking backwards across the lawn, and only dared to start screaming again when he had got to the entrance door. I was glad, but I hid the flowers, for I sensed that once again I had done something that was forbidden.

By the time I got home the manager had already telephoned. I had, he said, threatened to assault the caretaker with a dog. Instead of a kiss from my mother, which I thought I would get in return for the flowers, I got a jolly good hiding from my father.

Sometimes in the summer the heat would be unbearable. Concrete, asphalt and stones seemed to store up the heat and then reflect it back. The few puny trees provided no shade. And the tall buildings kept off the wind. There was neither a swimming pool nor a paddling pool. Only a fountain right in the middle of our concrete playground. Sometimes we paddled and splashed about in it. Needless to say, this was forbidden and they would quickly chase us away.

Then the time came when we wanted to play marbles. But where in Gropiusstadt do you find somewhere to play marbles? It just can't be done on concrete, asphalt, or on lawn of the 'keep off the grass' kind. Not in the sandbox either. For in order to play marbles you need a fairly firm base into which you can dig small holes. We found an almost ideal spot under the maple trees they had planted. To prevent the young trees from choking under all this asphalt, they had left a circular opening in it. The circle round the stem consisted of firm, clean, smoothly raked soil. Simply ideal for marbles.

However, by digging our little holes we got into trouble not only with the caretakers but also with the gardeners.

They always chased us away, uttering dire threat/
day they had a good idea: they no longer raked (
forked it up instead. And that was the end of our ga.
marbles.

When it rained the entrance halls of the houses provided
a great roller-skating alley. At least they could have been
great. Since there were no flats down there, the noise
wouldn't have disturbed anyone either. In fact, nobody
complained when we tried it a couple of times. Except for
the caretaker's wife. She said roller-skating marked the
floor. That was the end of that one. Except for the usual
tanned backside from my father.

When the weather was bad, things were really fucking
awful for us kids. None of us was really allowed to take
friends up to the flats. Besides, the box rooms were far too
small. Like my sister and I, nearly all the other children had
been allocated the box room. When it rained I sometimes
sat by the window remembering what we used to do in the
village. We carved bits of wood, for instance. We were properly prepared for rainy weather. We used to collect from
the woods thick pieces of bark off the oak trees, and out of
them we carved little boats whenever the weather was bad.
Then we would put on macs and boots and walk down to
the stream to try out our boats. We built harbours and
organised proper races.

You can take it from me: it isn't much fun hanging about
in the rain between high-rise blocks. We simply had to think
of something to do. Something which was really forbidden.
And there was something: playing with the lifts. At first it
was just to annoy other children. We grabbed a child, shut it
in a lift and pressed all the buttons. The other lift we held
downstairs. So the person in the lift had to slog all the way
up to the top, stopping at every floor. This was done to me
quite often. Just when I was returning with my dog and supposed to be back in time for tea. Then they pressed all the
buttons, and it took an awful long time before we got to the
eleventh floor. It always made Ajax nervous.

It was really mean to press all the buttons for someone

who wanted to go upstairs because he needed to do a pee. But it was even meaner to take away a kid's wooden spoon. All small children would come out with a long-handled wooden spoon. For this was the only way we could reach the lift buttons. Without a wooden spoon you were really stuck. If you lost it or the other children took it away, you would have to foot it all the way up eleven flights of stairs. For the other children didn't help you — no fear — and the grown-ups were convinced all you wanted to do was to play in the lift and damage it.

The lifts were often out of order, and we weren't altogether blameless for this. For we organised proper lift races. Although they all went up at the same speed, there were a few tricks by which one could save a couple of seconds, like shutting the outer door quickly but with a certain touch. For if you banged it shut too hard, it would open again just a little. The safety door shut automatically but if you helped it along with your hands it shut more quickly. Or, occasionally, broke down. I was rather good at lift racing.

Soon the thirteen floors in our block were not enough for us. Besides, the caretaker was, of course, forever breathing down our necks and so things were getting a little too hot for us. On the other hand, children weren't allowed to enter the other houses, and we couldn't get into them because we didn't have a house key. But there was always a second entrance which was used for furniture and similar bulky stuff. This entrance was barred by a grille. However, I discovered a way to get through this grille. First the head. One needed to be clever about it, turn your head first this way and then that, in order to get through. Once the head was in, we squeezed our bodies through somehow. Only the fatties couldn't manage it.

In this way we managed to enter a real lift paradise — a house with thirty-two floors and fantastically sophisticated lifts. Only then did we find out all the things you can do with lifts. One game we liked very much was jumping. If we all jumped together when the lift was moving, it would stop and the safety door opened. Or the safety door hadn't shut in the first place. At any rate, a jump ride like that was quite thrilling.

Next: a sensational trick. If one pressed the emergency switch sideways instead of downwards, the safety door would remain open while the lift was travelling. It was then one noticed how fast the lifts went. Concrete walls and lift doors whizzed past us at a mad pace.

Pressing the alarm button was the stiffest test of courage. A bell would begin to shrill, and the caretaker's voice came through a loudspeaker. And then we had to beat it. In a house with thirty-two floors there's good chance of getting away from the caretaker. He was always lurking, but he didn't catch us very often.

The most thrilling game in bad weather was the cellar game. It was also the one that was the most forbidden. Somehow we discovered a way into the high-rise cellar, where every tenant had a mesh wire locker. However, the mesh wire didn't reach right to the ceiling. Therefore, one could climb over the top into the locker. We used to play hide and seek there. 'Hide and seek everywhere' we called it. In other words, one was allowed to climb into any of the lockers to hide. It was all fantastically weird. It gave me the creeps anyway, in the dim light, with all that weird grot. On top of it we were scared in case anybody came. We knew that what we were doing was just about the most dreadfully forbidden thing ever.

Then we played at who could find the kinkiest things inside the lockers. Toys, junk, or clothes which we would put on. Afterwards, we could no longer quite remember where we'd got the stuff from and chucked it just anywhere. Sometimes if there was something really kinky we would pinch it. They found out, of course, that someone had 'broken in' down there. But they never caught us. In this way, then, we were to learn that anything allowed is a big drag and only what's forbidden is really great.

The shopping centre opposite our house was also more or less out of bounds to us. They had a really fierce caretaker there who always chased us away. He used to do his nut when I came anywhere near with my dog. He said it was us that made all the mess in the shopping centre. Mind you, it really was a rotten, stinking place. The shops all vied with each other to be the most posh and with-it. But the dustbins behind the shops were always overflowing and stank. Everywhere was melted ice-cream or dog-shit and you would stub your toes against beer or coke cans.

It was the caretaker's job to clean everything up at night. You can't really blame him for lurking all day, hoping to catch someone who made a mess. He couldn't do anything about the shop owners who threw their rubbish outside the bins. As for the drunken teenage louts who chucked beer cans all over the place, he didn't dare start anything with them. And the old grannies with their dogs just told him to get lost. So the kids copped it from him every time. In the shops they didn't like us either. When one of our lot had been given his pocket money or conned some money out of someone, he'd go to the tobacconists where they also sold sweets. And the rest of us trooped in after him because it was quite an event. It wound the salesgirls up no end when half a dozen kids came into the shop and started arguing about what they were going to buy for their few coins. Somehow we really got to hate the shopkeepers, so that in our eyes nicking from them was a good thing.

One of the shops in the centre was a travel bureau. We often stood there with our noses pressed against the window until they chased us away. In the shop window there were fantastic pictures of palm trees, beaches, natives and wild animals. And a model aeroplane hanging from the ceiling. And we used to talk about sitting in the 'plane and flying to that beach and climbing up the palm tree to look down on the rhinos and lions.

Next door to the travel bureau was the 'Bank for Trade and Industry'. In those days it didn't strike us as odd for a bank for trade and industry to have a branch in Gropiusstadt of all places, since the people living there might at most get their wages from trade and industry. We liked the bank. The fine gentlemen in their posh suits were never unfriendly.

They weren't as busy as the women in the tobacconists' either. They changed the pfennigs I'd pinched from my mother's pfenning jar into larger coins for me. Because in the tobacconists' they did their nut if you offered them pfennigs to pay for sweets. And if we said 'please' nicely, the bank would give us another of those animal money boxes. Perhaps the nice gentlemen thought we needed so many money boxes because we were keen savers. For my part I never put a pfennig into one of those boxes. We used the money box pigs and elephants to play zoos in the sandbox.

When things got a bit out of hand with our carryings-on, they built something they called an adventure playground for us. I don't know what the people who design this sort of thing mean by 'adventure'. But probably these things aren't called adventure playgrounds because children are actually allowed to do adventurous things there, but because grown-ups are supposed to believe their children can have great adventures there. I bet the thing cost a packet. At least it took them a long time to get it finished. At long last when they allowed us in the place, we were greeted by friendly social workers: 'Well, and what would you like to do,' and that sort of shit. The adventure in this playground consisted of being under constant supervision.

There were real tools and well-planned boards and nails. And they kindly allowed us to build something while a social worker watched to see we didn't hit our fingers with the hammer. When a nail was hammered in, that was it. Mustn't change anything. When half-way through making anything, one had invariably changed one's mind and wanted it to look different.

One day I told one of these social workers how we used to build things, caves and proper tree houses. Without a hammer and without a single nail. From any old boards and branches we found. And every day, when we returned, we would tinker around with it and change everything. And that was fun. I'm sure the social worker got the message. But he has his responsibilities and his instructions, hasn't he?

At the start we still had ideas of our own about what to do in an adventure playground. Like once we wanted to play Stone Age family and cook soup over an open fire. The social worker thought it was a great idea. But unfortunately, he said, cooking soup wasn't on. Couldn't we build a hut? With hammer and nails — in the Stone Age. I ask you.

Soon the playground was shut down. They told us they were going to rebuild it, so that we could play there when the weather was bad. The place was awash with iron girders, cement mixers and building workers. They built a concrete bunker with windows. Seriously, a real concrete bunker. No log cabin or anything like that, but a lump of concrete. After only a few days the windows had been smashed in. I don't know whether the boys wrecked the windows because the concrete thing made them so aggressive. Or whether our playhouse was built as a bunker because in Gropiusstadt anything not made of iron or concrete was vandalised. This big concrete bunker occupied a large part of the adventure playground. Then they built a school right next to it with its own playground, and in it a slide, climbing frame and a few wooden boards which had been driven into the ground vertically; behind them was actually quite a good place to pee. The school playground was built on the adventure playground and they fenced it off with wire mesh. There wasn't much adventure playground left after that. The little piece still there was gradually taken over by older boys whom we called rockers. They would arrive in the afternoon stoned, terrorise the children and just vandalise. Vandalising was practically their only occupation. The social workers couldn't cope with them. So the adventure playground was closed most of the time, anyway.

In its place we kids were given a real attraction. They built a toboggan run. During the first winter it was really fantastic. We could choose our own courses. We had easy ones and one death run. The boys we called rockers made it dangerous. They formed chains with their sledges and were out to run us over deliberately. But you could dodge them by going down another run. Those days where there was snow on the ground were among my happiest days in Gropiusstadt.

It was almost as much fun on the run in the spring. We romped around with our dogs and rolled down the slopes. The most fantastic thing was messing about with our bikes. Going downhill was really great. It looked more difficult than it was. If you did occasionally fall, you fell in the soft grass.

It didn't take them long to forbid playing on the toboggan run. They said this was a toboggan run, not a romping ground, and certainly not a cycling track. The turf needed to recover, and so on. By now we were old enough not to care two hoots about what was forbidden, and we kept going to the toboggan run. So one day the men from the horticultural department arrived and put barbed wire round the toboggan run. They had beaten us, but only for a few days. Someone managed to get a pair of wire cutters, and we cut a hole in the barbed wire, big enough to get through with dogs and bikes. When they mended the hole, we cut it open again.

A few weeks later, more building workers turned up. They started walling up, cementing and asphalting our toboggan run. Our death run was made into stairs. Almost every run was crossed by asphalted paths. Concrete slabs were put down on the platform at the top. One strip of grass remained as a toboggan run.

After that you couldn't do a thing on the hill in the summer. In the winter the one run was really dangerous. But the worst was getting on to it. It meant walking on stone slabs and stairs. They were always iced up. We got bruised knees, bumps on our heads, and if really unlucky, concussion.

The trouble was that gradually everything in Gropiusstadt was becoming more and more perfect. When we had first moved there, this grand model estate was still unfinished. However, outside the high-rise block quarter many things weren't perfect at all as yet. Really great playgrounds were only a short walk away, and even we younger kids could get there by ourselves.

The best was by the Wall* which is not far from Gropius-stadt. There was one strip which we called the woods or no-man's-land. It was barely sixty feet wide and at least a mile long. There were trees, shrubs, grass as high as us, old planks, water holes.

We climbed about, played hide-and-seek, and felt like explorers, discovering each day another new part of this mini-jungle. We even lit camp fires and roasted potatoes and sent up smoke signals. The time came when they noticed that the Gropiusstadt kids were playing and having fun. So the workers returned and tidied up. Then they put up notices forbidding things. There was absolutely nothing left we were allowed to do, absolutely everything was forbidden: cycling, climbing trees, letting dogs run without a lead. The policemen who were always hanging around there on account of the Wall saw to it that all the rules and regulations were observed. Our no-man's-land was supposed to be a bird sanctuary. A little later they turned it into a rubbish tip.

Then there was the old rubbish tip which had been covered over with earth and sand. We often played on it with our dogs. That, too, was made secure from us, first with barbed wire and later with tall fences, before they began to build a restaurant there.

Another lovely spot was a few fields the farmers no longer cultivated, where corn, cornflowers, poppies, grass and nettles grew, so high that you disappeared inside them. The State had bought the fields intending to make them into real recreation spots. One by one they were fenced off. The riding stable spread itself over part of the old fields, another part was turned into tennis courts. And then there wasn't really anywhere we could go to get out of Gropiusstadt.

At least my sister and I worked and rode at the riding stable. To begin with, you could ride wherever you wanted. But later, riding was forbidden on all streets and country roads. They had constructed a special bridle path. All

*The Berlin Wall, dividing East and West Berlin

beautiful, with sand and just the way a proper bridle path ought to look. Bet it cost a bomb. This bridle path ran directly alongside the railway track. Between fence and track was a space almost wide enough for two horses. You'd be riding along when the coal trains came thundering past. There isn't a single horse that won't shy when a goods train is thundering past only a few yards away. At any rate, our horses almost always bolted. And all you could think about was: let's hope the horse doesn't run straight into the train. Still, I was really so much better off than the other kids. I had my animals. Sometimes I took my three mice along to the playground. At least it didn't say 'No mice allowed' on the playground board. We built passages and caves for them in the sandbox and let them run around in there.

One afternoon one of the mice ran onto the grass which we were not allowed to walk on. We couldn't find it again. I was a little sad, but I was comforted by the thought that the mouse would like it much better out of its cage than inside it.

It was in the evening of that day that my father came into our room, peered into the mouse cage and asked in a funny voice: 'Why are there only two? Where is the third mouse?' I still didn't suspect anything when he asked in that funny way. My father had never liked the mice and had told me again and again to give them away. I told him that the mouse had escaped in the playground.

My father looked at me like a madman. I knew that now he would go completely berserk. He screamed and let me have it immediately. He was hitting me and I was wedged in my bed, unable to get out. Never before had he struck me like this, and I thought he'd kill me. When he started on my sister, I had a few seconds' respite and tried instinctively to get to the window: I think I would have jumped — from the eleventh floor.

But my father grabbed me and flung me back on to the bed. I daresay my mother was again standing in the door weeping, but I didn't see her at all. I only saw her when she threw herself between my father and me. Then she pummelled him with her fists.

31

He was completely out of his mind. He beat my mother on to the floor. Suddenly I was more afraid for my mother than for myself. I went after them. My mother tried to flee into the bathroom and lock the door. But my father kept holding on to her by her hair. As usual, the dirty washing had been put into the bath to soak. So far we hadn't managed to buy a washing machine. My father forced my mother's head into the bath full of water. Somehow she struggled free. I don't know whether my father let go of her or whether she managed to free herself.

Deathly pale, my father disappeared into the living room. My mother went to the wardrobe and put on her coat. Without saying a word she left the flat.

That was one of the most dreadful moments in my life when my mother walked out of the flat just like that and left us. At first all I could think was, now he'll come back and then he'll start hitting me again. But in the living room all was quiet, except for the television which was on.

I took my sister into my bed. We clasped each other. My sister needed to pee. She didn't dare go to the bathroom and trembled. She didn't dare pee in the bed either, for she'd get a hiding if she did. At some point I took her by the hand and led her to the bathroom. From the living room my father said 'Good night' to us.

Next morning nobody woke us up. Some time during the morning my mother returned. She said hardly a word. She packed a few of our things, put Peter the cat into a bag and told me to put Ajax on his lead. Then we went to the tube. We spent the next few days in a small flat with a colleague of my mother's. My mother explained to us that she intended to get a divorce.

My mother's colleague's flat was too small for my mother, my sister, Ajax, Peter and me. At any rate, after a few days we seemed to get on my mother's colleague's wick rather a lot. So my mother once more packed our things, we took our animals and went back to Gropiusstadt.

My father came into the flat just as my sister and I were sitting in the bath. He walked into the bathroom and said

32

quite normally, as if nothing had happened: 'Why did you go away? You really don't have to sleep in other people's houses, you know. The three of us would have got on fine together.' My sister and I looked at each other, embarrassed. That evening my father pretended not to see my mother at all. Then he looked right through us as if we weren't there. And he didn't speak another word to us either. In a way that was worse than a hiding. My father never hit me again. But the way he now behaved, as if he was no longer one of us, was really much worse. I had never hated him, but only been afraid of him. I had always been proud of him as well. Because he loved animals and had a powerful car, his 62 Porsche. Now, although he still lived with us in our small flat, he was somehow no longer our father. And then something else very terrible happened: my dog Ajax got peritonitis and died. There was no one to comfort me. My mother was completely preoccupied with herself and the divorce. She cried a lot and didn't laugh at all any more. I felt very lonely.

One evening the doorbell rang. I opened the door and there stood Klaus, a friend of my father's. Klaus was calling for my father to take him on a pub crawl. But he had already gone out.

My mother asked the guy in. He was much younger than my father. In his early twenties. And then this Klaus suddenly asked my mother if she'd like to go out for a meal with him. My mother said immediately: 'Yes, why not?' She changed and went off with this man, leaving us by ourselves.

Other children might have been pissed off or frightened for their mother. I suppose for a moment I felt like that myself. But afterwards I was honestly pleased for my mother. She'd looked really cheerful when she left. My sister felt like me and said: 'Mummy was really pleased.'

From now on Klaus popped in more often when my father wasn't in. It was on a Sunday, I still remember it exactly, when my mother sent me downstairs to empty the dustbins. When I came back I was ever so quiet. Perhaps I was very quiet on purpose. As I peeped into the living room, I saw this Klaus kissing my mother.

I felt quite funny. I crept to my room. They hadn't seen me. And I told no one what I had seen. Not even my sister, from whom I didn't usually have any secrets.

I began to feel very uncomfortable about this man, who now started coming regularly. And yet he was nice to us. Above all, he was very nice to my mother. She laughed again and didn't cry at all. Also, she began to dream again. She talked about the room my sister and I were to have when we moved into a new flat with Klaus. But we didn't yet have the flat. And my father wouldn't move out. Not even when the two of them had finally been divorced. My parents slept in their marital bed hating one another. And we still had no money.

And when we did at last have a flat, one stop further up on the tube, in Rudow, things didn't run all that smoothly either. Klaus was there almost all the time now, and somehow he was in the way. He was still very nice, but he just came between my mother and me. Deep down inside, I couldn't accept him. I was not prepared to be told anything by this man in his early twenties. I reacted more and more aggressively towards him.

And then we started having rows. About trifles. Sometimes I provoked these rows. Usually it was about playing records. My mother had bought me a record player, just a little one, for my eleventh birthday, and I had a few records — teeny-bopper music. And at night I'd put on a disc and turn up the record player as loud as it would go. One evening Klaus came into our room and asked me to turn down the record player. I didn't. He came back and roughly pulled the arm off the disc. I put it back on and stood in front of the record player so that he couldn't get at it. He got hold of me and pushed me out of the way. When this man touched me, I really did my nut.

Mostly, when we had these rows, my mother would be cautiously on my side. That was embarrassing, too, for it would develop into a row between Klaus and my mother and somehow I felt guilty. There was one too many in the flat.

But the worst was not that we had the occasional row. What was really awful was when everything was dead quiet at home, and we were all sitting in the living room, with Klaus reading a magazine or fiddling around with the telly, and my mother trying to talk first to us and then to her boyfriend, and no one responding. Then it was really uncomfortable. My sister and I sensed that there were too many of us in the living room. And when we said we'd like to pop outside for a bit no one contradicted us. At least, so it seemed to us, Klaus was really glad when we went. That's why we stayed away so often and as long as possible.

Looking back, I don't blame Klaus a bit. he was only in his early twenties after all. He didn't really suss how attached we were to our mother and she to us. That, in fact, we needed her completely during the brief periods we saw her at night and at week-ends. Probably he was jealous of us, and certainly we were jealous of him. My mother wanted to be there for us, but at the same time she didn't want to lose her boyfriend: it was all too much for her.

I reacted noisily and aggressively to this situation. My sister, on the other hand, grew more and more quiet and suffered. Probably she didn't know herself what she was suffering from. But she did say now and again that she wanted to go and live with my father. I thought that a crazy idea after all we'd been through with him. But now he did actually ask us to come and live with him. Since he had left us, he had become a changed man. He had a young girlfriend. And whenever we saw him he seemed to be in a good mood. He made a show of being incredibly pleasant. And I suppose he was, really. He gave me another mastiff, a bitch this time.

I was twelve, my breasts started to develop and I began, in a very funny way, to become interested in boys and men. I thought them strange creatures. They were all brutal. The older boys in the street as well as my father and, in his way, Klaus, too. I was afraid of them. But then again they fascinated me. They were strong and they had power. They were as I should have liked to be. At any rate, their power, their strength attracted me.

I began to use a hair-dryer occasionally. With my nail scissors I shortened my hair a little in front and brushed it to one side. I messed about with my hair because people had remarked how lovely and long it was. I also wanted to wear jeans, not those silly check children's slacks. I got jeans. I had to have high-heeled shoes. My mother gave me an old pair of hers.

Wearing my jeans and high heels, I roamed the streets almost every night until ten o'clock. I felt that at home they wanted to get rid of me. But the freedom I enjoyed was really fantastic. Perhaps I even enjoyed squabbling with Klaus. It gave me a feeling of strength to quarrel with a grown-up.

My sister couldn't bear any of this. She did what was absolutely beyond me. She went to live with my father. She left my mother and, above all, she left me. Now I was even more lonely. But it was a tremendous blow for my mother. She cried again. She was torn between her children and her boyfriend — and once again she couldn't cope with the problem.

I thought my sister would soon come back to us. But she liked staying with my father very much. He gave her pocket money. He paid for her riding lessons and he gave her a pair of real jodhpurs. It was a bit tough on me. I had to go on earning the cash for my riding lessons by mucking out the stables. As that didn't always work out, my sister, with her swish jodhpurs, could soon ride better than me. But my father made it up to me. He invited me to go to Spain with him. At the end of the school year I'd had a very good report, good enough for them to suggest that I ought to go to a grammar school. My name was put down for Gropius-stadt comprehensive.

Before the start of this new phase in my life, which was to culminate in the Abitur*, I flew to Spain with my father and his girlfriend. It turned out to be a really fantastic holiday.

*University entrance exam, equivalent to A-levels

My father was great. I noticed that in a way he loved me, too. Now he treated me almost like a grown-up. I was even allowed to go out with him and his girlfriend at night. He had become really sensible. Now he was mixing with friends of his own age, and he'd tell them that he'd been married before. I didn't have to call him Uncle Richard any longer. I was his daughter. And he seemed to be really proud of that. Mind you, typical for him, he'd arranged his holidays to suit himself and his friends. At the end of my holidays. So I was two weeks late in arriving at my new school.

I felt very lost in my new school. In my form friendships and groups had been formed by the time I arrived. I sat by myself. But most important, during the two weeks I had spent in Spain, the others had had the comprehensive system explained to them, which is rather complicated for someone coming from an elementary school. The others had been helped in the choice of their courses. I didn't know whether I was coming or going. I didn't have a clue about this school. I never did get it either. There weren't any form masters, as in the elementary school, who could look after individual pupils. Every teacher taught a few hundred pupils in different classes and courses. If you intend doing your Abitur in a comprehensive school, you have to know what's what. You have to decide to study of your own free will, to see that you get into an extension course. Or you have parents who get to you, who tell you, do this, do that, that sort of thing. I simply couldn't get clued up at all.

I felt they didn't appreciate me at this school. All the others were two weeks ahead of me. In a new school that's a lot. I started behaving as at the elementary school. I interrupted the teachers by heckling, I contradicted them. Sometimes when I felt I was in the right, and at other times just for the sheer hell of it. Once again I fought. Against the teachers and against the school. I wanted to be accepted.

The greatest kid in our class was a girl. She was called Kessi. She already had tits. She looked at least two years older than the rest of us and she was more grown-up. She was fully accepted by everybody. I admired her. It was my

37

greatest wish that Kessi should be my friend.

Kessi had a boyfriend who was really tasty. He was in a parallel form, but he was older. Name of Milan. He was at least five foot seven with long black curly hair down to his shoulders. He wore tight jeans and fantastic boots. All the girls were gone on Milan. And Kessi was fully accepted, not only because of her tits and her carrying on like a grown-up, but also because she had Milan as a boyfriend.

In those days we girls had quite definite ideas about what a boy who was 'it' must be like. He mustn't wear baggies but skin-tight jeans. We thought boys who wore plimsols were a drag. They had to wear fashion shoes, preferably high-heeled boots with decorations. We didn't think much of boys who chucked paper balls or apple cores round the classroom. They were the same boys who drank milk during break and had a kick-about in the playground. The really tasty boys immediately disappeared to the smoking corner. And they had to be able to drink. I remember how impressed I was when Kessi told me Milan had been stoned out of his mind.

I thought all the time of how I could make myself become the kind of chick a boy like Milan would chat up or even go with. Or, and this really amounted to the same thing, that Kessi would accept me. Even her nickname was, I thought, really out of this world*. I wanted to make it, so that then I, too, would get a nickname that was something else.

I told myself, you're not really interested in the teachers, you only see them for the odd hour or so. Why bother to please them? It's important to be accepted by the crowd you knock about with all the time. The way I carried on with the teachers was a bit much, but I had no real personal contact with them. Most of them didn't seem to care a monkey's anyway. They had no real authority; all they did was to let rip. But I always let them have it. Soon I could get the whole class into an uproar just like that and fuck up a lesson. Naturally that got me appreciation.

*Kessi = Cheeky

I scraped together all my cash in order to buy cigarettes and go to the smoking corner. Kessi went to the smoking corner every break. And when I kept going there as well, I noticed that Kessi accepted me more and more. We started nattering after school. Finally she invited me to her house and we sat drinking beer until I felt a bit woozy. We talked about out homes. Kessi's story was rather similar to mine. Actually, if anything, hers was an even bigger fuck-up than mine.

Kessi was illegitimate. Her mother frequently changed boyfriends. And, of course, the men didn't accept Kessi. She had just been having a rotten time with one of her mother's boyfriends who'd done his nut. He used to go in for beating people up, and one day he had smashed the whole flat to smithereens, and for his final trick he'd flung the telly out of the window. Only Kessi's mother was different from mine. She tried to be very strict. Kessi had to be in before eight almost every night.

In the end I made it at school; what I mean is I got fully accepted by my schoolmates. There was scarcely any time left for studying. My day of triumph arrived when I was allowed to sit next to Kessi. It was from Kessi that I learnt about skiving. If she didn't fancy certain classes she'd simply stay away and meet Milan, or do anything else she fancied. At first I was scared. But soon I twigged that skiving was a piece of cake. You were scarcely ever found out. It was only in the first lesson that the names of those who were absent were entered in the register. During the lessons that followed, the teachers had far too many pupils to know who was or was not present. Many of them didn't care, anyway.

At this time Kessi used to allow boys to kiss and pet her. And she used to go to Centre House. This was a meeting place for young people, attached to the Protestant Church, with a kind of discotheque in the cellar called the Club. You had to be fourteen to get into the Club. But Kessi didn't look as if she was only just thirteen.

I nagged and nagged until my mother bought me a bra. I didn't really need one yet. But it made me look bigger in

front. I also started using make-up. And then Kessi took me
to the cellar which opened at 5 o'clock.

The first person I saw in the cellar was a boy from our
school. He was a third-former, and for me he had come to
be the greatest guy in our school. Greater even than Milan.
He was better-looking. Above all, he seemed fantastically
self-assured. In Centre House he moved about like a star. It
was obvious that he felt superior to everybody else. His
name was Piet. Piet belonged to a crowd that always stood
or sat apart. It gave one the impression that they didn't
belong to the other teeny-boppers who were hanging about
there. The whole group was the greatest. All the boys
looked great. They wore skin-tight jeans, boots with fantastically high platforms and embroidered jeans jackets, or fan-
tasy jackets, made from carpet or other beautiful materials.

Kessi knew the guys and introduced me to them. I was
excited and thought how really beautiful it was that Kessi
could get me in with these guys. For everybody else in Centre House respected this crowd. We were actually allowed
to sit with them.

Next evening when I got to the cellar, the crowd had
brought a huge hookah. At first I hadn't a clue what it was
they'd got there. Kessi explained to me that they were
smoking hashish and told me I could sit with them. I didn't
really know what hashish was. All I knew was that it was a
narcotic drug and absolutely forbidden.

They lit the thing and let the pipe go round. Everybody
had a suck. Kessi too. I declined. Actually, I didn't really
want to decline. For I wanted to be one of this crowd. But I
simply couldn't do it yet: smoke drugs. That still scared the
pants off me.

I felt very unsure of myself. I just wanted to crawl under a
stone. But I couldn't even leave the table, or it would have
looked as if I were giving the crowd the brush-off because
they smoked hashish. I told them that what I really fancied
just then was beer. I collected empty bottles that were lying
around everywhere. For four empty bottles one got 80
pfennigs or a bottle of beer. For the first time in my life I got

drunk while the others sucked their hookah. They were talking about music. About some music which I didn't yet know much about. I enjoyed listening to The Sweet. I was into all those teeny bopper groups. So, since I couldn't join in the discussion anyway, it was just as well that I was drunk. At least it stopped me from feeling all inferior.

I soon sussed what sort of music turned them on and straightaway was into their music myself — David Bowie and that sort of thing. For me, the guys themselves were stars. From behind they all looked exactly like David Bowie, although they were only around sixteen.

The people in this crowd were superior in a way which was quite new to me. They weren't noisy, they didn't have fights. Their superiority seemed simply to come from inside. Even among themselves they were really great. There were never any quarrels. And on arriving, each crowd member was greeted with a kiss on the mouth by everyone else. Although it was the boys who set the tone, the girls were accepted. At any rate, they had none of those grotty fights between boys and girls.

One day I was again playing hooky with Kessi. The last two lessons. Kessi had a date with Milan at Wutzkyallee tube station. So we were hanging around at the station, waiting for Milan and watching out for teachers who might turn up at this time of day.

Kessi was just lighting a fag when I saw Piet and his friend, Kathi, another guy from the crowd. This was a moment I had often dreamt about. I had always wanted to meet Piet or someone else from the crowd in the daytime. And then I was going to ask him whether he'd like to come home with me. Honestly, I didn't really mean anything by this invitation. I wasn't really interested in boys and men at all. I was only twelve, and hadn't even started my periods. All I wanted was to be able to say that Piet had been to my house. Then the others would have thought that I was really in this great crowd.

So there were Piet and Kathi. At this time, there was nobody in our flat. So I said to Kessi: 'Let's go over to the boys and have a little natter.' My heart was pounding. However, after a few minutes I asked Piet, quite confidently: 'Do you fancy coming to my place? Nobody's at home. And my mother's boyfriend has some really great discs, Led Zeppelin, David Bowie, Ten Years After, Deep Purple, and the Woodstock Festival Album.'

I'd picked up a lot. I knew not only the music they were into, but I'd also learnt their language. It was different, as was everything about them. I had been concentrating on the new expressions I'd heard them use. This was more important to me than my English vocabulary or mathematical formulae.

Piet and Kathi were all for it. I was terribly pleased. I was quite self-assured. When we got to our flat, I said: 'Shit, I haven't anything to drink.' So we scraped together all our small change and Kathi and I went off to the supermarket. Beer was too expensive. You needed quite a lot of money if you wanted enough to turn on a little. We bought a litre bottle of red wine for 1 mark 98. Plonk they called it. So we emptied the bottle and nattered. Mainly about the police. Piet said he had to be terribly careful just now with them on account of the pot. They were protesting about the cops, saying that this was a police state.

All this was terribly new to me. Up to now the only representatives of authority I knew were caretakers, whom you had to hate because they were always bugging you just when you were having fun. But the police were still an indisputable authority. Now I learnt that the Gropiusstadt caretakers' world was a coppers' world. That the cops were far more dangerous than caretakers. For me, anything Piet and Kathi said was the pure and unmitigated truth anyway.

When the wine was finished, Piet said he had some pot at home. There was great rejoicing among the others. Piet departed via the balcony. We now lived on the ground floor and most of the time I went out that way too. After all the years on the eleventh floor, I thought this was a hoot.

Piet returned with a dish almost the size of his hand, subdivided into gramme pieces at 10 marks each. He produced a chillum. That is a wooden tube about 20 centimetres long. First he filled it with tobacco so that you didn't have to smoke down to the wood. Then he mixed tobacco and pot and put the mixture on top. To smoke you have to bend your head back, holding the tube in a vertical position to stop the hot mixture from dropping out.

I watched carefully how the others were doing it. I realised that now, with Piet and Kathi here at home with me, I couldn't say no. So I said quite cool-like: 'Today I fancy some pot, too.' And I pretended that it was my umpteenth chillum.

We had let down the blinds. What little light still came through the blinds filtered through thick clouds of smoke. I had put on a David Bowie record and now took a puff at the chillum and held the smoke in my lungs until I got a fit of coughing. Everybody grew quite quiet. Everybody was somehow dozing, listening to the music. I was waiting for something to happen to me. I thought now that you've taken narcotic drugs something fantastically new is bound to happen to you. But actually I noticed absolutely nothing. I did feel a little tipsy. But I was sure that was the wine. I didn't know then that most people don't feel anything the first time they smoke pot. So you do need a little practice before you consciously get the feeling that pot gives you. I must say alcohol lights you up more vigorously.

I saw Piet and Kessi, who were sitting on the sofa, move close together. Piet was stroking Kessi's arm. After a while the two of them got up, went into my room and closed the door.

Now I was alone with Kathi. He came and sat on the arm of my chair and put one arm round my shoulders. At once I thought Kathi was even better than Piet. I was rather pleased that Kathi had come over to me and that he showed me he was interested in me. I was always afraid the boys could tell I was only twelve and wrote me off as a child.

Kathi began to fondle me. I no longer knew whether I ought to approve. I felt terribly hot. I believe it was fear. I sat absolutely petrified and tried to say something about the

43

record which was on the turntable. When Kathi put his hand on my breast, I got up, went over to the record player and started fiddling about with it.

By this time Piet and Kessi were returning from my room. They looked very strange. Upset and somehow sad. Kessi had a very red face. The two were no longer looking at each other. Nor did they say another word. I felt that Kessi had had a very bad experience. At least that she hadn't got anything out of it. That it must have been very unsatisfactory for both of them.

At last Piet asked whether I was coming to Centre House that evening. This made me happy again. I had achieved so very, very much. Things had turned out exactly as I had dreamt they would. That I would invite Piet and Kathi to come to my house and that then I should really belong to their crowd.

Piet and Kessi left via the balcony. Kathi was still standing about in the room. Once more I felt something like fear. I didn't want to be alone with Kathi. I told him straight that I had to clear up and do my homework. Suddenly I didn't care what he thought. He left after that. I lay on the bed in my room, staring at the ceiling and trying to understand what it was all about.

True, Kathi was really goodlooking, but somehow I no longer liked him. An hour and a half later the doorbell rang. Through the spy-hole in the door I saw Kathi. I didn't open it and tiptoed back to my room. I was really scared to be alone with the guy. At this moment he really made me throw up and I was ashamed somehow. I didn't know why. Whether it was on account of the pot or because of Kathi. But there hadn't been anything at all.

I felt rather sad. Now that I had been accepted into the crowd, I thought that I wasn't really one of them. I was much too young for messing about with boys. Now I knew for certain that I just couldn't do it. And what they'd said about the police and the state and all that, I found very strange and, besides, it wasn't anything that directly concerned me.

Nevertheless at five o'clock I was at Centre House. We

didn't go to the Club but to the cinema. I wanted to sit between Kessi and a boy I didn't know, but Kathi forced his way in between. While the film was on, he began to fondle me again. At some stage he put his hand between my legs. I didn't struggle. I was really paralysed. I was terrible afraid of something. There was a moment when I wanted to run outside. But then I thought: 'Christiane, this is the price for being in the crowd.' I submitted to everything and never said a word. But when he said I was to fondle him too and then tried to pull my hand over, I put my hands in my lap and kept them there tightly clenched.

I was terribly glad when the film was finished. I left Kathi immediately and went over to see Kessi. I told her everything and said I didn't want anything more to do with Kathi. I'm sure Kessi told him, for a little later it turned out that she was really gone on Kathi herself. So she started to blub because Kathi didn't take more notice of her than of the other girls in the Club. At one time she told me how gone she was on him and how she always felt like blubbing whenever Kathi was about.

In spite of the business with Kathi, I now belonged to the crowd. They called me 'Kid', it's true. But I was one of them. None of the boys tried to touch me. I suppose word had got round and was fully accepted that I felt I was too young for messing about. We were altogether different from the 'alkies'. That's what we called kids who turned on with alcohol, beer and shorts, and that sort of thing. They treated any of their girls who made a fuss with terrible brutality. They took the mickey out of these girls, insulted them and then gave them the push. In our crowd brutality didn't exist. We all accepted each other as we were. For in a way we were all alike, or at least on the same trip. We understood each other. No one in the crowd was ever noisy or filthy. The yakking of the others didn't concern us a great deal. We felt above that sort of thing.

Apart from Piet, Kessi and me, everybody else went to work. They all felt the same. They thought their homes were a drag, and work was a drag, too. Unlike the alkies, however, who were hung up about their stress, and aggressive even when they were in the Club, the guys in our crowd could switch off completely. After work, they got tarted up, smoked pot, listened to cool music, and all was sweetness and light. We forgot all the shit outside that we had to wade through during the rest of the day.

I didn't yet feel quite like the others. For that, I thought, I was still too young. But the others were my models. I desperately wanted to be or to become like them. I wanted to learn from them because I thought they knew how to live the cool life and how not to let yourself be got at by all those cunts and the whole shit. As far as I was concerned, parents and teachers had had it. For me the crowd was everything in life that was important — except for my animals.

The reason why I was so completely into this group was partly due to the way things were at home. It had become quite unbearable. And what was most unbearable was that Klaus, my mother's boyfriend, really hated animals. At least that was what I believed in those days. It began by Klaus continually going on about how it wasn't on to have animals in such a small flat. Then he said the new dog my father had given me was not to lie down in the living room.

It made me go absolutely berserk. Our dogs had always been part of the family. They were treated like every other member of the family. And now, there was this guy telling me the dog mustn't come into the living room. But worse was still to come. He tried to stop the dog from sleeping by my bed. He seriously suggested that I ought to build some kind of dog kennel in my tiny room. Of course, I did nothing of the sort.

Then Klaus made his final scene. He declared the animals would have to go. My mother actually backed him up and said I no longer looked after the animals. I thought this was the end. It was true that now I was often not at home in the evenings and that meant one of them had to take the dog out before going to bed. But for the rest, I thought, I spent every spare minute looking after the dog and the other animals.

I could threaten, shout or cry until I was blue in the face. They gave my dog away. At first to a woman whom I thought okay because she really liked the dog. But the woman fell ill with cancer quite soon and had to give the dog away. I heard it had gone to a pub. This dog was a terribly sensitive animal — he almost went round the bend every time there was a noise. I knew it would go to pieces in a pub and I put the blame on Klaus and my mother. I no longer wanted to have anything to do with the people who hated animals like that.

All this happened during the period I began going to Centre House and smoking pot for the first few times. All I had left were two cats. But they didn't need me during the day. At night they slept on my bed. After the dog had gone there was no longer any reason for me to be at home. I had no place there. Neither did I enjoy going for walks by myself any more. I only waited for 5 o'clock to come round when the Club in Centre House would open. Sometimes I'd spend the early afternoons with Kessi and others in the crowd.

I smoked every night. Any of the crowd who had money shared with the others. I no longer thought it wrong to smoke pot. After all, in Centre House we did it quite openly. Occasionally, the social workers of the church who were supervising the Club tried to talk to us when we smoked. They didn't all have the same attitude, but most of them admitted immediately that they had smoked too. They came from the universities, from the student movement, and among them smoking pot had probably been quite normal. And these guys said we oughtn't to overdo it or use it as a means to flee from reality, and all that. Above all, we weren't to change to hard drugs. It went in one ear and out the other with us. Why were they talking so far back when they admitted to having smoked themselves?

One of us told one of these guys: 'You seem to think if students blow dope, that's okay. They know what's what. But when apprentices or workers blow dope, that's dangerous. We don't wear those sort of arguments.' The guy didn't know what to reply. He had a really bad conscience.

I not only smoked pot, but I also drank wine and beer when I had no pot. It began when I came out of school or even in the mornings when I played hooky. I had to turn myself on somehow. I was continually sort of spaced out. And I wanted to be so that I needn't be confronted with all that shit at school and at home. School was a big drag anyway. My average marks dropped quite quickly from Bs to Ds and Es.

Outwardly, too, I changed completely. I became terribly thin because I scarcely ate anything. All my trousers were miles too big. My face became haggard. I stood in front of the mirror a lot. I liked the way I was changing. I came to look more like the others in the crowd. At last my innocent child's face had gone.

I was totally absorbed with my appearance. I made my mother buy me high-heeled shoes and skin-tight trousers. I parted my hair in the middle and brushed it into my face. I wanted to look mysterious. Nobody was to see through me. Nobody was to notice that I wasn't the together chick I wanted to be.

One evening in the Club Piet asked me whether I'd ever been on a trip. I said: 'Sure thing, old man.' I'd heard a lot about LSD, which they called acid or tripping. I'd often heard people talk about their latest trip. When Piet grinned and I could see that he didn't believe me, I began to talk rubbish. I gathered together what I remembered of the tales I'd heard and improvised a story about my own trip. I noticed that Piet still didn't believe me. You couldn't put anything over on him. I'd not done it very well either and I was ashamed of myself. Piet said: 'If you'd like to try, next Saturday I'll have really good trips. You can have some if you like.'

I was looking forward to Saturday. I thought once I'd really tripped I would belong totally with the rest. When I arrived at Centre House, Kessi had already had her trip. Piet said: 'If you're sure you want to try, I'll give you half a one. That'll be enough for the first trip.' Piet gave me a bit of

48

crumpled cigarette paper with a crumb of acid inside it. I couldn't swallow it just like that in front of the others. I was terribly excited. Also I was scared of being found out. Besides, I wanted to do it somehow solemnly. So I went to the toilet, locked myself in and swallowed the crumb.

When I returned Piet thought I'd thrown the acid down the loo. I waited impatiently for something to happen to me to make the others believe that I'd swallowed it.

By the time the Club closed at ten I still hadn't noticed a thing. I walked with Piet to the tube station. At the station we met two of Piet's friends, Frank and Paul, dressed like twins. They were terribly calm. I liked them. Piet told me: 'They're on H.' This meant they were on heroin. At that moment it didn't register. I was preoccupied with myself and the acid which was gradually having an effect.

We got into the tube train and as it went off, I nearly blew my mind. It was absolute madness. I thought I was inside a tin and someone with a gigantic spoon was stirring it. The noise of this tube train inside the tunnel was madness. I thought I couldn't stand this noise. The people in the tube train had dreadfully distorted faces. That is to say, they actually looked the way they always do, the creeps. Only now I could see even more clearly in their faces what revolting creeps they were. I imagined that these fat creeps had come out of some fucking pub or from some fucking work. Then these pig faces went to bed and then they went to work and then they sat in front of the box. I thought, aren't you lucky that you're not like them. That you've got the crowd. That you're tripping and that you know what gives and that you can see what fucking creeps are sitting in this tube. That's roughly what I thought. On later trips, too. Then I started to be afraid of the distorted faces. I looked at Piet. He, too, was uglier somehow than usual. His face was quite small in contrast to the pig faces. But somehow he still looked normal. When we got out in Rudow I was glad. Now I was really freaking. All the lights were terribly bright. A street lamp above us was brighter than I'd ever seen the sun. In the tube I had been cold. Now I was feeling really hot. I thought I was somewhere in Spain and not in Berlin. It was just as on one of those lovely posters in the travel bureau in Gropiusstadt. The trees were palm trees and the street the beach. Everything was terribly bright. I didn't tell Piet I was freaking. Somehow I wanted to be alone during this fantastic trip.

Piet, who was freaking too, said we might go to see his girlfriend if her parents weren't there. He had a girlfriend whom he loved very much. We went to the underground garage in his girlfriend's house. He wanted to see if her parent's car was there. In the garage I got the horrors a bit. The low ceiling was coming down all the time. It really sagged quite alarmingly. The concrete pillars were rocking to and fro. The parents' car was there.

Piet said: 'Man, this is a bloody garage.' And then he obviously thought suddenly that he was freaking by himself and asked me: 'Well, and where did you throw the acid?' He looked at me, and after a while he said 'Man, I'm sorry I spoke. You've got pupils like pinpoints.'

Outside everything was beautiful again. I sat down in the grass. The wall of a house was intensely orange as if the rising sun was reflected on it. The shadows moved as if they meant to make room for the light. The wall bulged out and suddenly seemed to disintegrate in flames.

We went to Piet's house. Piet could paint terribly well. In his room he had a picture he'd done. It was of a terribly fat horse. Sitting on the horse was a skeleton with a scythe. I was gone on that picture. I'd seen it before a few times, and just thought that it was meant to be Death. Now the drawing didn't frighten me at all. My thoughts were quite naive. I thought this skeleton can never control this strong horse. It's already lost its power over the horse. We nattered for a long time about the picture. Piet lent me a few records. He said: 'It's fantastic freaking on a trip.' I went home.

Of course my mother was still up. There was the usual cross-examination. Where had I been? I knew things couldn't go on like this. And anyway, I found my mother terribly ridiculous. Fat and dumpy in her white nightie, her face all distorted with rage. Like the creeps in the tube.

I didn't say a word. I no longer talked to her, anyway. At least only about trivial things. I didn't want affection from her. I didn't want to be touched by her. I imagined — at least sometimes — that I no longer needed a mother or a family. My mother with her boyfriend, and I, we now lived in very different worlds. They had not the least idea of what I was doing. No doubt they thought I was quite a normal child who was going through puberty. What should I have told them, anyhow? They wouldn't have understood. So I thought. Now I only felt sorry for my mother. The way she came in from work all tensed up and went straight into her housework. But I thought it's the old girl's fault if she leads such a creepy life.

CHRISTIANE'S MOTHER

I have often asked myself why I did not notice sooner what was the matter with Christiane. The answer is simple, yet I could only accept it after I had talked to other parents who had similar experiences with their children: I simply did not want to face the fact that my daughter was a drug addict. I fooled myself for as long as possible.

My boyfriend, with whom I have lived since my divorce, suspected early on. But I always said: 'You're imagining things. She's only a child.' That is probably the greatest mistake, imagining one's children aren't ready. When Christiane began to isolate herself, when more and more often she avoided contact with her family, preferring at weekends to go off with her friends rather than doing things with us, I ought to have commented on her behaviour and questioned her. I've taken too many things too lightly.

Probably when one is a working mother, one does not look after one's children with sufficient care. One wants to have some peace and quiet and is relieved when the children go their own way. It is true, there were times when Christiane came home late. But she always had an excuse, and I was only too ready to believe her. I considered such irregularities as well as her, at times, quite recalcitrant

51

behaviour as quite a normal phase in her development, and I thought it would pass.

I did not want to force Christiane into anything. I had myself had the worst experience in this respect. My father was extremely strict. In the village in Hesse where I grew up, he was a respected man, the owner of a quarry. But his idea of educating his children consisted entirely of Don'ts. If I as much as talked about boys, he would box my ears.

I remember clearly one Sunday afternoon when I was out walking with a friend. More than a hundred yards behind us walked two young men. My father happened to come past on his return from the football ground. He stopped and slapped my face right there in the street. He dragged me into his car and took me home. And all this merely because the two young men were walking behind us. It made me very obstinate. I was sixteen when it happened, and I thought: how on earth can I escape this?

My mother was kindness itself, but she had no say in our family. I was not even allowed to choose the profession I wanted, which was to become a midwife. My father insisted that I trained as an office worker so that I could do his book-keeping. It was at this time that I got to know Richard, who was later to be my husband. He was a year older than I and a trainee farmer. He was supposed to become a farm bailiff. At his father's wish. At first we were just friendly. But the harder my father tried to break up this friendship the more stubborn I became. I saw only one way out: I had to get myself pregnant so that I could marry and in this way obtain my freedom at last.

When I was eighteen it happened. Richard immediately broke off his training, and we moved to North Germany to where his parents lived. The marriage was a fiasco right from the start. Even during my pregnancy I could not depend on my husband. He left me by myself for nights on end. All he could think of was his Porsche and his high-falutin plans. No work was agreeable to him. He was determined to become someone superior, to impress people. He liked to talk about the fact that before the war his family had

had standing. His grandparents in East Germany had owned a newspaper, a jeweller's shop and a butcher's shop. And on top of that they had owned land.

He was determined to be independent, to be a business-man like his forebears. Sometimes he dreamt about a for-warding business, then it was a car-dealing business, and then he wanted to open a garden and landscaping business with a friend. In fact he never got further than the prelimi-nary stages. He took out his anger on the children at home, and if I intervened he would turn on me.

It was mostly I who earned the money we needed to live on. When Christiane was four I landed a very good job in a marriage bureau. If at the week-end there were contracts to tie up, Richard would help. All went fairly well for two years. Then Richard quarrelled with the boss and I lost my job. Now Richard planned to open a marriage bureau of his own in grand style. He chose Berlin as the best place to start his new venture.

We moved in 1968. I had hoped that a change of scenery would mean a new beginning for our marriage. But instead of impressive private and business premises we ended up in two rooms and a box room in Gropiusstadt on the outskirts of Berlin. Richard had been unable to raise the necessary capital to start up his new business. Everything was as before. Richard took out his anger on me and on the children. At best, he obtained odd jobs as a dealer. He simply could not come to terms with the idea that he was just one of many lower middle-class people who live in Gropius-stadt.

I often thought about a divorce but did not have the cour-age. What little self-confidence I had saved from my father, was smashed to pieces by my husband.

Fortunately, I soon found a steady job as a shorthand-typist for 1000 marks net a month. The feeling of being appreciated and able to hold down a job gave me new strength. I no longer put up with everything from my hus-band. I began to regard him and his boasting as ridiculous. The quarrels between us became more and more intolerable. Several attempts to separate did not work out. I was, after all, still very fond of him. Perhaps because he had been my first man. And also on account of the children. I could not get nursery school places for my two girls. I could not have paid for them either. So it was preferable that Richard should be at home, at least now and then. And in this way I kept putting off the divorce until, in 1973, I was strong enough to correct my mistake. I went to see a solicitor.

What I had gone through was something I wanted to spare Christiane. When she was born I had sworn to myself: I shall bring her up in such a way that she will never just have to drift into a disastrous marriage. I want her to develop freely, without being pressurised in one direction, I want her to have her freedom — a freedom I never had — as is right and proper. I daresay that with these ideas I later let her get away with far too much.

After the divorce I had to find another flat, because Richard refused to move out. The rent of this new flat was 600 marks a month inclusive of garage, although I had no car. It was really far too expensive for me. But I had no choice. I wanted to get out of this marriage at long last. I wanted a new beginning for myself and the children — at any price.

Richard was not able to pay for the children either. I told myself: there is only one thing you can do, you must pull yourself together, work overtime so that you have something to offer your children. They were now ten and eleven, and during all those years when they were small they had only ever had the absolute minimum of comfort. There was not even a decent settee, everything was just thrown together. It hurt me deeply that I couldn't even offer my children a comfortable home.

After the divorce I wanted to make up for this. I wanted, at long last, to have a pretty flat where we could all be comfortable. That was my dream. That was what I worked for. But also so that I could indulge the children a little, with pretty clothes and weekend jaunts together where we wouldn't have to count every penny.

I pursued this goal enthusiastically. They were allowed to choose their own wallpaper and they had a room furnished with pretty furniture. In 1975 I bought Christiane a really first-rate record player. These were things that made me happy. I was so glad that at last I could afford to buy things for the children.

And when I came home from work in the late afternoon I often brought them back some little present. I enjoyed going to one of the big stores to buy something for them. Mostly cheap offers. Some unusual sweets or a fancy pencil sharpener or some other trifle. Then they would fall round my neck. And I felt as if it was Christmas.

Today I realise that in giving these presents I was trying to ease my conscience because I spent so little time with the children. I should not have bothered about money. I should have looked after the children instead of going out to work. Today I can't understand myself: why on earth did I leave the children alone? As though lovely presents could possibly compensate for their mother's company. It would have been better if I had lived on social security for as long as the children needed me. But social security was something I could not bring myself to accept. From my early childhood days I had it dinned into me that one mustn't be a burden on the State. Perhaps I ought to have taken my former husband to court for maintenance. I don't know. At any rate, I was so busy trying and trying to get a nice home together, I completely forgot what really mattered. I can twist and turn it all whichever way I like, in the end I always reproach myself with the same thing. I did leave the children on their own far too often. And Christiane, particularly, needed support and guidance. She is more unstable and sensitive than her younger sister. At that time nothing was further from my mind than the possibility of Christiane going wrong. Despite the fact that I saw daily what went on in the families of this satellite town where we lived. Brawls by the dozen; the consumption of alcohol was unbelievable; it was not uncommon to see a woman or a man, or even a youngster, lying drunk in the gutter. But I imagined, if you set an example to your children, if you don't slop around or let yourself go, they will follow your example.

I really thought we were on the way up. In the mornings the children went to school. At midday they got their own lunch. And in the afternoon they often went to the riding stables in Lippschitzallee. They're both very fond of animals.

All went well for quite a while. Apart from little jealousies between the children and Klaus, my boyfriend, who had moved in with us. In addition to my work, the house and the children, I had him, and I wanted to be there for him, too. He was a source of tranquillity for me. And I may have made another serious mistake in wanting to have more time for my boyfriend: I allowed Christiane's sister to go and live with her father who had enticed her with all sorts of promises because he felt lonely.

Now Christiane was alone when she came home from school. At this point she fell into the hands of friends who were to lead her astray. But I never noticed anything. Kessi, her schoolfriend, who lived not far from us, and with whom she often spent her afternoons, seemed to me a very sensible girl for her age. And Kessi's mother would keep an eye on them now and then. Sometimes Christiane was at Kessi's, and sometimes Kessi came to our house.

They were both of an age — about twelve, thirteen — when their curiosity is aroused and they want to try out everything. And I had no objection when, in the evening, they went to the youth club in Centre House, which is run by the Protestant Centre in Gropiusstadt. Naturally I felt certain that Christiane was in safe hands with the church people. That the youngsters in Centre House were allowed to smoke hashish was something that would never have occurred to me in my wildest dreams.

On the contrary, I was reassured that Christiane was developing into a cheerful teenager and no longer missed her sister so much. Since Kessi had become her friend, she had started to laugh more often. Sometimes the two of them were so boisterously silly that I had to laugh with them.

56

How was I to know that their laughing fits were caused by hashish or some narcotic pills?

The crowd was my family. Between us there existed friendship, affection and somehow love as well. Even the way we kissed when we met was something I liked terribly. We all kissed one another tenderly and affectionately. My father had never kissed me like this. Problems didn't exist in the crowd. We never talked about our problems. No one bothered the others with their mess at home or at work. When we were together, the rotten world of the others did not exist at all. We talked about music and pot. Sometimes about clothes, and sometimes about people who kicked this coppers' society up the arse. We approved of anybody who ripped somebody off, like knocking off a car or cleaning out a bank. After my trip I felt like the others in the crowd. The trip had been really beautiful. I was glad that I didn't get the horrors. Most people have a horror trip the first time. But I had coped with it beautifully. I felt I had proved myself. Now I tripped whenever I had a chance.

Somehow I had a new attitude to everything. I went out into the country again. In the old days I had gone into the country with my dog and somehow I had experienced the countryside through the dog. Now I first smoked some pot if I wasn't on a trip. Nature as I experienced it now was quite different. It was no longer as before. It dissolved into colours, forms and sounds which were reflected in my moods. I thought the life I was leading was really together. There were a few months when mostly I was pleased with myself.

But eventually things in the crowd came to a halt. Shit, that is to say, hashish, or trips no longer provided a proper kick. We had got used to it. Somehow being high on shit or trips was one's normal state. It no longer gave us any new experience.

One day someone in our crowd came into the Club and said: 'People, I've got something really new, ephedrine. It's really beautiful.'

I took two tabs of this ephedrine — they're uppers — without knowing what I was gulping down. I washed them down with beer, bottoms up, because I'd seen someone else doing it like that. It wasn't easy. For I'd come to hate beer because I hated the people who filled themselves up with it until it came out of their ears. Suddenly there was any amount of tabs in the club. That same evening I took a mandrax, a strong sleeping tablet. Once again I found everything really terrific and loved the people in our crowd. During the next few weeks we checked out all the drugs available.

At school I had more and more difficulties. I no longer did any homework at all and in the mornings I couldn't wake up. Nevertheless I was moved up into the next form*. There were times when I did quite well in subjects like German or Social Studies because they interested me occasionally and somehow I was good at them.

And yet it was precisely in subjects with which I wasn't completely pissed off that I got into difficulties. Not only with the teachers, but also with the class. I thought it simply incredibly lousy the way people treated each other at school. I remember a huge row with a teacher who wanted to discuss the conservation of the environment with us. As it was, the whole form was completely apathetic. Not a soul was interested. Because there was nothing to write down and swot up. But the way the teacher kept rabbitting on really wound me up. So I did my nut and shouted at him, something like: 'What sort of shit are you talking about? What the fuck do you mean by conservation of the environment? I'd have thought for starters people have to learn how to treat each other. That's what this fucking school ought to teach us. How one person ought to be sort of interested in the other person. How it isn't right for everybody to try and talk bigger and be stronger than the other person; and for people to rip each other off and cheat each other only so that they can get better marks. And for teachers to learn

*In German schools pupils are not moved up automatically, but may have to repeat a form (very ignominious) if their academic standards fall short.

58

how to get clued up and assess pupils fairly.' And so on. This was a teacher I still liked, relatively speaking. That's why I was so furious and thought there was some point in shouting at him.

I was terribly pissed off with this school. There simply was no personal contact at all with the teachers. And even in our form the bond became increasingly weaker because we all took different courses. Again, it was always a question of taking it out on each other. Nobody helped anybody, everybody wanted to be ahead of everybody else. The teachers took it out on pupils because they had it in their power to mark their work. And the pupils joined forces to take it out on teachers who were goodnatured and unable to wield authority.

I saw all that, and yet somehow I continued to join in whenever I had reason or even just fancied interrupting the lesson. By now most people in the form only understood me if I shouted some rubbish and not if I tried to talk about the fact that school was fucking awful.

This didn't worry me any longer. I only wanted to be accepted by my crowd and there wasn't any of this fucking fighting and fucking rubbish. But even in the crowd I often sat by myself. Less and less often I took part in the conversation. At any rate it was always the same: pot, music, the last trip, and then, more and more often, about prices on the scene for shit, acid and various tabs. Most of the time I was so cooked up that I didn't want to talk: I just wanted to be alone.

However, now I had a new objective. It was called the Sound. It was a discotheque in Genthiner Strasse in the Tiergarten quarter. All over town there were posters proclaiming: 'The Sound — Europe's most modern discotheque.' The people in the group often went there. But you only got in if you were over sixteen. I had only just had my thirteenth birthday. And I was always afraid they wouldn't let me in, although I had already faked my date of birth in my bus pass.

I knew that the scene was in the Sound. You could buy

anything there. From shit through mandrax and valium to heroin. So the people there must be really together guys, I thought. For a little girl like me, going backwards and forwards between Rudow and Gropiusstadt, this was some sort of dream place. I imagined the Sound to be like a real palace, all glitter, fantastic light effects, and the most fantastic music. And those really together guys, too.

A few times I'd planned to go with the others. But it had never worked. Now Kessi and I drew up a plan of action. One Saturday I told my mother that I wanted to stay overnight at Kessi's place. And Kessi told her mother she was staying with me. Our mothers were taken in. A friend of Kessi's was supposed to be coming with us. She was a little older than us and her name was Peggy. We met that Saturday evening at Peggy's. We were waiting for Peggy's boyfriend, Micha. Kessi told me very gravely that Micha was on H, in other words that he was shooting heroin. I was looking forward to meeting him. I had never yet consciously met a junkie.

When Micha came in I was very impressed by him. Somehow he was even more together than the guys in our crowd. But I immediately had an inferiority complex. Micha treated us very condescendingly. Once again I remembered that I was only thirteen and that this junkie was much too sophisticated, far too grown-up, for me. I felt inferior. Incidentally, a few months later Micha was dead.

We took the tube and went to Kurfürstenstrasse station. In those days it was rather a long journey for me. I felt very far from home. Kurfürstenstrasse where it crosses Potsdamerstrasse looked rather seedy. Some girls were hanging about there. Of course, I had no idea that they were prostitutes waiting to be picked up by cars. There were also a few guys slouching around. Peggy said they were dealers. If anybody had told me at that moment that one day I, too, would have been hanging about this grotty stretch of Kurfürstenstrasse, I'd have told them they were round the bend.

We went to the Sound. When I got inside I nearly had a

fit. This had nothing whatever to do with what I had imagined it to be. 'Europe's most modern discotheque' was a very lowceilinged cellar. It was noisy and filthy. On the dance floor everybody was doing his or her own thing. Somehow there was no contact between people. You could have cut the air with a knife. Now and then a ventilator would whirl the fug about a bit.

I sat on a bench, not daring to move. I felt as if people were staring at me because they noticed that I didn't belong in here. I was the complete outsider. It grabbed Kessi at once. She was running around all the time, looking for tasty boys. She thought she'd never seen so many tasty guys in one place. I sat there like a dummy. The others had brought some tabs and were drinking beer. I didn't want anything. All through the night I hung on to two glasses of peach juice. I'd have liked very much to go home. But I couldn't because my mother thought I was staying with Kessi. I was waiting anxiously for five o'clock when this joint would shut. For a moment I wished that my mother would find me out and suddenly stand in front of me and take me home. Then I fell asleep.

At five the others woke me up. Kessi said she was going home with Peggy. I had a terrible tummy ache. No one took any notice of me. All by myself I walked up Kurfürstenstrasse to the tube station at five o'clock in the morning. There were a lot of winos in the station. I felt like puking.

I hadn't been so pleased for a long time when I opened the door to our flat and saw my mother coming out of her bedroom. I told her Kessi had woken up very early and I'd decided to come home to have a nice long kip. I took my two cats to bed with me and snuggled down. Before going to sleep I thought: 'Christiane, that isn't your bag. What you're doing is wrong.'

When I awoke at midday, I still felt awful. I needed to talk to someone about my experience. I knew that no one in the crowd would understand. It was something I could only talk to my mother about.

I didn't know how to begin. I said: 'Listen, mummy, last

night Kessi and I went to the Sound.' My mother looked horrified. I said: 'Actually, it was quite good. It's a terribly big place. They've got a cinema in there.'

Straightaway my mother started her usual whingeing. I waited for the questions. But my mother didn't ask many. This Sunday lunchtime she was once again under stress. Housework, cooking, trouble with Klaus. I suppose she didn't want to add to her troubles by starting something with me. Perhaps she wasn't all that keen on knowing everything in great detail.

I didn't have the courage to talk. Nor was I really aware that I wanted to talk. At this time I wasn't really conscious of anything. I lived out of the subconscious of my moods. I never thought of tomorrow. I had no plans. What plans? None of us ever talked about the future.

On the following week-end Kessi had to stay with me, because that was the tale we had told my mother. I had to drag her to our house. She was bombed out. On acid. I'd dropped some myself, but still had a clear head. Kessi stood in the road outside our house and thought it absolutely great that there were these two lights coming towards her. I had to drag her away off the road, otherwise she'd have got run over.

I quickly pushed her into my room. But, of course, my mother came trotting after us. As she stood in the doorway, Kessi and I saw the same crazy picture: that my mother was too fat to get through. We began to giggle and simply couldn't stop. I saw my mother as a fat, kindly dragon with a bone in her hair. We laughed, and my mother joined in quite cheerfully. She must have thought what a pair of silly teenagers we were.

From now on Kessi took me to the Sound almost every Saturday. I went with her if only because otherwise I shouldn't have known what to do with my Saturday nights. Gradually I got used to the Sound. I did tell my mother that we were going to the Sound, and she allowed me to stay until the last tube train.

All went well for a few weeks, until one Saturday in the

summer of 1975. We intended staying away all night and had once more told them at home that we would be staying with our friend. We still got away with it, for at that time my mother hadn't yet got a telephone. So the mothers couldn't check up on us. For a kick-off we went to Centre House and knocked back two bottles of wine. Then we prepared ourselves a really fantastic joint. Kessi dropped a few ephedrine tabs as well and at some stage started to wail. I knew all about that. After ephedrine you do sometimes get all hung up.

When Kessi suddenly disappeared I got worried. I had an idea where she might be and walked to the tube station. There she was, draped over a seat, fast asleep, a bag of chips on the floor in front of her. Before I had time to wake her up a tube train came in. Kessi's mother got out. She worked in a sauna parlour and came home from work at this time, around ten o'clock. As soon as she clapped her eyes on her daughter, whom she believed to be in bed at my house, she landed the still sleeping Kessi a couple of resounding smacks. Kessi threw up. Her mother took her firmly by the arm, using a sort of police hold, and carted her off.

Those smacks on Wutzkyallee station probably saved Kessi a lot of aggravation. Without them she might have ended up on the scene, even before me, and wouldn't be taking her *Abitur* now.

From now on Kessi was forbidden to associate with me and she was no longer allowed out at night. I didn't get much out of the crowd at Centre House any more, although during the week I still met people at the Club. But I couldn't imagine a weekend without the Sound. I found the Sound and the people there were more fantastic — the greatest. They were my stars now. Greater than these guys who never really got out of Gropiusstadt. I was always very short of cash now. For Kessi had had 100 marks a month pocket money which we spent on hash and acid. Now I had to scrounge or nick my cash.

I went to the Sound on my own. Next Friday afternoon I

63

went to the chemist's and bought a box of ephedrine. You didn't need a prescription for that. Now I no longer took two ephedrines but four or five. I stopped off at Centre House and scrounged a joint. I walked to the tube station feeling fantastically charged up. I didn't think about Kessi, I never thought about what was. I was simply there. I was simply floating in a very fantastic, intoxicating world. Travelling in the tube I thought it great how at every station new people got in, and one could tell from a hundred yards off that they were going to the Sound. Fantastic get-up, long hair and four-inch platforms. My stars, the stars of the Sound. I was no longer the least bit scared of going to the Sound by myself. I really was fantastically charged up. The joint at the Club had been far out.

On the stairs into the Sound I collided with a boy. He looked at me and said something. I thought he seemed really together. Still going up the stairs, I started to rap with him. After all, I was really charged up. With every sentence we understood each other better. We were into the same music and even had had similar experiences when tripping. His name was Atze. He was the first boy that I found really great. I was gone on him that very evening. It was the first time in my life that I was gone on anybody.

Atze introduced me to his friends. They were a really together crowd. I immediately joined in the talk. It was about drugs and how best to turn oneself on. And that was a subject in which by now I really had as much experience as they. They also talked about H, that is to say heroin. Everybody agreed that this was a fucking awful drug, that starting on H was the same as committing suicide. I said: 'People who shoot must be out of their tiny minds.' Then we talked about how to make trousers tighter. Another subject where I was experienced. For I was growing thinner at such a rate that I had to keep making my jeans tighter. Skin-tight trousers were another trade mark of the people in the Sound. I was able to give them sewing tips. Tightening trousers was the only kind of needlework I had ever done.

Atze's crowd accepted me at once. Without any struggle.

64

But then, charged up as I was, I was so calm and self-possessed, I surprised myself. There was another boy in the crowd whom I also liked very much. His name was Detlef. He was quite different from Atze. He looked very sweet, was very soft and somehow almost child-like. They called him Dolly. He was sixteen. With him I talked most freely of all. Then there was also a fantastic chick-Astrid. She was the greatest. She said things that made everybody fall about laughing. She always said exactly the right thing. I admired her for that. Blacky was the only one you had to watch it with. He could be very hurtful if you said something wrong. When I told them that once while on a trip I had played with a small child in the tube, and that child had been a genuine angel, Blacky immediately made a stupid remark. So one had to be very careful as to what one said. Then there was Bienenstich*, of whom I didn't think much. He was one of those superstuds. And, ever since my experience with Kathi, guys like that pissed me off. But anyway Bienenstich only half belonged to the crowd.

So we nattered and in between we went outside to smoke hash. When the Sound shut up shop at five in the morning, I went with the others to the Kurfürstendamm. Sitting in the tube to Rudow, I felt terribly happy. I came down very gently from tabs and hash. I was pleasantly tired, and for the first time in my life, in love.

Now I longed for the week-ends. Atze was all gentle affection. When we met for the third time in the Sound, he kissed me and I kissed him back. It was a very innocent kiss. I did not want more. Atze felt this without us having to talk about it. This was the difference between alkies and druggies. Most druggies knew instinctively what was the matter with the other person. At least if he belonged to his crowd. Alkies, when they were drunk, would make a beeline for the girls. All they cared about was a good fuck. For us, however, quite different things were important.

Atze and I were like brother and sister. He was my big

*Literally means bee's sting. Biene is slang for girl. The meaning of the nickname is obvious from the text.

brother. We always went arm in arm. For me this meant being protected. Atze was sixteen, a glazier's apprentice, and terribly pissed off with his job. He had certain ideas as to what a together woman ought to look like. I combed my hair the way he liked. Because he was kinky on coats I went to a junk shop and bought myself a long coat with a slit up the back. I could no longer imagine life without Atze.

By now I no longer went straight home when the Sound closed at five, but stayed with the crowd. Together we came down and loafed around in town all morning. We went to exhibitions, to the Zoo or to the Kurfürstendamm. Sometimes we all stayed together all of Sunday. I told my mother the Kessi story and invented a few new friends with whom I was supposed to be staying. I developed an incredible talent for invention when it came to telling my mother where and how I was spending my week-ends.

During the week I still saw the old crowd at Centre House. I would sit, all mysterious, a little way off. Sometimes I told them what had happened in the Sound. I believed they were full of admiration for me. I had simply gone a step further than they. I didn't know then that it was a step further into a complete and utter fuck-up. Nor did I know that many from the old crowd were to follow me a little later.

On the scene at the Sound you could get all types of drugs. I took everything except H. Valium, mandrax, ephedrine, cappis — that's captagon — any amount of shit, of course, and a trip at least twice a week. Uppers and downers we dropped by the handful. Various tabs would fight each other in your body, and this gave you the great feeling. You could give yourself any mood you fancied. You could swallow more uppers or downers. So if I fancied dancing off my aggressions in the Sound, I swallowed more cappis and ephedrine; if all I wanted was to sit quietly in the Sound cinema, I dropped a lot of valium and mandrax. Once again I was blissfully happy for a few weeks.

Until this totally evil Saturday. As I arrived at the Sound I met Uwe, one of our crowd, on the stairs. Uwe said: 'Have you heard? Atze's chucked his job.' For a moment Uwe was silent, then he said: 'Atze's here every night, you know.' He said it in a funny voice, and I got it at once. If Atze was in the Sound every day, he must have got to know other girls.

I asked: 'Anything up with Atze?'

And Uwe replied: 'He's got a woman — Moni.'

It was a terrible blow when Uwe said that. All I could hope was that it wasn't true. I ran down into the discotheque. Atze was standing around by himself. It was as always. He gave me a kiss and put my things in his locker. At the Sound everybody put their things in lockers because an awful lot of nicking goes on.

A little later this Moni arrived — someone I had never been aware of until now. She sat with the crowd without batting an eyelid. I kept a little apart and watched her surreptitiously.

She was quite different from me. Short and chubby, and pretending to be cheerful. She seemed positively to mother Atze. I kept thinking: 'It can't be true. Surely, he's not going to ditch me on account of this silly fat cow.' I had to admit to myself that she had a very pretty face and really lovely, very long, blonde hair. And I thought: 'Perhaps he needs a girl like that who is always cheerful and mothers him.' Another suspicion struck me more and more forcibly: 'Atze needs a girl with whom he can go to bed. This one will go to bed with him.'

I was completely sober. I didn't want to take anything that evening. When I could no longer bear to watch those two together, I went on the dance floor simply to work off my temper. When I returned the two had disappeared. I stormed through the place like a lunatic. I found Atze and Moni in the cinema. Locked in each other's arms.

Somehow I found my way back to the crowd. One guy noticed immediately what was up with me — Detlef. He put his arm round my shoulder. I didn't want to start snivelling. I always thought it was terribly sloppy to cry in front of the crowd. Don't know why I thought it sloppy. When I couldn't hold back my tears any more I rushed outside, across the street and into the park opposite the Sound. I cried buckets. Suddenly Detlef was standing next to me. He gave me a tissue and then another one. I was far too pre-occupied even to notice Detlef at all. Only much later it struck me how sweet it was of him to look for me outside.

I never wanted to see Atze again. I thought I would not be able to look him in the eye again. Not after I had cried in front of everybody and shown how dependent I was upon him. But Detlef drew me back into the Sound.

I had to get back, anyway, because Atze had the key to the locker. I really pulled myself together, tore into the cinema, made Atze nearly jump out of his skin and got the key. Once I'd got my things out of the locker, however, I hadn't the nerve to take the key back. Detlef, who seemed to be hanging around me all the time, did it for me.

It was almost two o'clock. The last tube had gone. I stood outside the Sound and didn't know where to go. I really needed to turn on badly. I needed it right now. But I hadn't any cash left. Just then Panther, a boy from the Centre House crowd, came past. I knew that Panther dealt a bit with LSD and that he always had very good stuff. I tried to touch him for a trip. He gave me something. One of those terribly good crystal tabs. He didn't even ask why I had to trip at this late hour.

I dropped the tab at once and went down on to the dance floor. While I was dancing I freaked out completely. I danced like crazy for at least an hour. When I stopped I still noticed nothing from the acid. I thought Panther had ripped me off. Fortunately, a few people from Centre House had arrived. I went over to Piet. He was tripping too. I told him the story of Atze. But of course Piet was gone on something else and all he said was: 'Forget it, girl,' or: 'Don't get all hung up about it,' and a few more draggy things like that.

I ate a vanilla blancmange and said: 'The whole world is a drag and a lot of shit.' I wanted to return the bowl and get my deposit back, for in the Sound you have to pay a deposit for every glass and bowl to stop people from pinching them. And then suddenly I was bombed out. It was like a flash. I keeled over with the bench I was sitting on.

Then I danced until they shut up shop.

Outside I met the crowd with Atze and Moni again. I didn't give a fuck. I was gone on some Sound poster. Atze and Moni went to Atze's room.

The rest of us walked in the direction of the Zoo. Someone suggested going to the Europa Centre. We ended up on the ice skating rink at the Europa Centre. It was a fairly warm night. It had been raining and there was water where the ice had melted.

I slid across the water and thought I was walking across the sea. Suddenly I heard the sound of breaking glass. The boys were busy with the ticket office kiosk. One of them was reaching through the broken glass in the door. He forced open a drawer and threw out rolls of money*. Before I had really cottoned on, they were all running. The first thing I did in my high-heeled boots was to fall flat on my face on the ice. I was wet through. Detlef waited for me and took me by the hand.

On the Kurfürstendamm outside Kranzler's, the loot was divided. I got two rolls. Everybody was terribly happy. Not so much because of the money, but because we had ripped off the two private coppers who guarded the Europa Centre at night and who had been after us for a long time. We were crazy with joy. We opened the pfennig rolls and threw the money into the air. Outside Kranzler's it was raining pfennigs. The pavement was strewn with pfennigs.

We went to a café in Zoo station. It really turned me off. It was the first time I had gone to Zoo station. This was a really evil station. Dossers were lying in their own puke. Winos were hanging about everywhere. How was I to know then that in a couple of months I was to spend every afternoon here?

Towards six o'clock I went home. In bed I almost got the horrors for the first time on a trip. On my wall I had a poster with a negress smoking a joint. There was a little blue spot in the bottom right hand corner. Suddenly it changed into a terrifying mask, a real Frankenstein face. Just in time I

*In Germany coins are put in rolls by banks, not in bags as England.

managed to concentrate on something else.

Towards midday I awoke feeling totally apathetic. I was quite numb. Like dead. I only thought: 'What an old cow you are for your first boyfriend to ditch you like this.' I went to the mirror, peered at my reflection and hated myself. Only yesterday my face had been so calm, so mysterious, but now it was just like the face of a druggy woman. I looked a terrible wreck. There were black rings round my eyes. My skin was pasty and greasy. I discovered several pimples.

I said to myself: 'Now then, Christiane, you'd better pack in this Sound number. Better keep out of sight of Atze and the crowd.' During the next few days I tried to deaden any feelings for others inside me. I didn't drop any tabs and didn't do a single trip. All day long I drank tea with hashish and rolled one joint after the other. A few days later I'd got myself together again. I'd got so that, apart from myself, I neither loved nor liked anyone nor anything. I thought that now I had my feelings under control. As for the Sound — I never wanted to go there again.

The following Saturday night was the longest in my life. I stayed at home. It was the first Saturday night in weeks that I had not gone to the Sound. I couldn't look at the telly, I couldn't sleep. I no longer had enough of anything to get cooked up. I realised that I could not live without the Sound and the people there. Without them my life became totally meaningless.

Then I began to look forward to next Friday when I would go to the Sound again. In my mind I got ready for the Sound. I messed about with my hair and decided not to comb it at all any more. I thought that would give me an even more mysterious air.

On Friday I started off with a few valiums. I washed them down with beer and then swallowed a mandrax before leaving for the Sound. By then I was no longer scared of Atze or the crowd. I hardly noticed a thing. I borrowed a large jeans hat, sat at a table, put my head down and kipped nearly all night.

Once I awoke, Detlef had pushed the hat out of my face

70

and was stroking my hair. He asked what was up. I said nothing was up. I was very distant, but I did think it really sweet of him the way he looked after me.

By the following week-end I spent almost all my time with Detlef. Now I had a new reason for going to the Sound: Detlef.

It was a very slow business with him. This wasn't the big bang like with Atze. For a kick-off we were just together at the Sound. We talked a lot. I got on with Detlef in a totally new way. Neither one of us was superior to the other, at least not when we talked. I could rap to Detlef about anything without being afraid that he would take advantage of my weaknesses. Neither of us stuck to his point of view. Each could occasionally talk the other round. From the very start I had always liked Detlef very much. But he had never been a really tasty guy for me, not like Atze. He was too sweet and too much like a child for that. However, gradually I realised that I got far more out of my friendship with Detlef than I did with Atze. I grew fonder of him from one week-end to the next, although I baulked at again being dependent on a boy as I had been on Atze. But somehow I had to admit to myself that I was really in love with Detlef.

I grew very calm. That was partly due to the fact that I was dropping more and more downers and only occasionally uppers. All my fidgetiness had gone. I only went on the dance floor occasionally. Actually I only needed to work it off whenever I hadn't been able to pick up some valium.

At home I must have been a pleasure to have around for my mother and her boyfriend. I did not contradict, I never fought with them. I no longer rebelled against anything because I had given up trying to change things for myself at home. And I noticed that this made the situation a whole lot simpler.

By Christmas 1975 — I was now thirteen and a half — I believed my relationship with my mother had become so relaxed on account of my resignation that I could risk telling her part of the truth. So I told her that I had not always stayed with Kessi, but occasionally, when the last tube had

71

gone, in the Sound. Of course, she wasn't exactly over-joyed and gave me a right mouthful. I argued that it was better if I stayed in this disco for a night and then came home, instead of leaving home and crashing out as other children in Gropiusstadt did. And I told her it was better she should know the truth and know where I was rather than me telling her a pack of lies. She swallowed it.

To be honest I no longer felt a strong urge to tell my mother anything about myself. But this constant telling of whopping great lies had got on my wick. Besides, it was growing steadily more difficult to invent credible stories. The reason for my confession was that I wanted to go to the Sound over the Christmas holidays and on New Year's Eve, and couldn't think of a suitable story. My mother actually gave me permission to stay away every night during the holidays. I was flabbergasted. But then I had told my mother what a respectable, harmless teenage disco the Sound was, and that all my friends went there. Moreover, I pointed out to her that she must have noticed how much more calm I was after I had had a chance of letting off steam once a week.

Meanwhile the scene in the Sound became increasingly hard. Heroin hit it like a bomb. In our group, too, all the talk was about H. Actually everybody was against it. We had already seen many examples of people who had been ruined by H. But then one after the other tried their first fix, and most of them stayed with it. Heroin destroyed our crowd. Those who had tried H immediately belonged to quite a different crowd.

I was really scared of H. Whenever it was a question of H, I suddenly was conscious of the fact that I was only thirteen. On the other hand I once again had this respect for crowds where they fixed. For me they were the next higher crowd. The junkies looked down on us hash smokers and tab drop-pers with immense contempt. Hashish they called baby drug. Somewhere I felt depressed at the thought that I should never get into the junkie crowd, into the real scene. That there was no move up for me. I did have a true horror of this drug, knowing as I did that it was the end.

It didn't matter all that much to me that our crowd was breaking up over H because I had Detlef. The others weren't all that important any longer. Things between Detlef and me got better and better. One Sunday, early in 1976, I took him to our flat. I knew in advance that my mother and her boyfriend wouldn't be there. I cooked a proper lunch for Detlef. We sat at the table, eating our Sunday lunch like husband and wife. I thought it was really fantastic.

After that I thought only about Detlef all week and really looked forward to Friday and the Sound. This Friday I arrived at the Sound quite sober but really happy. There was Detlef sitting with a real old bag of a girl. I sat down with them but Detlef hardly took any notice of me. I realised he was into something else. For a moment I thought it would be like that time with Atze all over again. But that was rubbish, of course, with this old bag.

At first these two didn't talk, and then only in snatches, which didn't make real sense to me. At any rate it was something to do with H. And suddenly I somehow got the message. Either Detlef wanted to score some H from this bag or she wanted to palm some off on him. I panicked. I shouted: 'Are you off your rocker, old man? You're sixteen, you can't seriously want to take H.'

He didn't appear to be listening. I said: 'Go on three trips all in one go tonight. I'll get them for you. But please, no fuck-up.' I really implored him.

When he didn't seem to react I made a big mistake, which I often thought about later. I went completely to pieces and screamed. 'If you take H, I don't want anything more to do with you. You can fuck off as far as I'm concerned. I don't want to see you again.' After that I went straight on the dance floor.

I'd done it all wrong. I shouldn't have made such a fuss. I should have talked to him calmly as soon as we were alone. He would have listened to me. Above all, I shouldn't have left him alone for a second, for he was already quite spaced out when he was talking to the bag. Two or three hours later

73

someone told me that Detlef and his best friend Bernd had been fixing. They hadn't started by snorting. They'd fixed straightaway.

I did see Detlef again that night. He smiled at me from a long way off. He seemed very happy. He didn't even want to natter to me. I didn't want to go to him. This night was even heavier than the Saturday when I'd lost Atze. Detlef was gone. Into a world in which I didn't belong. Just like that, one fix and we no longer had anything in common.

I continued going to the Sound. Detlef soon had another girlfriend. Called Angie, she was ugly and insensitive. I realised that there was nothing at all between those two. Actually I never saw Detlef talking to her. She was a junkie, that was it. Sometimes Detlef came over to speak to me. We were like strangers. Most of the time he came because he wanted to scrounge money for his next fix. Whenever I had money I gave him some.

Sunday mornings were very bleak. I crept to the tube station, feeling fagged out and thinking: 'What a fucking mess.' I no longer understood what it was all about. I didn't know why I went to the Sound, I didn't know why I took drugs, I didn't know what else I was supposed to do, I knew fuck-all. Didn't get much out of hash any more either. When I was high, I was completely isolated and couldn't talk to anybody. But at sometime I had to talk to someone, now that I no longer had Detlef. I kept taking more and more tablets.

One Saturday when I was flush, and there was every tablet on the scene you might care to mention, I overdid it. Because I was feeling low I washed down two captagons, three ephedrines and a couple of caffies, or caffeine tablets, with beer. But when I was completely worked up, I didn't like them either. So I dropped some mandrax and any amount of valium.

I can't quite remember exactly how I got home. At any rate, on the way from the tube to our flat I flaked out. I crawled to some steps leading to a shop and doubled up. At some time I pulled myself up and kept making for the next point to hold onto. From a street lamp to the next tree, and from there again to the next street lamp. It was an endless road. I thought I'd die if I didn't get home. The worst thing was this pain in my chest. It was as though someone was twisting a sword in my heart.

Next morning was Monday. My mother couldn't get me to wake up. When she returned from work that night I was still lying there motionless. She kept forcing honey down my throat. It was not until Tuesday afternoon that I managed to get up. I told my mother I had 'flu and bad circulation. In fact my circulation did break down from time to time. I told my mother that others in my class had the same thing. I said it was due to puberty and rapid growth. I wanted to stop her from calling a doctor because I was afraid he might realise what was wrong with me. In fact, my mother didn't call a doctor. She always seemed to be glad when I could come up with an explanation for what was wrong with me.

For the time being I had had it up to here where tabs were concerned. Up till next Saturday I was sober almost all the time. I felt very low.

On Saturday I went on a trip in the Sound. It was total horror. The first time I really got the horrors properly. This Frankenstein mask from the spot on my poster was there again. Then I thought I was bleeding to death. It went on for hours. I could neither speak nor walk. Somehow I got into the Sound's cinema and sat there for five hours thinking I was bleeding to death.

So nothing worked any longer. No tablets, no LSD. I no longer fancied hash anyway. So, apart from a few valiums now and then, I stayed off drugs. I believe for three weeks. It was a bloody awful time. We moved to Kreuzberg near the Wall. It was a grotty district but the rent was cheaper. It took me half an hour by tube to get to my school in Gropiusstadt. But the Sound was nearer.

The Sound was evil without drugs. Absolutely nothing ever happened. Until the morning when I was walking to the tube and saw the posters which had been put up everywhere. They were fantastic pop posters. 'David Bowie is coming to Berlin', they said. I couldn't take it in. David Bowie was our star of stars, the greatest of them all. His music was the best. All the guys wanted to look like David Bowie. And here he was, coming to Berlin.

My mother got me two complimentary tickets for the concert through her firm. Funnily enough, I knew at once to whom I was going to give the second ticket: to Frank. I never thought why Frank of all people. Frank was one of our old Sound crowd. Somehow he looked exactly like David Bowie. He had even dyed his hair red with henna. Perhaps that was why I thought of him.

Frank had also been the first junkie in our group. He was the first to become completely physically dependent on H. They used to call him Chick. But by now everyone called him Corpse because he had come to look like a walking corpse. Like almost all the boys in the crowd he was about sixteen. But for his age he was really clued up. He was above everything. He was so confident that even with little hash-smoking me he never put it on.

So it was with an out-and-out junkie of all people that I intended going to this David Bowie concert which, I imagined at that time, was one of the most important events of my life. How important I didn't yet know when I offered Chick the ticket. After all, I lived only out of my subconscious. But somehow, in the weeks during which neither tabs, nor shit, nor LSD could no longer do anything for me, my attitude to H must have changed. At least the insurmountable barriers which had existed between me and the junkies had obviously vanished.

On the day of the concert I met Chick at Hermannplatz. He was incredibly tall and fantastically thin. It had never struck me so forcibly before and I told him so. He said he weighed nearly ten stone. He had just weighed himself when giving blood. Chick earned some of his money for stuff as a blood donor. Although he looked like a corpse and his arms were covered with scars from the needle, and although junkies have jaundice rather often, they still

76

kept accepting him as a blood donor.

In the tube I realised that I had forgotten my valium. I said to Chick: 'Shit, I meant to bring it, in case I might freak out at the concert;' I had in fact dropped a few valiums at home. So that I should remain perfectly cool at the David Bowie happening. Chick was immediately gone on the idea of going back to fetch the valium. I asked: 'Why are you so dead keen on valium?' He said again that he wanted to go back. When I looked at him carefully I got the message. He was doing cold turkey. That's the expression used among old junkies when the effect of their fix wears off. There are other expressions, but we mostly use cold turkey.

I told him that we hadn't time to go back because we should then be late for the concert. He said he had no stuff left and no cash either. Because of the concert he hadn't time to pick anything up. It was fucking awful to go to a David Bowie concert doing cold turkey, and not even to have some valium. Now he was no longer cool and confident. I'd often seen people doing cold turkey, but never experienced it so consciously.

In the Deutschlandhalle where the concert took place, the atmosphere was great. There were practically only our sort of people there — all Bowie fans — that was why. Next to us sat some American soldiers smoking a joint. We only had to look at them and they passed the joint on to us. Everyone was in a fantastic mood. Chick took a long drag. But he was getting steadily worse.

When David Bowie started it was almost as fantastic as I'd imagined. It was terrific. But when he came to the song *It's Too Late* I came down just like that. All at once I felt terribly hung up. During the last few weeks when I no longer knew where I was, this *It's Too Late* had got on my wick. I thought the song accurately described my situation. Now this *It's Too Late* got me in a state. I could have done with my valium.

After the concert Chick could scarcely walk any more. He was doing cold turkey really badly. We met Detlef's friend, Bernd. He had had a fix before the concert. He said we

77

must do something for Chick here. He himself could do with another fix.

Bernd had two trips left. We sold them quite quickly outside the Deutschlandhalle for twelve marks. The rest I was going to scrounge. I was an accomplished scrounger. In the Sound I had scrounged most of the money I needed for drugs. We needed at least twenty marks. There was nothing to be scored on the scene for under that. Scrounging outside the Deutschlandhalle was a piece of cake. There had been many people with cash at the concert, guys who hadn't already been touched every five minutes by someone who only wanted the cash for stuff. I trotted out my usual 'no money for my tube fare', and the money was positively rattling in my plastic bag. Bernd scored H with it. More than enough for two fixes. In those days stuff was comparatively cheap.

All of a sudden the thought struck me: 'Now that you've scrounged the money for it, why shouldn't you at least try some? Let's see if it is really as good as it ought to be, judging by the junkies' happy expressions after their fix.' I really didn't think any further. It didn't occur to me that during the past few months I had systematically got myself ready for H. At this moment I wasn't even aware that I was in a fantasic low, that this *It's Too Late* had knocked me sideways, that no other drug would help me come out of it, that on my road H was now the logical conclusion. All I could think of was that I didn't want those two junkies to go off and leave me alone in my fucking mess. I told them at once that I wanted to try some. Chick could hardly speak any longer. But he became really furious. He said: 'Oh, no, you don't. You've no idea what you're doing. If you do that it won't be long before you'll be exactly where I'm now. Then *you* will be a corpse.' He knew very well that they called him Corpse.

So it wasn't at all that poor little me was being deliberately tempted by a wicked fixer or dealer, as the papers always report. I know no one who was led into temptation literally against his will. Most youngsters get to H of their own accord

78

when they're ready for it — as I was.

Chick's painful stammering made me really stubborn. After all, he was doing cold turkey, now no longer the cool and confident guy but a poor sod who was dependent on me. I had no intention of taking orders from him. I said: 'For starters most of that stuff is mine, anyway, because I scrounged the cash. Besides, don't talk so far back. I shan't get hooked like you. I got myself completely under control. I'll just try it once, that's all.'

I didn't yet know how weak one is when doing cold turkey. Chick, at any rate, seemed really impressed by what I said. He didn't bother to say anything. Bernd muttered something, however. I didn't listen but told them if they didn't want to let me try they should give me all of my share. We went into a doorway and Bernd divided the stuff fairly into three portions. By now I was lusting after it. There was no thinking about it, no pang of conscience. I wanted to try it at once to get myself really well charged up. I was scared of the hypodermic. I told the two of them. 'I don't want to fix. I'll snort.'

Immediately I sniffed powder up my nose. All I felt was a sharp, bitter taste. I had to suppress a feeling of nausea; however, in the end I spat out quite a lot of it. But then it came awfully quickly. My limbs became terribly heavy and at the same time they were quite light. I was very tired and that was a really fantastic feeling. The whole shit had gone all at once. I felt as great as never before. That was on 18th April, 1976, a month before my fourteenth birthday. I shall never forget the date.

Chick and Bernd had their fix in the car of a junkie. I went ahead to the Sound. I no longer minded being alone. I was terribly strong. In the Sound I sat on a bench. Astrid came up, looked at me and asked immediately: 'Man, are you on H?' At that time Astrid was my best friend. I went berserk when she asked such daft questions. I shouted: 'Fuck off, man. Piss off, can't you.' I didn't know why I carried on like that.

Chick and Bernd came and they were high, too. Chick

was once again the totally together guy. Detlef wasn't in the Sound.

At five in the morning Bernd asked whether we'd like to go to his place for a cup of tea . We went. I took Chick's arm, quite happy. I felt as if I was part of a fantastic new family. I didn't say much, but I had the feeling that I could speak to these two about anything. The H made us like brothers and sisters.

I slept with Bernd in his bed. He never touched me. We were all members of the H family. Chick lay on the floor with his head against an armchair. He lay like that until two in the afternoon. Then he got up, because he was doing cold turkey again and needed to get a fix together for himself.

I was plagued by an insane itch all over. I stripped naked and scratched with my hairbrush. I scratched until I bled, particularly on my calves. This didn't annoy me. I knew that fixers scratched. The backs of Chick's legs were so badly covered with scratches that there wasn't a place where the skin was unbroken, and in some spots he'd scratched himself down to the raw flesh. Chick didn't use a hairbrush but his pocket knife.

Before he left, Chick said to me: 'The stuff you gave me, you can have it back tomorrow.' For him, then, it was as clear as daylight that I had now become a proper fixer who, by the next day, would want another fix, Somehow I twigged what he was saying so matter-of-factly. I pretended to be quite cool and said: 'Leave it. It'll keep. It'll do if you'll return it in a month's time.'

I had another sleep, perfectly happy and content. In the evening I went home. There were moments when I told myself; 'Man, you're thirteen, and you've already been on H. Fucking awful, somehow.' But it was gone again just like that. I was feeling far too well to ponder. There are no withdrawal symptoms at the start. With me, the terrific feeling stayed all week. Everything went first class. No rows at home. I took school in my stride, quite relaxed, joining in at times and getting good marks. During the week I went to Centre House again. There four people of our old crowd had meanwhile changed over to heroin. Within a few weeks the number of fixers in Centre House increased by leaps and bounds. In Gropiusstadt, too, H struck like a bombshell.

JÜRGEN QUANDT, DISTRICT YOUTH CHAPLAIN AND MINISTER OF THE PROTESTANT CENTRE HOUSE

For years Centre House, the Protestant centre's youth cellar, was the central meeting place of youngsters from Gropiusstadt and Neukölln. Every night up to 500 young visitors came to the cellar until December 1976, when, due to the rapid increase in the use of heroin among the young people, we closed the cellar so as to draw public attention to the disastrous situation. What surprised us as educationists who, at the time of the student movement, had discussed the use of so-called soft drugs and their effect on human consciousness, was how quickly a scene for hard drugs was created in Gropiusstadt. Within a few months young people from our catchment area had changed to heroin. Our attempts up till then to persuade youngsters with arguments rather than disciplinary measures of the danger of drug use, resulted only in encouraging them to carry on, and an admission of our own helplessness in the fight against drugs.

Our Open Youth Work at Centre House brought to light what the authorities were still steadily denying: that there could be no question of a decrease in the so-called drug wave. On the contrary, the drug problem had reached dimensions which quantitatively as well as qualitatively were comparable to those in the United States of America. The market for these drugs was provided by unemployed and unskilled working-class youngsters. All we education-ists could do was to protest publicly against offical igno-rance. The closure of the youth cellar was intended to bring to light what, no doubt, many would have preferred to remain in the dark. It has had the desired effect: there is today in West Berlin an intensive discussion concerning drug problems as well as official admission that these prob-lems do exist.

In the meantime the youth cellar has been reopened. A few of the demands attached as a condition of the reopening have been fulfilled. There now exists in Neukölln a state-financed drugs advisory bureau; in Gropiusstadt there is the 'Clean Bus', a meeting place for drug endangered youngsters, as well as extended availability of therapy. After two years there has been no decrease in the problem of drug addiction, even if now we are dealing with a new generation of young people. Some of the young people from Gropiusstadt, who began using heroin two years ago, are no longer alive.

Meanwhile the living conditions of the young people have not improved. In addition to the old problems new ones have cropped up: more and more young people in Gropiusstadt possess arms and, if necessary, are prepared to use them.

The majority of young people whom we meet in Centre House come from working-class families. In spite of apparently increasing prosperity, their situation is characterised by a steady deterioration in their living conditions during the last few years: increasing demands for achievement and stress at school, overcrowded classes, lack of vacancies for apprentices, unemployment and family conflicts are the concrete expression of this deterioration.

In addition, a new housing estate like Gropiusstadt, where approximately 45,000 people live, any problem automatically occurs many times over due to the concentration of people in a comparatively small area: in other words, there are many out-of-work youngsters, many family problems, frequent failures in school, etc. Besides, by now the 'natural' environment offers little by way of nature and thus little scope for development. The weakest groups in society — children, young people and the aged — are most immediately exposed to such destructive living conditions. After completion of the building programme — and that means after the utilisation of every available building site — Gropiusstadt lacks suitable play facilities for children, recreational facilities for young people and adults, and, most of all, space for rest and relaxation. There are no large parks, no meadows, no woods, simply nowhere for children to romp or adults to take a walk.

The logic of towns such as Gropiusstadt rests on the profitability of capital and is not orientated according to the needs and vital necessities of human beings. The consequences — so far only suspected — of a prefabricated way of life are revealed more and more clearly.

Material need is still the cause of many conflicts and problems. High rents and an ever increasing cost of living demand a steadily increased workload and the necessity for both husband and wife to go out to work. And thus the life of the people here is subject to a seemingly irresolvable constraint: the constraint of having to produce more and more stamina for the daily grind without becoming really happy and prosperous.

From time immemorial drug taking has been one of the most reprehensible means of allowing men to forget that they are the victims of social development. Among workers, alcohol has for a long time had this function. During the last few decades other addictives have been added: tranquillisers and pep pills, a legal and lucrative business; and narcotic drugs, like heroin or cocaine, no less lucrative, although illegal.

What is astonishing is not, basically how many people use them, but how many refrain from using them despite massive existential problems. This applies particularly to young people. In view of their situation we should not really be surprised at rising drug misuse, increasing criminality, growing brutalisation, and the spread of fascist ideas among working-class youngsters.

It cannot be denied that there exists an immediate connection between the increase in drug abuse among working-class youngsters, and the massive deterioration in their living conditions.

The week-end after my first snort of H, I met Detlef in the Sound. He got at me immediately: 'Got yourself into a

83

fucking mess, haven't you,' he said. 'You must have gone completely off your rocker.' He'd already heard from Astrid that I had snorted.

I told him: 'Why don't you screw off, you bastard. After all, you started it, and now you're a proper fixer. I don't intend to get like that, anyway.' That shut him up. He wasn't doing cold turkey, because he wasn't yet physically dependent. But he wanted a fix badly. At last he told me that he had no cash and would like to buy a little stuff.

I said: 'What did I tell you?' And then I proposed that he and I should scrounge money for stuff. He agreed, although he must have known what that would boil down to. In twenty minutes outside the Sound I had scrounged twenty marks. Detlef had much less. However, it was enough for both of us since we could still turn on with a small dose. We didn't bother to discuss whether I would be getting my share. That went without saying. This evening Detlef had his fix and I snorted. So nothing had come of my vague resolve not to try H again for four weeks.

Detlef and I were back together. It was as if we had never been apart. Neither of us spoke about the weeks during which we had passed one another in the Sound. It was just as beautiful as on that Sunday when I'd cooked for Detlef and we had eaten Sunday lunch together. I was, I believe, happy about the way it had turned out. If I had not tried H, I should never have got together with Detlef again. I imagined I would stay a joy popper. Everyone who starts on H imagines he will, although, needless to say, he doesn't know anybody who has remained a joy popper. What was more, I imagined I could save Detlef from becoming a proper fixer. Those were the kind of lies with which I was happy.

Probably my subconscious did not believe these lies. Whenever someone got at me about H, I blew my top. I screamed and shouted 'Fuck off'. Like after my first snort when Astrid wound me up. And I began to hate every girl of my age who looked to be on the same road as me. I picked them out in the tube or in the Sound, those little amateur experimenters with hash and trips who tried to dress like real fixer chicks, those twelve-and thirteen-year-old kids, crashed out and hanging around in the Sound. I always told myself: 'That grotty little bag will end up using H.' Although as a rule I was very easy-going, these girls made me really aggressive. I hated them. It never occurred to me then that it was really myself I hated.

After I had been snorting for a few weeks, I actually packed it in for a couple of weeks. It didn't make any difference, I imagined. And physically I didn't feel worse either. But we were back with the whole fucking business as before: I no longer fancied anything, I started arguing with my mother again. That was in 1976, shortly before the Easter holidays.

On the first Saturday of the holidays I was sitting on the bench by the stairs in the Sound, once again not really knowing why I was sitting there. Two girls came down the stairs, about twelve years old, but with make-up and brassieres and got up to look sixteen. I also told everybody who didn't know me very well that I was sixteen and I, too, tried to slap on enough make-up to make me look it. At once I took a terrible dislike to these two girls. But then they interested me. I kept my eyes riveted on them.

By the way they moved across the Sound I sussed immediately that they were trying to make friends. Those two wanted to get into a crowd. And for them the greatest would be the H crowd, I thought. They had already got to know Ritchie, the Sound's chief. He was the only one of the Sound staff who was older, around the late thirties. He fancied girls of this age group. The kind uncle of all little girls who were dossing around. The two, then, were talking to Ritchie across the counter. They knew very well that I was watching them. They kept looking across to me. Probably because I was their age. One of them came over to me. She really had the innocent face of an angel. Her name, she said, was Babsi, and then she asked whether I had got a trip for her.

I said: 'Do me a favour. What d'you want with a trip, kid?'

I enjoyed being so vastly superior to her. Let her learn that it wouldn't do to come scrounging trips just like that from one who'd had experience with H. I suppose she found me as together as, a few months earlier, I had found the guys who were further on in the drug scene. She said she'd stand me a cherry juice and would be right back.

When this Babsi had gone, the other one came over at once. She was called Stella. Stella asked what Babsi wanted. I said: 'A trip.'

Stella said: 'Did she give you any money? I've lost five marks, actually. I bet the old bag's pinched it.' That was just typical of Stella. Soon I was to be in her company almost every day. For Babsi and Stella became my best friends. Until Babsi made the headlines in the papers because she was the youngest child in Berlin to have died of heroin.

So Babsi returned with her cherry juice. I despised her, but on the other hand, I also somehow liked her with her angel face and her naive, uncomplicated ways. We got talking. Babsi and Stella had been expelled from their grammar school because they'd played truant a few times too many. They'd played truant because they'd got into a crowd where there was a lot of hash smoking. Now they had cleared out from home and were dossing around, besides which they were determined to see a little more of life than they had done in their hash crowd. Babsi was twelve and Stella thirteen.

I invited Babsi to come to my house the next day. Because she had nothing at all, I gave her two of my old T-shirts and a pair of briefs. Then she slept in my bed and I cooked a meal. Now I really liked her. On the following day I also made friends with Stella. She and Babsi were as I had been only a short while ago. Somehow I felt more at ease in their company than with those totally fucked-up fixers. They smoked shit and went on trips, and through them I got away a little from the people who thought and talked only about H. Only on Saturdays I had my little snort. The others of the crowd took the mickey because I wasted my time with teeny-boppers. But I didn't mind.

We three had a lot to rap about. We'd all had similar trouble at home. Babsi's father had killed himself when she was still a small child. Her mother had been a dancer in East Berlin and a photographic model in the West, Babsi told us. Her stepfather was a distinguished pianist. A world-famous artist, Babsi said. She was mighty proud of her stepfather. Especially when we went into a record shop and there were any amount of record sleeves with her stepfather's name and picture. This pianist, however, did not seem to take a great deal of notice of her. Babsi lived with her grandparents who had adopted her. She lived there like a princess. Later I once went to her house. She had a fantastic room with the greatest furniture. She had an incredible record player and loads of records. And gear, mountains of it. But she didn't hit it off with her grandmother who was a right evil-tempered old bag. She would have liked to go back to her mother. Babsi didn't want anything to do with her fantastic room and that's why she was dossing around.

Stella also had a very beautiful mother. And Stella loved her, too. But her father had died during a fire in their flat. Stella must have been about ten when that happened. And since then her mother had to fend for herself and had little time for Stella, and then she started to drink. In those days Stella used to have a crush on someone. It was Mohammed Ali. She used to go on about his strength. I think in her imaginings he was her father and lover all rolled into one.

So we three were on the same road. I knew from the first evening I met them that these two would also end up using H. But when the moment came when Stella asked me for H, I was truly horrified. Once again I blew my top and shouted at her. 'Keep your hands off the fucking stuff. Nobody will give you any H, anyway. I'll pack it in myself. There's nothing in it for the likes of us, I tell you.'

I didn't give Stella anything either and told the others not to give her any stuff. A few days later she did get some, after all, from Blacky, one of the Sound crowd, who was her boyfriend. And Babsi copied her, of course.

But for a while after that, they didn't have many opportunities of scrounging snorts. They were picked up during a rumble and taken back home. I didn't see them again for a few weeks.

Meanwhile spring had come and outside it was getting steadily warmer. For me the first few warm days in the year were associated with my feeling of happiness. I think this goes back to my early childhood days. Going barefoot, taking off all one's clothes splashing about in the water, flowers blossoming in the garden. This spring of 1976 I waited in vain for this feeling of happiness. I thought it couldn't possibly happen that life would fail to grow beautiful once the sun was growing warmer. But I was always making heavy weather of my problems, and I didn't really know what problems they were. I snorted H, and the problems were gone. But a snort like that no longer lasted a whole week.

In May I had my fourteenth birthday. My mother gave me a kiss and fifty marks. These fifty marks she had saved from her housekeeping money. She told me to buy whatever I wanted with it.

That night I went to the scene in Kurfürstenstrasse. I spent forty marks on two quarters of H. I'd never had so much H at a time. For six marks I bought cigarettes. By now I smoked like a chimney, always lighting one after the other. I easily managed to smoke a packet in two or three hours. Now I had four marks left for the Sound.

In the Sound I straightaway met Detlef. He gave me a very loving kiss and wished me a happy birthday. I wished him a happy birthday, too, because his was two days before mine. Detlef was a bit sad and told me that this time his parents hadn't wished him many happy returns. Only his granny. He really was much worse off than me. I tried to console him with a 'Don't let it get you down, old man,' and besides I had a really fantastic present for him, I stood him a fix. I had so much stuff that both of us could stay cooked up till past Sunday.

After this joint birthday party, with a fantastic snort for me and a proper fix for Detlef, we went together officially. Up till

88

then Detlef had occasionally been messing about here and there, while I'd been with Babsi and Stella. Now we were together almost all the time whenever I managed to get away. Detlef had just chucked in his apprenticeship as a pipe fitter and consequently had all the time in the world. When we had enough money we were both on H.

The summer holidays were here.

On the first day of the holidays, Detlef, myself and a few people of our crowd went to Wannsee open-air swimming pool. Once again we were skint. I quickly learnt how at this open-air pool one could come by certain assets which might be converted into ready cash. We hung around at the back near the woods where the old grannies lie. On account of the shade because they can no longer stand the sun.

We started in a modest way, just enough to get what we needed for the day. We sidled up to a rug with a cold box next to it whose owner had no doubt gone for a swim. I said quite loudly: 'Oh, what a shame, granny's not here.' Then I went to the cold box and took out a few cans of coke. On the next occasion I nicked a towel and a rug. That evening I had a portable radio and a few bits and pieces, and Detlef had a watch.

In the Sound I got rid of the portable at once for fifty marks. It was really a fantastic day. When I had the money I immediately said to Detlef: 'Here, listen, this snorting business, I'm bored with it. Today I'm going to fix.'

Detlef kept protesting one way or another. But that was bullshit. In principle, it was the same thing whether one snorted or fixed. Only, as long as one snorted one wasn't looked on as a genuine fixer, but still someone who played around.

We went to the scene round the corner in Kurfürstenstrasse. By now our regular dealer recognised us from afar. He started walking the minute he saw us and waited a few street corners away when the coast was clear. I scored two quarters from him for forty marks. So now, at last, I wanted my first fix. With snorting the effect comes slowly. With a fix it's like a hammer. At some time the others had compared it to a sexual climax. I wanted it, without reflecting for a minute that it was the next step to a total fuck-up.

We went to the public toilets at the Bülowbogen. Ever such a seedy district. Tramps were hanging round outside the toilets. It was a place where alkies went to sleep at night. We gave them a box of cigarettes. For that they keep a lookout. They knew the whole procedure and were dead keen on the fags.

Tina, a chick from the Sound, had come with us. Detlef took the syringe, a spoon and a lemon from out of his plastic bag. He put the stuff on the spoon, added a few drops of water and some lemon juice for the H, which was never quite pure, to dissolve more easily. He heated it with his lighter and drew it up into the syringe. This old cleanworks was completely gunged up, the point as blunt as a knitting needle. Detlef fixed first, then Tina. By then the needle was totally clogged. Nothing whatever went through. At least that was what those two maintained. But perhaps they just didn't want me to fix. However, now I was crazy to do it more than ever.

There was another fixer in this toilet who'd just finished fixing. A completely fucked-up guy, totally wrecked. I asked him if he could lend me his syringe. He said okay. But now I had the jitters about jamming the needle into the vein in the bend of my arm. I started, but simply couldn't manage it, although I'd watched others time and time again. Detlef and Tina pretended that the whole thing didn't concern them at all. So I had to ask this fucked-up guy to pick me up. Of course he knew at once that I was doing it for the first time. I felt rather daft, face to face with this old fixer.

He said he thought it was a fucking shame, but then he took the syringe from me. Since my veins can hardly be seen, he had difficulties hitting one. Three times he had to jam in the needle before he drew up a little blood, which told him he'd got a vein. He kept muttering that he thought it a fucking shame, and then he shot up the whole quarter.

It really did come like a hammer. But I must say I had

imagined a real sexual climax to be rather different. Immediately afterwards I was quite apathetic. I scarcely noticed anything and no longer thought anything. I went to the Sound and squatted in a corner drinking cherry juice.

Now I really was on a level with Detlef. We were together like a real married couple. Except that we didn't go to bed together or have any sexual contact whatever. I still felt I wasn't old enough for that, and Detlef accepted it without my having to do a great deal of explaining. I thought that was fantastic of him. He really was simply a great guy.

I was certain that one day I should sleep with him. And I was glad that I'd never had anything to do with any other boy. For me there was no doubt that we would stay together. When we had been at the Sound, Detlef walked me home. It was a two-hour walk. As a rule he would then hitch from Kreuzberg to Lankwitz where he lived with his father.

We talked a lot of unrealistic nonsense. I no longer had any contact with reality. What was real was unreal to me. I was interested neither in yesterday nor in tomorrow. I had no plans, only dreams. What I liked best to talk to Detlef about was what it would be like if we had a lot of money. We were going to buy a large house and a large car and the most terrific furniture. Only one thing was missing in these ravings: heroin.

Detlef came up with a real idea of how we might grow rich. He told me he could get a hundred marks' worth of H on tick from a dealer. This he wanted to bag into ten papers of twenty marks each so that we should have made a hundred marks from the sale. With this money we could buy fresh supplies and double our capital every time. I thought this was a really great idea. That's how simple we thought dealing was in those days.

Detlef did in fact get a hundred marks on tick. It seemed that a few small dealers on the scene had been rumbled, and they were looking for new street sellers. We didn't dare go straight to the scene with our stuff. We sold it in the Sound. Detlef, the silly tit, kept running into people doing cold turkey who didn't have a bean. So like a fool he gave them stuff on tick. Of course they never paid him. One half of the H went this way, the other half we fixed ourselves. When it was all gone, we didn't have a penny to show for it.

The guy from whom Detlef had got the stuff on tick wasn't half pissed off. But he didn't do anything about it. Probably he had only wanted to test whether Detlef was any use as a small dealer. And he had proved adequately that he had absolutely no knack whatever for dealing.

During the first three weeks of the summer holidays I spent every day with Detlef. We met at lunch-time. And usually we spent our time trying to get some cash. I did things I should never had managed to do in the old days. I nicked things from department stores like a magpie. Especially things you could convert first into cash in the Sound and then into stuff. There was rarely enough for two fixes a day. But at that time we didn't yet need that much. We could still manage to go without H for days because we weren't yet physically hooked. For the second half of the holidays I was to visit my gran in Hesse. My gran lived in a little village. And, funny thing, I was terribly looking forward to the village and my gran. On the one hand, I simply couldn't imagine three weeks without Detlef. To exist even for a few days without the Sound and the bright lights of the Kudamm was scarcely feasible. On the other hand, I was looking forward to the village children who had never heard about drugs, to paper chases, to splashing about in the stream, and to riding. I no longer knew myself who I was.

Without thinking a great deal about it, I had already split into two totally different people. I wrote letters to myself. That is to say, Christiane wrote letters to Vera. Vera is my second Christian name. Christiane was the thirteen-year-old who wanted to visit her gran, she was the good girl; Vera was the fixer. And so the two now argued with each other in letters.

From the moment my mother put me on the train I was only Christiane. And when later I sat in my gran's kitchen it was as if I had never been in Berlin. I felt really at home from the minute I arrived. My gran, simply from the way she sat

92

there all relaxed, gave me a feeling of being at home. I was terribly fond of my gran. And I was fond of her kitchen. It was like something out of a picture book. A real old-fashioned farmhouse kitchen. With an open fireplace and huge pots and pans, with something always simmering away on the stove. Really comforting. I immediately got on once again with my cousins and the others in the village who were of my age. They were all still real children. Like me. For the first time since I don't know how long I felt like a child again. I chucked my high-heeled boots into a corner. Depending on the weather, I borrowed sandals or welling-tons from the others. Never touched my make-up. There wasn't anybody here I had to prove things to.

I did a lot of riding. We went on paper chases on horse-back or on foot. Our favourite playground was still down by the stream. We were all older now, and the dams we built were huge. Behind them proper artificial lakes were created. And in the evening when we made a breach into the dam, a wave at least three metres high shot down the stream.

Of course, the others wanted to know what it was like in Berlin, what I did there. But I didn't tell them much. I didn't want to think about Berlin at all. It was crazy, but I didn't even think of Detlef any more. Actually, I'd intended writing to Detlef every day. I didn't write to him once. Sometimes, at night, I tried to think of him. But I could hardly imagine any longer what he looked like. Somehow he was a guy from another world, a world whose signals I no longer understood.

At night in bed, however, I kept getting the horrors more and more often. I saw the guys from the Sound like ghosts in front of me and I thought that soon I would have to return to Berlin. Then I thought about asking my gran whether she would let me stay with her. But how could I have justified this, to my mother, too? I would have had to tell them all about my experience with drugs. And that was something I simply couldn't bring myself to do. Besides, I thought my gran would drop dead if I were to tell her that her little grand-daughter was injecting herself with heroin.

So I was forced to return to Berlin. The noise, the lights, the whole hullaballoo, everything I had loved about Berlin, now got on my wick. At night I could hardly sleep with all the noise. And on the Kurfürstendamm, between cars and crowds of people, I got the horrors good and proper.

I didn't even try to get used to living back in Berlin again. For a week after I got back we went away with my form at school. Although my grandmother had given me fifty marks, it didn't for a moment occur to me to score with it. Nor did I go looking for Detlef. I'd heard he wasn't going to the Sound any longer. I stayed totally off H until I went to the Black Forest with my form.

I had been looking forward to the trip, but after a few days I felt awful. After every meal I had tummy ache, and when we went on walking tours I could barely manage to keep up. In the coach, on our way to the Suchard chocolate factory in Lörrach Kessi who was sitting next to me said suddenly: 'Man, you're looking completely yellow. Jaundice.' She actually moved away from me.

I thought, well, stone the crows. Sooner or later, all fixers get jaundice through the filthy old hypodermic needles they use, which, on top of it, they lend to others. It was the first time for ages that I thought of H again. And immediately I remembered the filthy syringe which the fucked-up guy in the toilet at Bülowbogen had used to shoot my first quarter for me. Then I noticed that Kessi hadn't really been serious when she said that about jaundice. And I thought it couldn't have possibly happened after the few shots I'd had, and anyway that was weeks ago.

From a stall outside the Suchard factory I got a plastic spoon. Then into chocolate dreamland we went. I dipped my plastic spoon into every vat containing anything reasonably appetising-looking. If it was especially nice, I distracted the guide's attention with questions and had another few spoonfuls. Also, at the end I had swiped so many sweets that they were overflowing from my jacket which I had knotted into a bag.

Back in the coach I swore that I would never touch another piece of chocolate again. When we got back to our quarters I collapsed. My liver capitulated before the fatty cocoa gunge I had spooned up by the pound.

Now even our teacher noticed that I was looking rather yellow. A doctor came, and then I was taken by ambulance to university hospital in Freiburg. The isolation room in the children's ward was small and spotlessly white. No picture on the wall, nothing. Nurses came with food and pills, not saying much. At times the doctor came and enquired how I was. This went on for three weeks. I was not allowed to leave the room, not even to pee. No one visited me, no one talked to me. I had nothing decent to read and no radio. I often thought I would go bananas.

My mother's affectionate letters were the only thing which kept me sane. I wrote to her, too. But most often I wrote to my two cats, the only animals I still had. They were minute letters in tiny envelopes which I folded myself.

Sometimes I thought of my gran and the village children and the stream and the horses, and sometimes of Berlin and the Sound, of Detlef and H. I didn't know who I was. When I felt really pissed off, I thought: 'You're a fixer with her first bout of jaundice. And that's it.' When, in my imagination, I was with my cats I thought that I would make an effort at school and spend all my holidays with my gran. This went up and down, up and down. For many hours I thought nothing at all. I just lay there staring at the ceiling and wishing I was dead. And besides I was afraid the doctors might discover the cause of my jaundice. But the punctures had healed during the last few weeks. I hadn't got scars and thromboses on my arm. Who would have suspected a fixer in the children's ward in Freiburg?

After three weeks I had to learn to walk again. Then they let me fly to Berlin. It was all paid for by health insurance. At home I had to get back into bed again immediately. I was happy to be with my mother and my cats. I thought of nothing else.

My mother reported that Detlef had visited her a few

times to ask after me. He seemed to be really sad because I stayed away for so long, my mother said. Only now did I remember Detlef properly. I saw him before me, his beautiful curly hair, his face that was so terribly sweet. It made me really happy that someone had worried about me, that I was really loved by someone. By Detlef. And I had a really bad conscience that for a few weeks I had almost forgotten my love for him.

After a few days, Detlef had heard somehow that I was back and visited me. When he stood by my bed I had a real shock. I couldn't manage to say a word.

Detlef had grown so thin he was all skin and bones. His arms were so thin that I could easily span them with my hand. His face was all white and sunken. But it was still as handsome as before. His terribly kind eyes had somehow grown larger, but also sadder. I immediately loved Detlef again terribly. I did not in the least mind that he was all skin and bones. And I didn't want to think about why he had deteriorated so much physically.

At first we found it hard to talk. He only wanted to hear about me. But I had nothing to report that would have interested him. It wouldn't have occurred to me to talk to him about my holidays or our games at my gran's. At last I asked him why he didn't go to the Sound any more. He said the Sound was a lot of shit. I wanted to know where he was all the time and eventually he said: 'At Zoo station.' What was he doing there? 'Going on the game,' said Detlef.

Momentarily this did not shock me at all. I knew from other fixers that occasionally they went on the game. I had no clear ideas as to what this being on the game meant. Nor did I want to think about it. I only knew that in some way they sexually gratified queers without feeling anything themselves, and that they got a lot of money for it. This day all that mattered to me was that Detlef had come and that he still really loved me and I him.

Next Sunday I was allowed to go out for the first time. Detlef called for me in the afternoon. We went to a café in Lietzen-burgerstrasse. Most of the people there were queers and most of them knew Detlef. They were all very nice to me and paid me compliments. They congratulated Detlef on his pretty girlfriend. And I noticed that Detlef was really proud that I was his girlfriend, and that it was for this reason that he had dragged me to this café where everybody knew him.

In a way I liked the queers. They were nice to me and paid me compliments without chatting me up like other men. I went to the loo and looked in the mirror. I found they were quite right. I looked really good, now that I hadn't touched any drugs for more than two months. I found I'd never looked so good before.

Detlef said he must go to Zoo station because he'd arranged to meet his best friend, Bernd. He said today Bernd had gone on the game for the two of them. It was because of me that Detlef hadn't had time to go to the station. Of course I went with him. Besides I looked forward to seeing Bernd again.

Bernd had just left with a customer. We had to wait. This evening the station didn't seem as seedy to me as I remembered it. Most of the time I looked at Detlef. Once when Detlef was briefly talking to another boy and I was standing by myself for a moment, some wogs came and started chatting me up. I only caught something like 'sixty marks'. I took Detlef's arm and felt terribly safe. I persuaded Detlef to come to the Sound with me. And also to give me a little of his fix for a snort. Of course, at first he didn't want to. But I said to him: 'Only tonight. Only as a welcome. I'd like to be on it with you. Or you won't have a fix yourself.' Then he gave me some. He said he would never give me any again. I said there was no need for it. After all, hadn't I proved over two and a half months that I was not dependent on H. And during the last few weeks I'd really noticed that I felt much better without H.

Detlef was impressed. He said: 'Listen, sweetie, I'll pack it in, too. If you can do it, it'll be a piece of cake for me.' He had his fix; I snorted. We were terribly happy and talked about how happy we would be without H.

Next lunchtime I went to Zoo station and met Detlef. He gave me another snort. I met Detlef at the station almost every afternoon after school. I had my first fix again. It was as if I had never been away from Berlin, as if for me the two and a half months without H hadn't existed. We talked almost every day about packing it in and I told Detlef how easy it was.

Often I went to Zoo station straight from school. In my bag I had a hypodermic syringe and a large packet of sandwiches. My mother ought to have been puzzled as to why I was getting thinner and thinner when I took so many sandwiches to school. I knew Detlef and his friends were waiting for the lunch I was taking them.

To begin with Detlef was furious when I came to the station. He didn't want me to be there when he went on the game. He told me: 'I don't want my girlfriend to be at the Zoo where all this disgusting riffraff hangs about. I'll meet you anywhere, but don't come to the station again.'

I scarcely listened. I simply wanted to be with Detlef, no matter where. I had gradually come to feel quite at home in the filthy station hall, at least everything was familiar. I no longer noticed the stink of piss and disinfectant. The bumboys, the scrubbers, the wogs, bums, cops, winos, the whole puke, that was my natural environment between lunch and supper. That's where I belonged, because Detlef was there.

At first it got on my wick the way other girls stared at me — up and down. Somehow even more aggressive than the customers. Then I sensed that the girls, who went on the game at the station, were scared of me. Scared that being, as it were, farm-fresh merchandise, I would pinch their best customers. Well, yes, I was better-looking than they, well-groomed. I washed my hair almost every day. As yet no one could tell I was a fixer. I knew I was superior to the other girls. It made me feel good. As far as customers were concerned, I would have had it made. But then there was no need for me to go on the game. Detlef did it for me. As the others watched me, they were bound to think, what a together woman, she's got stuff without going on the game.

At the beginning the customers wound me up. Above all, those wogs with their everlasting: 'You fuck? . . . You go hotel?' Twenty marks some of them offered. After a little while it really amused me to take the mickey. I said: 'Hey, sunshine, you've got to be joking. Nothing under five hundred for the likes of you.' Or I just looked at one, cool like, and said: 'I don't pop my cork for just any guy, old man. Piss off.'

It made me feel good to see these randy pigs sneak away with their tails between their legs. I was superior even to the customers. If one of them tried to touch me up, Detlef was there immediately. When Detlef went off with a customer, he told his friends who were hustling at the station to keep an eye on me. They were like brothers to me. They told anyone trying to be funny to get lost.

Instead of going to the Sound now I went to the station terraces. I no longer had any friends other than our little Zoo crowd. Apart from Detlef and me, that included Bernd and Axel. Both of them were sixteen, both bangsters on H, both hustling. All three lived in Axel's flat.

In contrast to the other two, Axel was terribly ugly. Nothing in his face matched. His arms and legs somehow weren't part of his body. So he was the very last guy to turn a queer on. But he had his customers, some of them even regulars. Detlef could afford to scream at his customers and insult them whenever they pissed him off. They came whining back. Axel, looking like the rear end of a bus, had to pull himself together and pretend to be full of the joys of spring. Besides, he must have been kinky in bed, some special thing that queers thought really great. Otherwise he couldn't have kept up with the competition on the station.

However, he revenged himself on his customers whenever he could. If he found a sucker, he cheated him, ripped him off, did him. Axel was a great guy. He allowed himself to be insulted and humiliated. He never let on. He remained friendly at all times. He was incredibly helpful, a quality which I never found again among fixers. Altogether there wasn't another fixer like him. It was as if he didn't any longer live in this lousy world. A year later he was dead.

Axel's story was similar to ours. His parents were divorced. He had lived with his mother until she moved in with a boyfriend. At least his mother was generous. She left him a two room flat with some sticks of furniture, and she even provided him with a TV. Once a week she visited him and gave him a little money to live on. She knew that he fixed. And I think she told him several times that he ought to pack it in. She considered she had done more for him than other parents. Hadn't she given him a flat, complete with TV? I spent a week-end in Axel's flat. With my mother's permission. Once again I had told her something about staying with a friend.

Axel's flat was really the end. A real fixer's flat. The stench hit me from the door. Empty fish tins were standing around, fag ends floating in oil, tomato and mustard sauce, beakers and cups everywhere, all containing a little water, cigarette ash, tobacco, cigarette papers. When I tried to push a couple of yoghurts on to the one and only table, two fish tins on the other side of the table crashed to the floor, the sauce soaked into the carpet. Nobody took any notice.

As it was, a quite revolting stench rose from the carpet. When Axel shot up, I saw why it stank so. He drew the syringe with its residue of blood out of his arm, filled it with water and then squirted the pink juice straight into the carpet. That's how he always cleaned his works. With every shot another few drops of blood trickled into the threadbare Persian patterns. And it was that which caused this sweetish-musty smell, together with the fish sauces. Even the curtains were yellow and smelly.

In this whole stinking grotshop there was a dazzlingly white bed. I sought refuge in it at once. As I buried my face in the pillows there was a smell of Lux or Persil. I thought, you've never lain on so clean a bed.

Axel said: 'I've put on clean bedclothes for you.' During the next few weeks, every Saturday when I arrived, the bed had fresh bed linen on it. I never slept more than once in the same bedclothes, while the others, I felt sure, never changed their sheets at all.

The boys bought me food and drink, always whatever I liked best at the time. They simply wanted to give me a treat. Above all, they always bought fine stuff for me. I still had trouble with my liver. If I shot cut stuff I felt terrible. So they always bought the finest H for me, even if it was expensive. The three were always there for me. Somehow I was the only thing they had. And I had, first Detlef, then Axel and Bernd, and no one else.

I came to have a real feeling of happiness. As I had rarely experienced it before. I felt secure. In the afternoon on Zoo station and at the week-end in the stinking fixerpad.

Detlef was the strongest and I the weakest in the group. I felt inferior to the boys, physically, in character, and most of all because I was a girl. But for the first time I actually enjoyed being weak. I enjoyed the way Detlef, Axel or Bernd were always there whenever I needed somebody.

I had a boy who did what no other fixer did: who shared every bag of H with me. Who earned cash for me by doing the most disgusting job there was. He had to service one or two extra customers a day so that I should have stuff. With us everything was different. It was the boyfriend who went hustling for his girl. Perhaps we were the only couple in the world who did things this way round.

The thought of going on the game myself would not have seriously occurred to me during these weeks in the late autumn of 1976. That is to say, I did think about it for a few seconds. When my conscience pricked me about Detlef who was with some grotty fellow. But it was clear to me that Detlef would have clouted me for the first time, if I had so much as hinted that I wanted to go out on the game.

I still had no precise idea as to what exactly took place on these occasions. At least I did not think about it, nor did I want to imagine it. Detlef did not talk about it. From the conversations of the three boys I gathered that they brought the queers off, and, at most, sucked them off.

I believe that this had nothing to do with Detlef and me.

101

At least I felt no revulsion for what Detlef had to do. If he touched the customers, it wasn't so bad. That was his filthy job, without which we wouldn't have got any stuff.

What I did not want was for these fellows to touch Detlef. For he belonged only to me.

To begin with I thought some of the customers quite okay. Sometimes the boys said this one or that one was all right, one ought to keep him sweet, and I accepted this. Some of them were really nice when they met me with Detlef in the station. They really liked me. It's just one of those things that some queers were gone on me. Sometimes one of the boys would give me twenty marks and say they were from this or that customer because he liked me. Detlef never let on to me that some of these guys were always at him with the suggestion to do it to them together with me.

I watched the other girls on the station, almost every one of them still half a child, like me. And I saw that they were in a bad way. Especially the ones who were on H and simply had to go on the game. I saw their revulsion when a customer chatted them up, although they must give him a nice smile. I despised the customers. What sort of idiots or perverted pigs were they who skulked across the station hall, randy and mean, looking out of the corner of their eye for fresh baby flesh? What fun was there in it for them to go off with some absolutely strange girl who was disgusted by them and whose misery was clear to see?

Gradually, I too came to hate the queers. I began to realise what Detlef had to put up with from them. Often it took him every last ounce of willpower to go to work: nauseated and feeling like throwing up. When he hadn't fixed he couldn't do it anyway. When he was doing cold turkey, in other words, precisely when he needed the money most urgently, he ran away from the customers. Then Axel or Bernd did a customer for him. Using every last ounce of their willpower: nauseated and feeling like throwing up. These two could only do it if they'd had a shot beforehand. The way these queers ran after Detlef really got up my nose.

While I was actually standing next to him, they stammered funny confessions of love and slipped him love letters. All the guys who chatted Detlef up were pitifully lonely. But I couldn't feel sorry for them. I would have liked to shout at them: 'Here, you bastard, don't you understand, Detlef belongs to me and to nobody else, and certainly not to a bloody queer!' But it was these very guys we needed, because they supplied the cash, because you could fleece them like sheep.

I noticed that there were men on the station who knew Detlef quite intimately, far more intimately than I. It made me really sick. And when from a conversation of the three boys I detected that some customers would only pay after the bumboy had had an orgasm too, I nearly did my nut.

I saw less and less of Detlef, for he was constantly busy with some queer pig. I was afraid for him. Someone had told me that in time bumboys may become queers themselves. But I could not reproach Detlef. We needed more and more money. And half of it went on my stuff. Since I was in their crowd, I wanted — unconsciously, perhaps — to become a real fixer like them. I fixed every day. And I saw to it that I always kept enough for my fix next morning.

And still we were not yet physically on the stuff. When you start to fix it does take quite a long time before you become physically dependent on heroin unless you shoot every day. We still managed occasionally to last for one or two days without a shot, turning ourselves on a little with something else, and it hadn't yet come to be hell. Then we made ourselves believe that we were different from those fucked fixers, that we could break at any time if we wanted.

Frequently I was still quite happy. Every Saturday in Axel's flat I was happy. Detlef joined me in the freshly made-up bed. He gave me a good-night kiss on the mouth and then we turned round. We slept back to back, my behind snuggling up to his. When I woke up, Detlef gave me a good-morning kiss.

In the six months we went together these were the only physical caresses we exchanged. When I first met Detlef I'd

103

already had experience of the brutality of boys. And I'd told him at once: 'Listen, I'm a virgin. And I'd like to take my time. I'd like to wait until I'm a little older.'

He had understood at once and never tried it on. For him I was not only a girlfriend who he could rap and be in perfect harmony with, but also, I'm sure, being all of fourteen, still a child. He was simply incredibly sensitive. He sensed what I wanted, what I could and could not do. Some time in October I had asked my mother to let me go on the pill. She'd arranged for me to get it prescribed because she had discovered that I slept in Detlef's flat. And she didn't believe that there was nothing between us any way. She was very suspicious for once.

So I took the pill, but didn't tell Detlef. I was still afraid. One Saturday towards the end of October when I arrived at the flat Axel had made up his own bed. It was wider than the one which we had shared up till now. Axel thought it was stupid that he should be wallowing in the big bed while the two of us bunked, squeezed together uncomfortably. He invited us to take his bed.

There was a very good atmosphere in the flat. And suddenly Detlef said why don't we clean the place up. The rest of us were all for it. For a kick-off, I tore open every window in the flat. As a breath of fresh air came in, I realised once again the sort of stink we were living in. Any normal person would have been whisked straight out of the front door by this evil stink of clotted blood, ash and mouldy fish tins.

Two hours later there was total and utter chaos in the flat. We swept up entire rubbish-tipfuls and put them in plastic bags. In the end I even switched on the Hoover. And then I cleaned the birdcage, inside which a sleepy budgie was surveying the chaos all round him. Axel's mother had left it behind in the flat. Her boyfriend didn't like birds. Axel hated the budgie, too. When in its loneliness the poor thing began twittering and chatting, Axel banged his fist against the cage and made the wretched bird flap about like mad. None of the boys looked after the bird. But once a week Axel's

104

mother dropped in with food for it. Every Saturday I gave it enough for the whole week. I'd also bought it a little glass tube which always contained enough clean water for six days.

This night when we went to bed everything was different. Detlef didn't give me a good-night kiss and didn't turn round either. He began to talk. Very loving things. I felt his hands. They were very affectionate. I wasn't a bit afraid. I fondled Detlef too. For a long time we fondled one another without saying anything. It was terribly beautiful.

I think an hour must have passed before Detlef spoke again. He asked: 'Would you like to sleep with me next Saturday?'

I said: 'Okay.' I'd always been afraid of this question. Now, when Detlef asked, it made me happy.

After a while I said: 'Okay. On one condition. Next Saturday we'll both be sober. Not a bit of H. I mean, otherwise I mightn't like it. Or I might like it terribly only because I'm high, and then, when I'm sober I shan't like it at all. I really would like to be quite sober. And I'd also like you to know what it's like with me when you're sober.' Detlef said: 'Okay.' He gave me my good-night kiss. We turned round and went to sleep, backside to backside.

Next Saturday we did stay sober. The flat was filthy and smelly again. But our bed was freshly made up and white as usual. As we got undressed I was a little scared, after all. At first we lay quite still side by side. I had to think of girls in my form who had told me how the boys had got on top of them for the first time. How they'd thrust their thing inside full force and not stopped until they'd got their gratification. The girls had said that it hurt like hell the first time. Some of them didn't go again with the boyfriend who'd deflowered them.

I told Detlef that I wanted to experience it differently from the girls in my form. He said: 'Okay, sweetie.'

We caressed each other for a long time. He went into me a little and I hardly noticed it. When it hurt Detlef felt it without my saying anything. I thought: he has a right to hurt you a little. After all, he's waited for six months.

But Detlef didn't want to hurt me. At some stage we were completely together. At that moment I loved him terribly. But somehow I lay quite stiff and motionless. Detlef didn't move either. He must have sensed what at that moment I could not think myself. That I was totally shattered with fear and happiness.

Detlef withdrew and put his arms round me. Everything was one crazy feeling. I thought, why do you of all people deserve a boy like him? Who thinks only of you and never of himself. Who, the first time he sleeps with you, doesn't want to get to his climax because this first time he's doing everything only for you. I thought of Kathi, how in the cinema he had simply put his hand between my legs. I was glad that I'd waited for Detlef. That I really belonged to Detlef. I loved this boy so terribly that suddenly I was afraid. Afraid of death. I kept thinking the same thing: 'I don't want Detlef to die.'

I said, while he was caressing me: 'Listen, Detlef, we'll stop fixing.'

He said: 'Yes, you must never become a fixer.' He kissed me. Then we turned round slowly. Backsides pressed together, we went to sleep.

I woke up because I felt Detlef's hands. It was still fairly early. But grey light was already coming through the curtains. We caressed each other, and then we slept together properly. All my feeling was in my head and not yet down below. But I knew now that it was fantastically beautiful to sleep with Detlef.

On Monday I went to Zoo station straight from school. Detlef was there. I gave him my sandwiches and an apple. He was hungry. I had a terrible craving for H, having not had any for three days. I asked Detlef: 'Have you got a shot for me?'

He said: 'Nope. And you won't get any more from me. Leave it alone. I'm too fond of you. I don't want you to become a fixer.'

I nearly blew my top. I had this craving and I shouted: 'You sod — that's great coming from you. Your pupils are

106

like pin-points. You're completely bombed out. And you've got the nerve to get at me about leaving it alone. Why don't you kick the habit and then I'll kick it myself. Meanwhile don't talk so far back. Why don't you come out with it and confess you want to shoot it all yourself.'

I really shattered him. He couldn't say anything, for, of course, he'd scored immediately on Sunday night. In the end he gave in and said: 'Okay, sweetie, we'll kick together.' He did his next customer to pay for my shot.

The fact that we had slept together changed many things for us. I no longer felt very comfortable on the station. Now I suddenly had a more precise idea of what was involved in going on the game. Only now did I really know what these fellows were after who kept chatting me up. Exactly what Detlef and I were doing. Fucking. Of course I'd known before what happened, but it had been something quite abstract for me. Now it was the most beautiful and intimate thing between Detlef and me. The customers disgusted me. What went on at this station made my mind boggle: fancy having to go to bed with one of these repulsive, stinking wogs, having to fuck a drunk or a potbellied, sweaty bald-head. It was no longer fun when customers tried to chat me up. I simply couldn't think of a snappy answer any longer. I turned away, disgusted, and sometimes I actually kicked them on the shins. Now I also felt a new hatred for the queers. I could have murdered the poor sods. Again and again I had to struggle against the idea that Detlef had to act affectionately towards them.

Still, every lunchtime I went to the station from school because Detlef was there. When he had finished with a customer we went to the station café and I had a cup of cocoa. Sometimes business at the station was slack. There were days when even Detlef had a job making enough cash for stuff for the two of us.

It was in the station café that through Detlef I gradually met all the other bumboys, from whom, at first, he had tried to keep me away. They were a great deal more fucked than us and had a harder time than the boys in our crowd to get customers. They were old fixers — the sort I used to admire in the old days.

Detlef said that they were all his friends. And then he said I must be careful, for they were, after all, old fixers, and your old fixer was a thoroughly nasty piece of work. They were always wanting a fix and never had any cash. You must never show or reveal to these friends that you had cash or stuff. Otherwise you risked a knuckle sandwich. They ripped off not only customers but each other as well.

I began to get an inkling of what it was really like, this fixer scene that had so attracted me. Now I was almost in it myself.

Sometimes friends of Detlef would say to me: 'Pack it in, girl. You're too young. You can still do it. You'll have to get away from Detlef, though. He'll never kick now. Stop messing about, give up Detlef.'

I put up two fingers to them. Parting from Detlef, that was the last thing. If he wanted to die, so did I. But that wasn't what I said. I said: 'Dont talk out of the back of your neck. Neither of us is on H. We can kick whenever we fancy.'

The days of November 1976 were very much alike. From two to eight I was on the station. Then we went to the Hothouse, a discotheque at the top end of the Kurfürsten-damm. The Hothouse was the scene Detlef was into in those days. It was even more fucked-up than the scene in the Sound. I would often stay there until the last bus at twenty past midnight. Basically I lived for the Saturdays when I slept at Detlef's. Sleeping with him became more beautiful each Saturday as long as we hadn't shot too much stuff.

December came. It grew chillier all the time. And I was cold. In the old days I never used to feel cold. Now I was always cold. I realised that physically I was in a bad way. I knew it ever since one Sunday early in December. I woke up in Axel's flat, lying next to Detlef. I felt bloody cold. I looked at some box. All at once the writing on the box came leaping out at me. It was the colours which were terribly bright and hurt my eyes. Above all, there was a certain red which scared me. On my trips I had always been afraid of red. On H, red was a very gentle colour. Like all colours on H, red became beautiful through a soft veil.

And now there it was once again, that aggressive red on this damned box. My mouth was full of spittle. I swallowed it but it was back again immediately. Somehow it seemed to come back up. Then the spittle had gone, after all, and my mouth was dry and sticky. I tried to drink something. But I couldn't. I was shaking with cold until I got so hot that sweat was pouring down me. I woke up Detlef and said: 'Listen, something's the matter with me.'

Detlef peered into my face and said. 'You've got pupils like saucers.'

There was a long pause and he whispered: 'Well, girl, this is it.'

I trembled again and said: 'What? What's the matter?'

Detlef said : 'Cold turkey.'

I thought: Aha, so this is what cold turkey is like. You're really doing cold turkey, you old fixer. Not so bad, is it, this cold turkey. Don't know why the others always make such a fucking fuss about it. In fact I felt no real pain. I trembled, and the colours and the spittle in my mouth were driving me slightly bananas.

Detlef didn't say anything. Out of his jeans pocket he fished a bag and some ascorbic acid. Then he fetched me a spoon, cooked up the stuff over a candle and handed me the works all ready. I shook so much I had a job hitting the vein. But then it worked quite quickly. I felt well again. The colours were gentle and the spittle had gone. For the moment there were no problems and I fell asleep next to Detlef who had shot at the same time. At lunch-time when we got up I asked Detlef how much stuff he still had.

He said: 'Of course you'll get another shot before you leave tonight.'

I said: 'But I'll need some for tomorrow morning.'

Detlef: 'I haven't got that much left. And I really don't fancy the station today. It's Sunday and there's fuck-all on the station, anyway.'

I was in a panic and hopping mad. 'Don't you understand, man. If I can't have a fix tomorrow morning, I'll be doing cold turkey and then I can't go to school.'

Detlef: 'I told you, girl. Now you're in the soup.'

In the afternoon we went to the station. I had plenty of time to think. My first cold turkey. Now I was dependent on H and on Detlef. It was being dependent on Detlef that bugged me more. What kind of love was that when one was totally dependent? What would happen if at night Detlef made me beg and implore him for stuff? I knew how fixers begged when they were doing cold turkey. How they humiliated themselves and allowed themselves to be humiliated. And how they collapsed into nothingness. I could not beg. And certainly not Detlef. If he made me beg and grovel, everything was over between us. I had never yet been able to beg anyone for anything.

In the end Detlef found a customer and I waited for what seemed to be ages for him to come back. Now I would always have to wait until Detlef gave me the stuff for the morning.

This afternoon I felt really gloomy. I talked to myself in a low voice: I said: 'Now, Christiane, now you've got what you were always so keen on. Did you think it would be like this. Not on your life. But you wanted it, didn't you? You always admired them, didn't you, those old fixers. Now you're one yourself. Now nobody'll pull a fast one on you. Now you needn't look incredulous when others talk about cold turkey. Now nobody'll rip you off. Now you're the one to do the ripping off.'

I didn't really succeed in comforting myself. I had to keep thinking about cold turkey. I remembered how I had shattered fixers who were doing cold turkey. I'd never really bothered to find out what was the matter with them. I only noticed that they were terribly sensitive, easily hurt and without any strength.

A fixer doing cold turkey will hardly dare contradict, he's such a weakling. Sometimes I used them to give vent to my hunger for power. If you went about it the right way, you could really hammer them into the ground, give them the treatment. All you needed to do was to pounce on their real weaknesses, to keep on probing their wounds, then they collapsed. After all, it was while they were doing cold turkey that it dawned on them what miserable sods they were. The whole superior fixer stance was gone just like that, they no longer felt superior to anybody.

I told myself: now it's your turn. Now they'll hammer you into the ground when you're doing cold turkey. They'll find out the grotty sort of bag you really are, never you fear. But you really knew all that beforehand, didn't you? Funny, isn't it, that it only strikes you today.

These conversations with myself did absolutely nothing for me. I should have talked to someone else. I could simply have gone to one of the fixers on the station. Instead I went and hid myself in a corner by the station post office. Didn't I know only too well what the others would have told me? Hadn't I listened often enough in those days when I was just a bystander: 'Don't work yourself into a lather, old lady. See how it goes. It'll all come out in the wash. If you really want to, you can kick the habit. There's methadone on the market, see.' When it was to do with H, even Detlef began making with the clichés.

I only had my mother I could talk to. But I couldn't do that either. I hadn't the heart to do this to her, I thought: She loves you, and in a way you love her, too. She would do her nut if you were to tell her. And she couldn't help anyway. Perhaps she'll put you in a home. And that would help even less. No one can kick the habit under pressure. And certainly not you. You'll get even more pigheaded, and then you'll clear out from the home and doss around. And that would only make things worse.

Once again I muttered to myself: Put a sock in it, man, can't you? Just stand a bit of cold turkey at the beginning, you'll do it with your hands tied behind your back. When Detlef gets back, you'll say to him: 'I don't want any stuff. I'm through. And either you're packing it in this minute or we'll split up. You've got two halves in your pocket? Okay,

111

old man. We'll shoot one last time and from tomorrow: no more.' I noticed how, while I was talking to myself, I'd worked myself up towards a fix. Then I whispered as if I were telling myself a great, great secret: Detlef won't wear it, anyway. And you'll split up with Detlef? Not bloody likely, Christiane, my girl. Now simmer down and talk sense, do. It's curtains, you know. The end. Really and truly curtains. Didn't get much out of your life. Ah, well, you've got what you wanted.

Detlef returned. In silence we went to Kurfürstenstrasse and located our regular dealer. I got half a half, went home on the tube and hid away in my room.

Two Sundays later Detlef and I were alone in Axel's flat. It was in the afternoon. We both felt foul. On Saturday we'd been unable to find our regular dealer and had been ripped off by another dealer. The stuff we scored was so cut that in the morning we'd had to shoot double the quantity, all we had, in fact, to get a proper fix. Detlef was already beginning to sweat again, and I realised that cold turkey wasn't far off.

We scoured the whole flat for something we might turn into cash. But we knew there was nothing left. From the coffee perculator to the radio everything was gone, all of it on fixing. Only the Hoover was knocking around. However, it was so old that nobody would have given us tuppence for it.

Detlef said. 'Listen, girl, we've got to make some money and we've got to make it fast. In two hours at the most we'll be doing cold turkey and by then we shan't be able to do a thing. On a Sunday night I just can't get enough money by myself. You must give a hand. The best thing will be if you go on the scrounge to the Sound. You've got to scrounge forty marks. If I do a customer for forty or fifty we'll have something left for tomorrow morning. How's that grab you?'

I said: 'Fine. You know I'm good at scrounging.' We arranged to meet again in two hours at the latest. I'd often scrounged in the Sound before. Often just for fun. It had always worked. But this evening there was nothing doing. I was in a hurry, and scrounging takes time. You have to consider carefully who would be an easy touch. You have to attune yourself to them, be ready to have a little chat, and be relaxed. What it amounts to is this: you've got to enjoy scrounging.

To crown it all, I was doing cold turkey and didn't do as well as usual. After half an hour all I had was six marks eighty. I thought, you'll never make it. I thought of Detlef who had to hang around the station, where on a Sunday evening there were only families with children. And on top of it he was doing cold turkey. He'd never do a customer in that state. I got into a panic.

Without a definite plan I walked out into the street. Somehow I still had a hope that scrounging outside the Sound might be easier. A flashy Merc was parked at the entrance. Flashy cars parked there quite often or crawled along the kerb. For nowhere is baby flesh as cheap as outside the Sound. There are girls who haven't the cash to get inside, because their pocket money is gone. They do it for the entrance fee and a few cokes.

The guy in the Merc beckoned me. I recognised him. He was often outside the Sound and had tried to chat me up before. Would I like to earn a hundred? I'd asked him what he wanted for it and he'd said: 'Nothing much.' I'd laughed at him.

I don't quite know what I was thinking at that moment. Probably not a great deal. Perhaps: go on, find out what this guy wants. Perhaps he'll be a good touch. At any rate he was beckoning frantically and suddenly I was standing by the car. He asked me to get inside. He couldn't stop here any longer, he said. And I got inside.

To be perfectly honest I knew exactly what was up. That scrounging wasn't on at all. After all, by now customers were no longer creatures from another planet for me. I knew the routine. From my observations on the station and from the stories the boys told. So I knew that it was not the customer but the tart who laid down the conditions. I tried to be ever so cool. I didn't tremble. The only trouble was I kept

113

gasping for air whenever I spoke and had a job finishing my
sentence in the same cool tone in which I had started. I
asked: 'Well, how about it?'

He said: 'How about what? A hundred marks. Okay?'

I said: 'Now, fucking or anything like that's out.'

He asked: 'Why?' And I was so agitated that I couldn't
think of anything but the truth: 'Now listen. I've got a boyfriend. And he's the only one I've ever slept with. And I
want to keep it that way.'

He said: 'That's fine by me. Well, suck me off, then.'

I said: 'No, I won't. It makes me throw up.' By now I had
regained my cool.

He wasn't in the least put out. He said: 'Okay. Do a hand
job then.'

I said: 'Of course. You're on. For a hundred.' At this
moment I wasn't really aware of anything. Later I realised
that this guy must have really fancied me. A hundred marks
for a hand job, and that on Kurfürstenstrasse where the
cheap b.p.'s* did their hustling. Well, it wasn't really on. It
must have been my fear which turned him on, for I couldn't
really hide it. He knew I wasn't pretending, the way I sat
there squeezed against the door, my right hand on the door
handle.

As he drove off I got really bloody scared. I thought: bet
he wants more, he'll try to get his hundred-marks-worth by
force. Or he won't pay at all. He stopped at a park nearby.
I'd walked through this park before. A real tarts' park.
French letters and tissues everywhere.

Now I was really shaking and I felt a bit sick. But the
guy remained quite calm. And then I plucked up my
courage and said what, according to tarts' rules, I had to say
at this point: 'Money first.' He gave me a hundred-mark
note. I was still scared. I'd heard enough stories about
customers who afterwards force you to give back the
money. However, I knew what I had to do. Of late the boys
in our crowd had talked of almost nothing else but their
experiences with their customers, for they didn't have

*Baby prostitutes.

much else left to say to each other.

I waited for the moment when he was busy undoing his flies. Then I slipped the banknote into my boot. He was ready. And I was still in the furthest corner of the seat trying not to move. I no longer looked at him and slid my left hand forward. My arm wasn't long enough and I was forced to slide a little closer to him. And then I had to dart another quick look before I'd got his thing in my hand.

I felt as sick as hell and I shivered. Looking through the windscreen I tried to concentrate on something else. On the light from the headlamps of cars filtering through the bushes and a neon sign which I could see. It didn't take very long.

Once more the guy took out his wallet. He held it so that I could look inside. I saw five-hundred-mark notes and hundred-mark ones. I suppose he wanted to show off or else put out a bait for the next time. He gave me another twenty. As a tip.

Once I was out of the car I calmed down. I drew up a sort of balance sheet: so that was your second man. You're fourteen. Less than four weeks ago you lost your virginity. And now you're a tart. And then I no longer thought of the guy and what I'd done. I really felt quite happy. On account of the hundred and twenty marks in my boot. I'd never had so much money at a time. I didn't think of Detlef and what he'd say. By now I was doing cold turkey and wanted a fix badly. I only thought of this fix. I was lucky. I found our regular dealer straightaway. When he saw the money he asked: 'Hello, where'd you get that from? Been on the game?' I replied: 'Shut up, you're crazy. Me on the game? I'd rather stop fixing then go on the game. Honest. No, its just my father who happens to have remembered that he's got a daughter and slipped me some pocket money.'

For eighty marks I bought two half halves. These half halves were new on the market. One paper contained about a quarter of a gramme. Three of us used to manage on a quarter. By now Detlef and I only just managed on that.

I went to the toilet in Kurfürstenstrasse and shot up. This was fine stuff. I slipped the remaining H together with the

115

forty marks I had left into the plastic cover of my season ticket.

Hustling and scoring had taken fifteen minutes. I'd only been away for three quarters of an hour. I was certain Detlef would still be standing at the station and took the tube to the zoo. Detlef was there. Looking really miserable. Needless to say, he hadn't got a customer, what with it being Sunday and him doing cold turkey. I said to him: 'Come along, I've got some.'

He didn't ask where from. He said nothing at all. He wanted to get back to the flat quickly. We went straight into the bathroom. I took my season ticket out of my pocket. He opened a paper and emptied the stuff on to a spoon. As he was cooking up he stared at the plastic cover which still contained half a half and two twenty-mark notes. Then he asked: 'Where did you get the money from?'

I said: 'Scrounging was no good. Impossible. There was a guy there with plenty of cash. I brought him off. Honest, I only brought him off. What else could I do? I did it for you.'

Detlef blew his top while I was speaking. His face looked quite awful. He shouted: 'You're lying. No one pays a hundred for bringing them off. You're telling lies. In any case, what do you mean you only brought him off?' He was at the end of his tether. He was doing cold turkey really badly. He was trembling all over, his shirt was wet with sweat, he had cramp in both legs.

He tied off his arm. I sat on the edge of the bath blubbing. I thought Detlef was completely entitled to blow his top. I blubbed and waited for his shot to take effect. I was sure that then he would hit me in the face. I shouldn't have struggled.

Detlef pulled out the spike and said nothing. He walked out of the bathroom and I followed him. At last he said: 'I'll take you to the bus.' I bagged some of the second half and gave it to him. He put it into his jeans without saying anything. We walked to the bus stop. Detlef still wasn't saying anything. I wanted him to shout, to hit me for all I cared, anything, as long as he made a sound. I said: 'Hey, old man, say something.' No response.

When we stood at the stop and the bus came, I didn't get on. When the bus had gone, I said: 'Listen, what I told you was God's truth. Honestly, I only brought him off and it wasn't too bad. You must believe me. Or don't you trust me any more?'

Detlef said: 'Okay, I believe you.'

I said: 'Listen, I really did it only for you.'

Detlef's voice rose: 'Who do you think you're kidding. You did it for yourself. You were doing cold turkey and you managed it. Great. You'd have done it even if I didn't exist. Don't you understand, man? You're a fixer now. You're physically, completely hooked. Anything you do, you do for yourself.'

I said: 'You're right. But listen. We'll have to go on like this. You can't manage it by yourself. We need too much stuff now. I don't want you to do all the hustling, anyway. We'll do it the other way round. I'm sure at first I can make a lot of cash. Without fucking and all that. I promise you I'll never fuck a customer.'

Detlef said nothing. He put his arm round my shoulder. It had started to rain and I wasn't sure whether the drops on his cheeks were rain or tears. Another bus stopped. I said: 'Oh God, everything is pretty hopeless. Do you remember when we were still on tabs and hash? Then we felt totally free. We were totally independent. We needed nobody and nothing. That's how we felt. Now we're pretty dependent.'

Three or four more buses came. We talked sad talk. I cried and Detlef held me in his arms. At last he said: 'It'll get better, you'll see. Soon we'll simply kick. We'll manage it, the two of us together. I'll get some valeron*. Tomorrow I'll talk to someone about valeron. We'll be together when we kick.'

Another bus came and Detlef pushed me up the steps.

At home I did everything quite mechanically as every night. I went into the kitchen and fetched a yoghurt out of

---

*The English drug used during withdrawal is called methadone. The correct name for the German substitute is said to be valeron, although valeron is used by Christiane throughout the text.

the fridge. I really only took the yoghurt into bed to avoid drawing attention to the fact that I also took a spoon. I needed one for cooking up in the morning. Then I fetched a glass of water from the bathroom. For cleaning the syringe next morning.

Next morning was like any other. My mother woke me up at a quarter to seven. I stayed in bed pretending I hadn't heard her at all. Every few minutes she nagged me again. In the end I said: 'Yes, I'm getting up.' She came in again and nagged, while I counted the minutes till a quarter past seven. By then she had to leave the house if she didn't want to miss her tube to work. And she never missed her tube. Actually I ought to have left the house at a quarter past seven in order to get to school on time.

When at long last the door banged shut, everything went quite automatically. In front of my bed lay my jeans, from which I now fished the foilpaper with the powder. My plastic bag was next to it with my make-up, my cigarettes, a small bottle of citric acid and the works wrapped up in loo paper. This syringe was almost always clogged. The damned cigarette tobacco drifted all over the plastic bag and mucked up the works. I cleaned the syringe in the glass of water, put the stuff on the yoghurt spoon, squirted a little lemon juice on it, cooked up, tied off my arm, and so on. For me this was the same as the habit of lighting the first cigarette of the morning in bed. After the fix I often went back to sleep and only arrived at school in time for the second or third lesson. I was invariably late whenever I shot up at home.

Sometimes my mother managed to get me out of bed and drag me along to the tube. Then I had to fix in the toilet at Moritzplatz tube station. That was quite unpleasant, for this toilet was particularly dark and smelly. The walls were riddled with holes. Squatting behind them were wogs and voyeurs who got a kick out of watching a girl pee. I was always afraid that they would go and fetch the cops because they were disappointed that all I did was to shoot.

I almost always took my works to school with me. Just in case. In case for some reason we had to stay on, or there

118

was something happening in the assembly hall, or I wasn't going home after school. On these occasions I had to shoot at school. None of the doors of the school loos could be locked any longer. For this reason my friend, Renata, had to hold the door shut while I had a fix. Renata knew about me. Most people in the form did, I believe. However, they didn't mind. In Gropiusstadt, at any rate, it was no longer a sensation for anyone to be hooked on drugs.

During those school lessons in which I still took part I would doze, completely apathetic. Often I was almost asleep, my eyes closed, my head on the desk. If I had fixed a heavy shot in the morning I could barely manage to utter a few words. The teachers were bound to notice what was up with me. But during all this time only one talked to me about drugs and actually asked about my problems. The others pretended that I was simply a lazy, dozy pupil and gave me E grades. In any case, we had so many teachers that most of them were pleased with themselves if they could remember our names. There was hardly any personal contact. Before very long they stopped commenting on the fact that I never did any homework. And they only fetched out their marks list when during tests I wrote, 'Can't do it' on the paper, handed it in and sat the rest of the time doodling. I believe most of the teachers were no more interested in the school than I. They, too, had become totally resigned and were, like me, bloody glad when another lesson was over without a row.

After the evening that I had gone on the game for the first time, everything continued as before. To begin with.

I kept nagging Detlef that I ought to make some cash as well — it would be better than the few marks which I managed to scrounge every day. Detlef's immediate reaction was one of jealousy. But on the other hand he had come to realise that things couldn't go on like this and suggested that we ought to join forces.

By now he knew all about the various customers and that there were a few bisexuals among them, and also queers who would have liked to try doing it with a girl — as long as a boy was there, just in case. Detlef said he'd choose customers who wouldn't touch me and who definitely wouldn't want to fuck. Customers, in other words, who were kinky. Deltef liked them best, anyway. He thought together we might earn a hundred marks or more. The first customer Detlef had selected for us was Max the Stammer. That's what we called him. He was one of Detlef's regular customers whom I had got to know quite well. Detlef said that this one only wanted to be flogged. If need be I might have to take off my top. That was all right with me. In fact, I considered this flogging business a really good idea, because I thought it would give me a chance to get rid of my aggressions against Detlef's customers. Max the Stammer was all for it when Detlef suggested that he might bring me. For double the price, of course. We arranged to meet at Zoo station on a Monday at three o'clock.

As always I was late. Max the Stammer was already there. Not Detlef, though, needless to say. Like all fixers he was terribly unreliable. I immediately assumed, correctly, that he had got a customer who paid well and with whom he had to spend more time. Max and I waited for almost half an hour. Detlef didn't show up. I had the wind up and no mistake. But Max was quite obviously even more afraid. He kept trying to explain that he hadn't had anything to do with a girl for more than ten years. He could barely finish a word. His stammer was pretty bad normally. Now he was almost unintelligible.

I found it hard to stand around on the station with him. Somehow I wanted to get the whole thing over with. Besides, I had no stuff left and was scared of cold turkey before this business with Max was finished. However, the more I sensed his fear, the more self-assured I became. I realised that in this situation I was superior to him. At last I said to him, quite casually: 'Come on, old man. Detlef's stood us up anyway. You'll be satisfied with me by myself, I promise you. But it stays the way you've agreed with Detlef. A hundred and fifty marks.'

He actually stammered 'yes' and started to go. He seemed

totally without willpower. I took his arm and really had to lead him. Detlef had told me Max the Stammer's sad story. He was an unskilled labourer, in his late thirties, and came from Hamburg. His mother was a prostitute. As a child he had had terrible floggings. From his mother and her pimps, and in the various homes in which he had been dumped. They walloped him silly so that from sheer terror he had never learnt to speak properly, and now needed floggings in order to get sexual satisfaction.

We went to his flat. I demanded the money, although he was a regular customer with whom, strictly speaking, one didn't need to be cautious. He did give me a hundred and fifty marks, and I was rather proud of the competent way in which I had got so much money out of him.

I took off my T-shirt and he handed me a whip. Everything was just like in the cinema. I was not myself. At first I didn't hit hard enough. But he whimpered that I should hurt him. So at some stage I really gave it to him. He screamed 'mummy' and heaven only knows what else. I didn't listen. I tried not to look. But I did see how the bruises on his body kept swelling up until in some places the skin actually burst. It was so revolting and lasted for almost an hour.

When he had come at last, I pulled on my T-shirt and ran. I ran to the door, down the stairs and just made it. Outside the house I could no longer control my damned stomach and had to vomit. Once I'd thrown up, everything was all over. I didn't cry, I didn't have the least trace of self-pity. Somehow, it was quite clear to me that I had brought this situation on myself, that the whole thing was a right fuck-up. I went to the station. Detlef was there. I didn't say much. Only that I'd done the job with Max the Stammer on my own. I showed him the hundred and fifty marks. From out of his jeans pocket he fished a hundred-mark note which he had made from his customer. Arm in arm we went to the scene and scored plenty of stuff. Fine stuff from our regular dealer. It turned out quite a good sort of day really.

From now on I mostly earned the cash for my stuff on my own. The customers on the station were terribly gone on me and I could choose with whom I went, and lay down my conditions. In principle, I did not go with wogs, that is to say foreigners. All the chicks on the station thought wogs were the utter end. These wogs, they said, were often really mean bastards. They had no cash and, as a rule, paid only twenty or thirty marks, and for that they expected a proper fuck and without Durex, too.

As far as I was concerned, fucking with customers was out. That was the last little bit of intimacy I gave only to Detlef. I did hand jobs and then also sucked them off. It wasn't quite as bad when I did things to the customers as long as they did nothing to me. Above all, they must not touch me. If they tried, I blew my top.

I tried to negotiate conditions while we were still on the station. With guys who pissed me off from the start, I didn't even bother to negotiate. My last remnant of pride did cost me a lot of time. It often took the whole afternoon before I had found a customer with whom everything was okay. And it was only rarely that we had as much money as on the day when I went to Max the Stammer for the first time.

Max became a regular customer of Detlef and myself. Sometimes Detlef and I went together, sometimes only one of us. Basically, Max the Stammer was all right. At any rate he loved both of us. Naturally he could not go on paying a hundred and fifty marks out of his labourer's wages, but forty marks — the cash for a shot — he somehow always managed to scrape together. Once he even smashed his piggybank and fetched small change out of a bowl, and then counted out forty marks exactly. When I was in a hurry I might just pop in and collect twenty marks. I told him I would come back next day at such and such a time and do it for him for twenty. If he had twenty left, he was game.

Max was always expecting us. For me he always had a supply of my favourite drink — peach juice. For Detlef he kept his favourite dish, blancmange, in the fridge. He made the blancmange himself. In addition, he always offered me a selection of yoghurt and chocolate because he knew that I enjoyed a snack after the job. The flogging business had become purely a matter of routine for me, and afterwards I would eat, drink and talk for a while with Max.

He was getting thinner and thinner. He really spent his last mark on us and didn't have enough left for his own grub. He had got so used to us and was so happy that he hardly ever stammered when he was with us. First thing in the morning he bought a couple of newspapers. Only to check whether they contained another report about someone who had died from heroin. Once when I popped in to swipe twenty off him, he stammered insanely and was really pale. There'd been a report in the papers that a certain Detlef W. had been the umpteenth victim of heroin addiction that year. He almost cried with joy when I told him that I had just come from my Detlef and that he was reasonably alive. As he had done quite often before, Max kept on at me that we should keep off heroin or we would die, too. I told him quite coldly that if we were to give up heroin we would no longer come to him either. That shut him up.

Detlef and I had a strange relationship with Max the Stammer. We hated all customers. So we also hated Max. But on the other hand we thought him somehow all right. Possibly it was because he was always good for an easy forty marks. But I'm sure we also felt something like pity for him. This was a customer who basically was even worse off than us. At any rate he was completey lonely and had only us. He ruined himself for us. But that was something to which we didn't give that much thought. Later we were to ruin still more customers.

Sometimes we spent a cosy evening with Max, watching the box and staying overnight. He'd let us use his bed while he slept on the floor. One night we were all in a crazy mood. Max put on a crazy record, put a long-haired wig on his head and dressed in a fur coat that was really something else. Then he danced like a madman and we fell about laughing. Suddenly he stumbled, fell and hit his head against his sewing machine. For a few minutes he was clean out. We were dead worried and telephoned for a doctor. Max had concussion and had to stay in bed for two weeks.

123

Shortly afterwards, he got the sack. He was completely up the spout without ever having as much as tried stuff. Fixers had finished him. Us. He implored us to come and visit him for old times' sake. But for a fixer friendly visits like that simply aren't on. Firstly, because he is incapable of raising that amount of feeling for anyone else. And then also because he is busy all day long raising cash and scoring stuff, and really hasn't time for such things. Detlef explained all this to Max the Stammer when he promised he would give us plenty of cash as soon as he got some again. Detlef was hard as nails. 'A fixer is like a businessman. Every day he must take care to see that his books balance. He simply cannot give credit out of friendship or feelings of sympathy.'

Shortly after I started going on the game I had a cheerful reunion. It was on the station. I was waiting for customers, and suddenly Babsi was standing next to me. Babsi, the little girl who a few months earlier had tried to scrounge some LSD from me in the Sound. Babsi, then aged twelve, crashing out because of trouble at school, who had quickly tried a few snorts of H before she'd been picked up and returned to her grandparents.

We looked at one another, got each other's number, fell round each other's neck and kissed. She was ever so pleased, and so was I. Babsi had grown terribly thin. No boobs and no bum. But she looked almost more beautiful than before. Her blonde shoulder length hair was sleek and her clothes put together just so. I had realised at first glance that she was now completely hooked. But I believe someone knowing nothing about fixing would never have guessed that this pretty child was a fixer.

Babsi was terribly calm. There was none of the hectic rushing after cash and stuff of the other fixers like myself. She told me straightaway I needn't go after customers, she would stand me a shot and something to eat.

We went to the station café. That we were both completely hooked and on the game went without saying. But at first Babsi wouldn't quite let on where she'd got all that stuff and cash from. She just told me that things were fairly strict at home since she'd crashed out. Every night she had to be in by seven or eight and attend school regularly. Her grandmother watched her like a hawk.

At last I asked her straight out, and she said: 'I've got a regular customer. Rather an elderly guy, but for all that really cool as a customer. In the afternoon I go to him in a cab. He gives me no cash but stuff. I get three half halves a day. He's got other chicks, they also get their stuff direct from him. But at the moment I'm the only one he fancies. It takes me an hour. Without fucking, of course. Only stripping, sometimes being photographed, chatting and, well, blow jobs. But fucking is not on.'

Her regular customer was called Heinz. He had a stationer's shop. I had heard of him. Just that, that he was really cool as a customer because he supplied H direct which cut out all the running around. I was really envious of Babsi who was home not later than eight, got a good night's rest and lived without all this rushing all over the place which really pissed one off.

Babsi had everything. Even plenty of works. These syringes, which one was supposed to use only once, were already hard to get in those days. Mine had got so blunt that I had to sharpen it on the rough surface of a matchbox in order to bang the thing into the vein at all. Babsi had plenty of syringes. She immediately promised me three pumps and two spikes.

A few days later I also met Stella on the station, Babsi's friend who had been dossing around with her and who had started using H even before her. Embrace, kiss-kiss, tremendous joy. By now Stella was hooked too, of course. She wasn't doing as well as Babsi. Her father had died two years ago in a fire at their flat. Her mother had opened a pub together with an Italian boyfriend and started drinking. Stella had always pinched money for stuff from the pub. When she pinched fifty marks out of the wallet of her mother's boyfriend, the whole thing came out. She no longer dared go home and was dossing around again.

Automatically we immediately began to talk about

125

customers. First of all, Stella enlightened me about her best friend Babsi. Babsi, Stella said, was completely fucked up. This Heinz of hers was an absolutely grotty guy. A grotty, old, fat and sweaty guy whom Babsi fucked properly. Stella said: 'That would be the end for me. To fuck a customer, any customer. You might as well go with wogs. A blow job, well, okay. But fucking really is the end.'

I was really shocked myself how far things had got with Babsi. At that moment I wasn't sufficiently clued up to twig why Stella was telling me this. It was only later that I learnt from Babsi that this Heinz had been Stella's regular customer before. That was why Stella was so well informed about what he demanded for three half halves. I was to find out myself later on.

Stella then announced that she thought it was the end to go on the game at Zoo station. 'Really, all the rest are the most fucked-up chicks. And wog customers. I wouldn't wear it, not me, constantly being chatted up by these disgusting wogs.'

Stella went instead to Kurfürstenstrasse where the kerb crawlers picked up b.p.'s, almost all of them fixers and mostly thirteen- or fourteen-year olds. I really had the wind up where these kerb crawlers were concerned; you couldn't really check whose car you got into. And I said: 'But I think these kerb crawlers are really the end. The chicks there do it for twenty marks. Two customers for one shot, I really couldn't do it.'

For almost an hour we argued whether one was more fucked-up as a child prostitute on Zoo station or in Kurfürstenstrasse. In between we agreed that Babsi, if she fucked this man, really was the ultimate and utter end and not worth a shit.

It was with a heated argument about out tarts' honour that our reunion began. It was an argument which Babsi, Stella and I were to continue almost daily during the next few months. It was invariably about which of us was deepest in the shit. Each wanted to prove to herself in front of the others that she had not deteriorated quite as far. When

126

there were only two of us, we said nasty things about the third.

The greatest thing was, naturally, to do without customers altogether. On the first day we met again, Stella and I kidded ourselves into believing we could do just that. We were going to scrape together our cash by scrounging and nicking. Stella had a large number of tricks up her sleeve.

We went immediately into one of the big department stores in order to try out one of Stella's supertricks. The place to give it a whirl was the ladies' loos. You wait until a few old dears have disappeared inside the loos. Most of the time they hang their handbags on the doorhandle. Now, when they've dropped their knickers and hoisted their corsets and are squatting on the loo seat, quick as a flash, you press down the doorhandles from the outside. The bags fall down and you can easily pull them out through the wide gap under the door. Naturally, with their bare behinds the old dears dare not rush outside. And by the time they've pulled their corsets down and their knickers up, you've scarpered.

So we hung around in this ladies' loo. But whenever Stella said now was a good moment, I got the wind up. She didn't want to do it on her own. Besides, knocking off all the handbags really was a four-handed job. So the great ladies' loo robbery was off. I had never had the right nerve for nicking and my nerves were getting steadily worse.

After several disasters while scrounging and nicking, Stella and I decided to go on the game together. I insisted that we did this on the station. From now on we only went with a customer together. This had several advantages. One which we would not admit to one another was that each could check on the other and knew how far the other one really went with customers. But besides this, we felt safer together. Together it was hard to rip us off and we were better able to resist if a customer refused to keep to the arrangements. And it was quicker when there were two. One kept the customer busy up top, the other down below, and in a jiffy it was all over.

On the other hand, it was more difficult to find customers willing to pay for two girls. And then there were experienced customers who were simply scared of two chicks. Of course, when there are two of you, it is easier to rip the guy off. While one keeps him really busy the other has a go at his wallet. It was Stella who liked to work with Babsi or me best. She found it more difficult than us to get customers because she no longer looked quite as much a child as we did.

Babsi was the one who did best of all. Even while she had Heinz, she earned extra cash just so that she could treat us to stuff. Her innocent child's face hadn't a trace of make-up. Without bum or boobs and barely thirteen, she was exactly the sort of b.p. the customers were looking for. There was one occasion when she achieved five customers in one hour for two hundred marks.

Babsi and Stella were immediately accepted into the crowd of Detlef, Axel and Bernd. Now we were three girls and three boys. When we set out together I took Detlef's arm and the other two boys grabbed the girls. There was nothing going on between them. But we were simply a really together crowd. Each of us could take almost all his worries to each of the others. Despite our many quarrels about trifles which, with fixers, is simply nothing out of the ordinary. During this phase, H and its problems still held us together. I'm not sure that among young people who are not drug addicts, there exists friendships such as we had in our crowd. And it is these really great friendships which spring up among druggies, at least at the beginning, which have an attraction for other young people.

Problems arose in my relationship with Detlef when the two girls joined the crowd. We loved each other as before, but we quarrelled more often. Frequently, Detlef was very irritable. I spent a lot of my time with Babsi and Stella and somehow he didn't quite like it. But what pissed him off most of all was that he no longer had any say about which customers I went with. I chose them myself or together with Stella or Babsi. Detlef began to accuse me of fucking customers. He was really jealous.

I no longer regarded my relationship with Detlef in quite as grimly determined a light. I loved him, of course, and would always love him. On the other hand, now I was independent of him. I needed neither his stuff nor his constant protection any longer. Strictly speaking, things between us were as in one of these modern marriages about which many young people dream. There was no such thing as being dependent on one another. More and more often it would happen that we girls treated each other to stuff when one had some to spare, while the boys looked after themselves.

But after everything was said and done our friendships were H friendships. All of us became increasingly aggressive as the weeks went by. Stuff and the whole carry-on, the struggle, day after day, for cash and H, the constant stress at home, the concealing and the lying with which we deceived our parents, destroyed our nerves. It was impossible to keep the build-up of aggression among ourselves under control any longer.

I got on best with Babsi, who was still the calmest of us all. We often went on the game together. We bought the same tight black skirts, slit up to the bum. Under them we wore black suspender belts with straps. This really turned customers on. Black suspender belts with straps — and with it our still rather childish figures and faces.

Shortly before Christmas 1976, while my father was on holiday, he allowed Babsi and me to stay in his flat with my sister. On our first evening in my father's flat we had a stinking row. When Babsi and I got at each other we were so foul-mouthed that my sister, who is a year younger than me, burst into tears. We had become fluent in tarts' slang. Of course, my sister had no idea of our double lives.

Next morning, Babsi and I were again as thick as thieves. It was always the same: after a good night's rest, when you are gently coming down, you are, as a rule, in rather a peaceable mood. Babsi and I agreed that we wouldn't shoot first thing in the morning, but try to put it off as long as possible. We'd tried this several times before. It was a right lark to wait as long as possible before shooting up. However, we talked only of the great shot to which we would treat ourselves eventually with this really fine stuff. We were just like schoolchildren on Christmas Day shortly before present time. Needless to say, my sister smelled a rat. She found out quite soon that we had some drug. But she didn't know, of course, that we were hooked. She thought we were trying out something. And she promised faithfully not to tell my mother or my father, and not to split on us in case someone of Babsi's family might unexpectedly turn up. Babsi was treated very strictly and neither her grandparents nor her parents had the faintest idea that she was a heroin addict and a prostitute.

Babsi went and fetched her strawberry-flavoured Quark-fein out of her plastic bag; this is some kind of flavouring you mix with cottage cheese, and Babsi was really gone on it. She lived almost entirely on cottage cheese and Quarkfein. My diet was hardly more varied. Apart from cottage cheese I ate yoghurt and blancmange and some cakes called Viennese Rings, on sale at Kurfürstendamm tube station. I could no longer keep anything else down. So there was Babsi, mixing her Quarkfein in the kitchen. This was something like a ritual act. My sister and I sat watching her with rapt attention, our mouths watering in eager anticipation of the enormous Quarkfein breakfast we were going to devour. Naturally, breakfast would have to wait until Babsi and I had had our fix.

By the time Babsi had beaten her cottage cheese to a really beautiful creamy consistency, we could stand it no longer. We told my sister to go and lay the table nicely and locked ourselves in the bathroom. No sooner were we inside than the row between us started all over again, because gradually we were getting to be on cold turkey.

We had only one usable syringe left, and I said I'd like to shoot first quickly. Immediately Babsi got frantic: 'Why always you, I'd like to know? Today I'll be first, just for a change. After all, I got the stuff.'

This really did get up my nose. It really wound me up when she tried to take advantage of the fact that often she had more stuff than we did and would stand us some. I said: 'Listen here, old lady, you know you take ages. Stop messing about.' It was true. This woman frequently needed half an hour before she was ready. She had hardly any veins left. And when she put in the spike for the first time without drawing blood, she would blow her top. In a frenzy she would plunge the spike into her skin, getting more and more hectic by the minute. By that time all she could hope for was a lucky hit, really.

At that time I still managed quite well. Unless Detlef picked me up — he was the only one I allowed anywhere near my veins — I would shoot into a spot in the crook of my left arm. That went on until I got a thrombosis there and everything was really fucked. Later, I, too, got to the point where I scarcely any longer knew where to shoot. But this morning I had my way. Babsi was pissed off. I got the syringe, immediately hit a vein and was finished after barely two minutes. It was quite a terrific shot, too. My blood was rushing like anything. I felt really hot. I went to the wash basin and let water run over my face.

Babsi sat on the edge of the bath, plunging the thing into her arm and doing her little nut. She screamed: 'Shit, there's no air in this dump. Open the fucking window.'

I said: 'You'll have to lump it then, there is no air in this dump. Stop getting at me, for Chrissake.' I really didn't care a shit what happened to this tart. I had my shot inside me, and all was okay as far as I was concerned.

Babsi was splashing blood all over the place but failed to hit a vein properly. She was really flipping her lid. She shouted: 'There's no light in this fucking loo. Get me some light, man. Fetch the lamp from the nursery.'

I was too bloody lazy to go and fetch the lamp for Babsi. Only when she wouldn't stop carrying on and I was scared my sister might cotton on, did I go and fetch the lamp. At some time Babsi managed it. She became calm at once. She cleaned her syringe properly and mopped up the blood from inside the bath and the floor. She didn't say another word.

We went into the kitchen. I was looking forward to the Quarkfein. But then Babsi took the bowl, put one arm firmly round it and proceeded to spoon. She actually forced the whole bowlful down her throat. Once she said: 'You know quite well why.'

Both of us had been looking forward terribly to our few days in my father's flat, and yet the first morning began with the row of the century. For nothing. But then we were fixers. And in the long run all fixers get to be like this. Stuff destroys relationships with other people. It was the same with us. Even if in our crowd, where, after all, everyone was still very young, we really clung to each other, with me still thinking there wasn't another crowd like ours anywhere.

My rows with Detlef became more and more heavy. Both of us had deteriorated physically quite a lot. I was one metre sixty-nine tall [approx. 5 feet 6 inches] and weighed 43 kilos [approx. 90 pounds], Detlef was one metre seventy-six [approx. 5 feet 9 inches] and weighed 54 kilos [approx. 120 pounds]. Often, when we felt physically very ill, everything got on our nerves and we were really beastly to one another. We tried deliberately to shatter the other completely, always brutally aiming at the other's weakest spot. And that was invariably to do with going on the game, although as a rule we pretended that this was an unimportant routine business.

Detlef would say: 'Do you think I fancy sleeping with a chick who gets fucked by all the grottiest customers?'

I replied.: 'And how d'you think I feel about you getting fucked in the arse?' And so on.

In the end I would be blubbing or Detlef would be utterly shattered, or we would blub together. When one of us was doing cold turkey the other had the power to shatter him to the point of incoherence. Matters weren't actually improved when at some stage we fell into each other's arms like two children. Things had come to such a state, not only between us girls, but also between Detlef and me that you saw in the other the sort of shit you were yourself. Hating your own grottiness, you attacked the others' grottiness, no doubt wanting to prove to yourself that you weren't quite as grotty as them.

Naturally this aggressiveness was also vented on strangers. I went berserk immediately when I went down into a tube station and saw the old grannies with their shopping bags. For starters, I would get into a non-smoker with my lighted cigarette. When the old grannies started getting at me I told them if they didn't like it they could go to another carriage. I particularly enjoyed snatching a seat from under an old granny's very nose. Sometimes the way I arsed about would bring the whole carriage into an uproar and, occasionally, I was kicked outside forcibly. The way I behaved got on my own nerves, actually. It also got on my nerves when Babsi or Stella behaved like that. I didn't want to have anything to do with these creeps anyway, and yet I just couldn't help myself and constantly had to wind them up.

I didn't care a shit what strangers thought of me. When that revolting itch began, when I itched wherever my clothes clung tightly or even in the spots where I wore make-up, then I scratched, irrespective of where I happened to be. Taking off my boots in the tube, or lifting my skirt up to my navel for a scratch, was nothing to me. All that concerned me was what the people in my crowd thought of me.

There comes the time when a fixer no longer cares. By then he no longer belongs to a crowd either. I knew a few of the old fixers who had been fixing for five or more years and survived. We had a very mixed attitude to these old hands. For us these total loners seemed to have very strong personalities. Also, it went down well on the scene when one was able to say one knew this or that old hand. On the other hand, I despised them all because they were all totally fucked up. Above all, we young ones were terribly scared of them. They really had not the tiniest vestige of morals, conscience or pity left. They would hit their fellow fixer over the head with a stone when they were doing cold turkey and wanting to get at a fix. The most ruthless of them was called Rip-Off Manne. Everybody called him that, for he was really the worst ripper-off on the scene. When the dealers saw him coming they ran faster than during a rumble. For if he got hold of a small dealer, he simply took away his stuff. No one dared struggle against him. Certainly no unimportant little fixer.

Once I had experience of Rip-Off Manne in full action. I had just locked myself in a ladies' loo ready to shoot when someone leapt over the partition wall, literally on top of me. Rip-Off Manne. I knew from stories that this was his dodge. Waiting in ladies' loos until a fixer chick with H arrives. And I knew how brutal he could be. So I gave him my works and my stuff. He went outside and stood in front of the mirror. That one was no longer afraid of anything. And then he banged the shot into his neck. He hadn't a spot left on the rest of his body where he might shoot. He bled like a pig. I thought he had shot into the main artery. But he just didn't care. He said 'many thanks,' and beat it.

At least one thing was clear to me, namely that I would never get that far. For in order to survive like Rip-Off Manne, you had to be totally ruthless. And I wasn't. I couldn't even pinch the old grannies' handbags in the department store toilet.

In our crowd it was increasingly a matter of going on the game and customers. The boys had the same problems as us. We still had mutual interests and were able to help each other practically. We girls swapped experiences with customers. In time the circle of customers came to be limited. A customer might be new to me, whereas Stella or Babsi had already had him. And it was of advantage to know their experience with him.

There were recommended, less recommended and absolutely unsatisfactory clients. In this evaluation of customers it was hardly ever a matter of personal likings. Neither were we interested in the customer's job, whether he was married, and so on. We never talked about the whole personal rubbish customers will tell you. All we cared

134

about in this evaluation of guys was our advantage, nothing else.

A customer had an advantage if he was terrified of catching VD and insisted on using a sheath for everything. Unfortunately, this type was rare, although sooner or later most girls who are amateur tarts, do catch something, and it is the drug addicts who are scared to go to a doctor.

It was of advantage if, from the start, the customer did not demand more than, at worst, a blow job. It meant you didn't have to spend hours haggling over conditions with him. It was also to a client's credit if he was reasonably young and not revoltingly fat, if he didn't treat you like a commodity but remained more or less friendly, perhaps even inviting us to a meal occasionally.

But the most important criterion for a customer was, of course, how much money he paid for which service. Unsatisfactory and to be avoided were guys who did not stick to agreements, and at the hotel suddenly tried to blackmail us into supplying additional services by threatening or tempting us.

But the ones we talked most about were those cheating bastards who afterwards demanded their money back and, at times, took it back by force because they were allegedly not satisfied. The boys had more trouble with cunts like that than us.

At some time the year 1977 began: I scarcely registered time. Whether it was winter or summer, whether it was Christmas or New Year's Eve that was being celebrated, for me one day was like the next. The only special thing about Christmas might be that I would be given some money and needed therefore to do one or two fewer customers. It was anyhow almost impossible to find customers over the holidays. During this phase I was completely apathetic. I didn't think. Not about anything. I no longer noticed anything. I was totally preoccupied with myself. But I did not know who I was. Sometimes I didn't even know if I was actually still alive.

I can barely remember details from this time. Probably

there wasn't anything worth remembering. Until a Sunday towards the end of January 1977. I came home in the early hours of the morning. Actually I was feeling quite good. I lay in bed imagining that I was a young girl who had come home from a dance where she had met a terribly sweet boy, and now she was really gone on him. Now I only felt good when I dreamt, and in my dream became someone quite different. What I liked to dream best was that I was a cheerful teenager, as cheerful as in a Coca Cola advert.

At midday my mother woke me up and brought me my lunch in bed. Whenever I was at home on a Sunday, and not with Detlef, my mother would bring me lunch in bed. I forced down a few mouthfuls. Actually I could no longer swallow anything except yoghurt, cottage cheese and blancmange. Then I got my white plastic bag. The plastic bag was rather tatty, no handles, torn everywhere because, in addition to syringe and cigarettes, I used to sling in my jacket all crumpled up. I cared so little about anything that I didn't even remember to get another plastic bag. I was too much past caring to worry as I slopped, carrying my plastic bag, past my mother into the bathroom. I locked the bathroom door behind me. In our family nobody else locked the bathroom door. I looked in the mirror as I did every day. I looked into a totally sunken, alien face. For a long time now I no longer recognised my face in the mirror. The face did not belong to me. Any more than the totally emaciated body. I no longer felt it at all. It did not even make itself felt when I was ill. Heroin made it insensible to either pain or hunger, or even a high temperature. All the body still registered was cold turkey.

I stood in front of the mirror, preparing my shot. I was particularly keen on this shot because I had scored what we called M-powder. In contrast to the white or brownish H which was on the market, this was a grey-greenish speckled powder. It is badly cut stuff, the sort fixers refer to as crap, but it produces a terrific flash. It hits the heart and one has to be terribly careful with the dose one takes. Too big a shot of M-powder and you've had it. But I was fantastically keen on this M-powder flash, regardless.

I slid the needle into the vein in my arm and drew blood immediately. I had filtered the M-powder several times, but, as I have said, it is totally cut. And then it happened. The spike got bunged up. This is about the worst thing that can happen to a fixer, his spike getting bunged up at this moment. For once the blood in the syringe clots, nothing more can be done. You have to throw the stuff away.

So I couldn't pull it out. I pressed as hard as I could in order to get this crap through the spike. And I was lucky. I got the shot in. I drew the plunger back once more to get the last remnant into the vein. And then the spike clogged up again. I was furious. I only had eight or ten seconds before the flash. So I pressed again as hard as I could. The pump came off and blood squirted around all over the place.

The flash was insane. I had to hold on to my head. In the region of my heart I felt a terrific cramp. My head buzzed as if someone had hit it with a sledge hammer, the skin on my head tingled as if pricked by a million needles. And my left arm was virtually paralysed.

When I was once more able to move, I used some tissues to mop up the blood. There was blood everywhere. In the wash basin, on the mirror and on the walls. Fortunately, everything was painted with gloss paint and the blood washed off easily. While I was still busy wiping, my mother banged on the door. She started gabbling immediately: 'Open up. Let me in. Why are you locking the door, anyway? What sort of newfangled ideas are these?'

I said: 'Shut up. I've nearly finished.' I was totally pissed off with her for getting at me now of all times. I wiped wildly with the tissues. In my panic I overlooked a few spots of blood and left a bloodstained tissue in the wash basin. Then I unlocked the door and my mother rushed past me into the bathroom. I still suspected nothing and thought she needed to do an urgent pee. I went back into my room with my plastic bag, got into bed and lit a cigarette.

No sooner had I lit the cigarette than my mother came running into the room. She shouted: 'You take drugs!'

I said: 'Oh, rubbish. Whatever gives you that idea?'

Then she virtually flung herself on me and forced my arms straight. I did not resist properly. She took my plastic bag and tipped everything inside on to the bed. Out fell the syringe, plenty of tobacco crumbs and a whole lot of small pieces of foil paper. The H had been in the foil paper. On occasions when I had no stuff and was on the point of doing cold turkey, I scraped up the last remains of dust with my nail file and used them for a shot.

All the stuff which had tumbled out of the plastic bag was plenty of proof of my drug addiction for my mother. She had already found enough evidence in the bathroom. Not only the bloodstained tissues and spots of blood, but also the soot from the spoon in which I had cooked up my stuff. She had read a great deal about heroin in the press and was quickly able to put two and two together.

I immediately stopped denying things. Although I had just banged a really terrific shot with M powder, I broke down. I blubbed and couldn't get out another word. My mother didn't say anything either. She trembled. She was totally shocked. She walked out of my room and I could hear her talking to her boyfriend Klaus. She came back. She seemed a little calmer and asked: 'Can't we do something about this? Don't you want to stop?'

I said: 'Mummy, there's nothing I'd like better. Honestly. Believe me. I really would like to break with this fucking shit.'

She said: 'Very well. Let's try to do it together. I'll take time off so that I can be with you while you stop taking drugs. We'll start withdrawing today.'

I said: 'That's really great. But there's another thing. I won't do it without Detlef. He wants to withdraw too. We've often talked about it. We were going to withdraw anyway. Together.'

My mother was completely thunderstruck and said: 'What, Detlef, he too?'

She had always found Detlef very nice and had been glad that I had such a nice boyfriend. I replied: 'Of course, Detlef

138

too. Do you think I'd do this by myself? Detlef would never have stood for it. But he won't stand for me withdrawing without him either.'

Suddenly I felt quite okay. I grew really cheerful at the thought of withdrawing together with Detlef. We had in fact intended to do it for a long time. However, my mother was completely shattered. Her face turned green and I thought she would have a nervous breakdown. This business with Detlef had shocked her all over again. I suppose she was shocked by her own lack of suspicion during the past two years. And now more and more doubts crowded in on her. She wanted to know where I got the money for heroin. Naturally she'd twigged straightaway: going on the game, hustling, and so on.

I could never have brought myself to tell her the truth. I lied: 'I just went on the scrounge. Asking people for the odd few marks here and there, you know. It worked most of the time. And then I did a bit of charring.'

My mother stopped asking questions. Once again she seemed very glad that she received an answer which failed to confirm her suspicions. What she had found out this Sunday was, after all, enough to shatter her totally. I felt honestly sorry for my mother and I had a bad conscience on her account.

We started at once to look for Detlef. He wasn't at Zoo station. He wasn't with Axel and Bernd either.

That evening we went to see Detlef's father. Detlef's parents were divorced, too. His father was a civil servant. He had known for some time what was the matter with Detlef. My mother remonstrated with him for not telling her about it. He almost burst into tears. He was terribly embarrassed that his son was a fixer and on the game. Now he was glad that my mother intended dealing with the matter. He said over and over again: 'Yes, we've got to do something.'

In his desk Detlef's father had a whole collection of sleeping pills and sedatives. He gave them to me to take away because I told him we had no valeron and that withdrawing without valeron was dead brutal. On the way home on the tube, I dropped a handful of these tabs because I could feel cold turkey coming on. With these pills inside me I felt quite well and slept through the night.

Next morning Detlef was on the doorstep. His father had found him at once. Detlef was doing cold turkey. I thought that was really great. I mean that he didn't have a quick shot but actually arrived doing cold turkey. He must have realised that I wouldn't have any stuff. And he said he wanted to be on the same level as me when we started withdrawing. That was really great.

So Detlef really wanted to withdraw, just as I did myself. He, too, was quite glad things had come to a head. Neither of us had any idea — nor did our parents — that it is sheer madness for two fixers to try kicking the habit together. For at some stage one will get at the other, they'll work each other up to the next shot. That is to say, perhaps we did know it at the time from tales we had heard. But then we cheated ourselves with illusions. We invariably thought that somehow what applied to other fixers didn't apply to us. We couldn't imagine, anyway, that we would do anything important and not do it together.

During the morning we kept our heads fairly well above water with the tablets Detlef's father had given me. We still talked to one another. We painted our life after withdrawal in rosy colours, promising each other to be dead courageous during the next few days. Although we were both beginning to be in pain, we were still quite happy.

In the afternoon we were full of it. We kept swallowing these tablets, washing them down with wine. But it was no use. Suddenly I could no longer control my legs. I felt a terrific pressure on the back of my knees. I lay on the floor and stretched my legs. I tried tightening and relaxing my leg muscles. But I no longer had any muscle control. I pressed my legs against the wardrobe. And there they stayed. I couldn't get my legs away from the wardrobe. I was thrashing around on the floor while my legs somehow stuck to the wardrobe.

I was wet through with icy cold sweat. I was cold and I trembled and this cold sweat ran down my nose and into my eyes. This sweat stank really awful. I thought this is the awful stinking poison which is now coming out of you. I really felt as if this was my own exorcism.

Detlef was in an even worse state than me. He was about to go berserk. He was trembling with cold and suddenly took off his jersey. He sat on my chair by the window. His legs were constantly in motion. He ran while sitting down. Up and down they went, these pencil-thin legs, twitching crazily. Over and over again he wiped the sweat from his face. He was really shaking. It wasn't just trembling any longer. Again and again he doubled up screaming. Stomach cramps.

Detlef stank even worse than I. The whole tiny room was filled with our stench. I remembered having heard that fixer friendships always break up after a successful withdrawal. But I thought that I still loved Detlef — even now when he stank so awful.

Detlef got up and somehow made it to the mirror. Then he said: 'I can't stand this. I can't do it. I really can't do it.' I couldn't answer. I hadn't the strength to give him courage. I tried not to think the same as he. I tried to concentrate on some silly story. Frantically I leafed through a newspaper and tore the pages. My mouth and my throat were completely dry. And yet my mouth was also full of spittle. I could not swallow it and started to cough. The more desperately I tried to swallow this spittle, the more violent grew my cough. I got a fit of coughing which didn't stop at all. Then I began to throw up. I threw up all over my carpet. I spewed white foam on to the carpet. I thought, just like my dog when it had eaten grass. Coughing and throwing up seemed to go on and on for ever.

Most of the time my mother was in the living room. When she came in to us she was quite helpless. She kept going off to the shopping centre to buy things we couldn't get down. One time she brought me malt sweets and they did help. The coughing stopped. My mother mopped up the puke.

She was so terribly sweet. And I couldn't even say 'thank you.'

At some stage the pills and the wine did have an effect. I had gulped down five valiums, two mandrax, followed by almost a whole bottle of wine. After that any normal person would have slept for a couple of days. My body was so badly poisoned that it scarcely reacted any longer to this poison. But at least I grew calmer and lay down on my bed. Next to my bed we had put a divan and Detlef lay down on it. We did not touch. Each was fully occupied with himself. I drifted into a sort of light sleep. I slept but, at the same time, I still felt the full impact of those damned pains. I dreamt and thought. All this was confused. I thought that everyone, most of all my mother, could completely see inside me. That everyone could read my terribly filthy thoughts. That everyone was bound to see what a revolting shit I was. I hated my body. I would have been glad if it had simply died on me.

That evening I once more dropped a few tabs. With any normal person it would have been enough to kick the bucket. As for me, it made me sleep tight — at least for a few hours. I woke up again, having dreamt that I was a dog that had always been treated well by humans, but which all of a sudden had been locked in its kennel and was being tortured to death. Detlef was flinging his arms about and hitting me. The light was on. Standing by my bed was a bowl of water and a flannel. My mother had put them there. I washed the sweat from my face.

Detlef's whole body was in motion, although he seemed to be fast asleep. His body moved up and down, his legs kicked out, and at times he thrashed his arms about.

I felt a little better. And I had enough strength to wipe Detlef's forehead with the flannel. He felt nothing. I knew that I still loved him terribly. Later, when I had dozed off again, I realised, half-asleep, that Detlef was touching me and stroking my hair.

Next morning we really felt better. Obviously, that old fixer rule that the second day of kicking the habit was the worst did not apply to us. But then it was our first withdrawal which invariably is not nearly as bad as subsequent ones. About midday we even started talking to each other. Unimportant things to begin with, and then, again, about our future. Our plans were no longer quite as bourgeois as at the beginning of our withdrawal. We swore never to take H again, nor LSD, and no tablets either. Instead we wanted to lead a peaceful life with peaceful people. We agreed that we wanted to go back to smoking hash as in our greatest time. Also, we wanted to have friends from the hash scene, for they were mostly very peaceable. We thought we'd never get close to alkies, and that we wanted to have nothing to do with these aggressive creeps. What we wanted was to get away from the H scene and back to the hash scene.

Detlef wanted to look for work again. He said: 'I'll simply go back to my old boss and say that I made a fuck-up of things after I left my job, and now have genuinely come to my senses. Actually my boss has always been very understanding. I'll start my apprenticeship as a pipe fitter all over again.'

I said that I wanted to concentrate completely on school, and that perhaps I might manage to get to grammar school and later even do my Abitur.

Then my mother came in with an enormous surprise which made us really happy. She had been to see her doctor who had prescribed a bottle of valeron. Detlef and I took 20 drops each, as the doctor had ordered. We didn't squander it, for it was meant to last the whole week. We really liked valeron. Now we could really cope with the withdrawal. My mother kept making blancmanges for us: we had a real craving for blancmange. She brought us ice cream, she fulfilled our every wish. She brought us stacks of reading matter. Any amount of comics. Before I had thought comics boring. Now I looked at them with Detlef. We didn't skim through as usual. We looked at every drawing in detail and, from time to time, fell about laughing over these witty drawings.

By the third day we felt quite well again. Admittedly we

143

were always turned on. Not only with valeron. We continued swallowing any amount of valium, washing it down with wine. We felt really good, although now and then our poisoned bodies revolted against the withdrawal of H. On the evening of the third day we slept together again, after a long time. For on heroin the desire to sleep together grows less and less. It was the first time since Detlef had deflowered me that we weren't on H when we were sleeping together. It was fantastic. We realised that we hadn't loved each other so intensely for a long time. We lay in bed for hours, stroking each other's bodies which were still sweating. Strictly speaking, we could very well have got up on the fourth day. But we stayed in bed for another three days, making love, enjoying having my mother to look after us, and swallowing valium and wine. We told each other that kicking the habit wasn't really all that bad and we were pleased that we had come off H.

On the seventh day we got up. My mother was delighted that we had got over everything. She kissed us happily. During this week I had developed a completely new relationship with my mother. I felt something like genuine friendship towards her, and gratitude, too. Also, I was again terribly glad that I had Detlef. Once more I thought there wasn't another boy like him in the world. It had been great, the way, immediately and without thinking, he had joined me in kicking the habit. And wasn't it really fantastic that our love hadn't died the way it does with other fixers after they have kicked, but had grown even more intense?

We told my mother we wanted to get a breath of fresh air after a week in such a tiny room. She approved. Detlef asked: 'Where on earth shall we go?' I looked at him, completely at a loss. I had absolutely no idea. Only now did we realise that we had actually no place left to which we could go. All our friends were fixers. And all the places we knew, the places where we felt at home somehow, were where the H scene was. We had no contact at all with the hash scene.

Once Detlef had asked where are we to go, I suddenly didn't feel so good any more. We had no valeron left, and that was doubtless the reason why we had become so restless and wanted to get out. That we didn't know where to go made me even more restless. I suddenly felt quite drained, quite empty. So now we were off H and didn't know where to go.

We walked to the tube without talking about where we were heading. Everything went quite automatically. We were drawn by an invisible thread without being conscious of it. And then we were standing on Zoo station. At last Detlef said something: 'We've got at least to say hello to Axel and Bernd. Otherwise they'll think we've been locked up or kicked the bucket or something.'

I said, greatly relieved: ' 'Course. We've got to tell them about the withdrawal. Perhaps we can persuade them to do one, too.' In fact, we ran into Axel and Bernd immediately. They carried plenty of stuff. They'd had a good day hustling. Detlef told them about our withdrawal. Both of them thought what we had done was really great. Then Axel and Bernd said they were now going back to the flat to shoot.

Detlef looked at me, I looked at him. We caught each other's eye and started to grin. I just had time to think: 'It would be insane, on the first day.' Then Detlef said: 'You know, just a little shot. We might treat ourselves to one now and then. It is quite something to be on H as long as one isn't hooked. Only we'll have to be terribly careful to avoid getting hooked again. To go through another withdrawal, it's just not on at all.'

I said: 'Well, a shot now and then, that's really great. Now we know very well that we mustn't get physically hooked again.' My reason and my thinking had gone out of the window. All I had now was shot-need.

Detlef said to Axel: 'Can you let us have some? You'll get it back as soon as possible, and that's a promise.' Axel and Bernd thought we ought to think about it carefully. Then they said next week they were going to do exactly what we had done, only they'd have to get some valeron first. They thought it was really great to go back to work and have a shot every now and then.

Two hours after we had left my mother's flat, Detlef and I were back on H and totally happy. Arm in arm, we sauntered down the Kurfürstendamm. It really was a terrific feeling to be on H and not to be in a hurry, but simply to stroll. We didn't need to worry about H for next morning. Detlef said quite cheerfully: 'Yes, and tomorrow morning we'll do a few exercises and we'll start the day really well without H.'

We believed all this quite seriously. Our self-deception had begun with our thinking that this one week of pains and puking had been a proper withdrawal. Certainly, we had got the poison out of our bodies, at least the H. But in its place we had filled ourselves up with valeron, valium, and so on. And we had not given any thought to what was to happen after we'd physically withdrawn. My mother was just as naive. She seriously hoped that we'd got over the whole thing. How could she have known better?

We really ought to have been sufficiently clued up, for we knew about experiences of all kinds from others who had made similar attempts to kick the habit. But we simply didn't want to know what really was the matter with us. Somewhere we were still terribly naive children. And all the experience we had made no difference at all.

For almost four weeks we actually almost managed to do what we had made up our minds to do. Neither of us went hustling. We only had a shot when someone stood us one, or when we had come by some cash. Only we were more and more keen to find someone who would stand us stuff or to lay our hands on some cash. Naturally we never admitted this to ourselves.

These weeks were a fantastic time. I didn't have to go back to school because my mother wanted my first few weeks without heroin to be especially pleasant. And Detlef was allowed to go on staying with me. I got to know Detlef from quite a new side and loved him even more if that was at all possible. He was lighthearted and cheerful and full of ideas. We were two teenagers who were always cheerful, or at least we pretended we were.

We went out to Grunewald and walked for hours. Sometimes we took my two cats along and let them climb trees. Almost every night we made love. Everything was out of this world. Sometimes we went without H for a couple of days in a row, sometimes we were high on H three days running. When we had scored, we cleared off as fast as we could from this awful H scene. The thing we liked to do best was to mingle with all the creeps on the Kurfürstendamm. Somehow we longed to be like them, only a little different. At any rate we wanted to demonstrate to ourselves and to everybody that we weren't old fixers — even if we had been shooting.

High on H, we went to teeny-bopper discos like Flashpoint and Big Eden. We used to sit there, bombed out, thinking we were almost like the others in the place, at any rate certainly no old fixers. Sometimes we stayed at home for days on end. We could look out of the window for hours, telling each other stories. We tried to pick leaves from the sickly trees which grew outside our house in Kreuzberg. I leant far out of the window while Detlef held on to my legs. In this way I could actually reach a few leaves. We kissed and cuddled, romped and read, and were most of the time really silly somehow. We never talked seriously about our future. On rare occasions I felt unwell. It was whenever some problem came up. When, for example, Detlef and I had a little row about some unimportant matter. When this happened I could not cope with the problem. I constantly pushed it to one side, and sometimes I was scared to have lost my temper over so trifling a problem. At times like this I had rather a craving for H, because with one shot any problem was gone.

Then a real problem arose. My mother's boyfriend, Klaus, made a great fuss on account of Detlef. He said the flat was too small to accommodate a visitor. My mother couldn't really argue with him. And I was once again powerless. It was something like the day Klaus had ordered me to give away my dog. In one fell swoop this whole fantastic life was at an end. After three weeks I had to go back to school and Detlef was no longer allowed to stay with me.

At school I did not feel as if I had been away for three weeks. I'd missed the bus long ago. Only now I had a new problem: cigarette-smoking. Whenever I wasn't on H, I smoked four or five packets a day: I had become a chain smoker. And now I really couldn't go through the first lesson without cigarettes. I had to go to the loo to smoke a few fags. During this first morning at school I literally smoked to the point of throwing up. I threw up in the wastepaper basket. I was hardly ever in the classroom.

This was the first day in three weeks that I hadn't seen Detlef. Next day at lunchtime I went to Zoo station after school, full of forebodings. There was my Detlef waiting for customers.

I thought it was revolting to wait around on this disgusting station for disgusting customers. But Detlef said he was absolutely broke. In any case, he had nothing to do. From now on Detlef slept most of the time at Axel and Bernd's and was on the station every day and had his shot every day. So I had to go back to the station when I wanted to see Detlef. Detlef was the only human being I had. I believed I could not live without Detlef. So I, too, went to Zoo station almost every day.

CHRISTIANE'S MOTHER

On the Sunday that I found the bloodstains in the bathroom and examined Christiane's arms, the penny really dropped. It was a severe blow. Christiane presented me, as it were, with the receipt for her education of which I had been so proud. Now I saw: I had done everything wrong, for the sole reason of not wanting to repeat the mistakes my father had made in my education.

For instance, when Christiane began to go to the Sound discotheque, I was not exactly overjoyed, but then her friend Kessi and other young people from Centre House went regularly to the Sound. I said to myself, oh, all right, why shouldn't Christiane go there now and again? All the young people raved about the Sound. I had to think of all

148

the harmless pleasures my father forbade me when I was a girl.

I continued with this liberal upbringing when Christiane introduced her boyfriend Detlef, whom she had met in the Sound. Detlef made a very good impression on me. He knew how to behave, had good manners and an open nature. All in all, a likeable fellow. And I considered it perfectly natural for Christiane at her age to have fallen in love for the first time. I thought the main thing is that he's a decent boy. I could see that he was really fond of Christiane.

If at that time anyone had told me that these two were even then injecting heroin, I would have said he was mad. For, apart from her crush on Detlef, nothing about Christiane struck me as in any way unusual. On the contrary, she seemed to me to be calmer and more balanced after she had been for some time exceedingly rebellious. Even at school things appeared to improve.

After school we always talked to each other on the phone, and she would tell me what she was doing. That she would be going to a school friend's house or fetching Detlef from work. I had no objections. As a rule, on weekdays, she was at home for the evening meal. And whenever she was late she rang up and was home an hour later. Sometimes she went out again to Centre House or met her friends, as she said.

She began helping around the house again, and I would show my appreciation by giving her a small present, a record perhaps or extra pocket money. My boyfriend Klaus did not approve. He thought I ought to think of myself for a change. Christiane was only going to take advantage of me. In a certain sense he may have been right. But then I always had this feeling of having to do something special for Christiane, to make up to her for something. However, in those days I wasn't yet able to see this quite accurately.

My boyfriend objected to my allowing Christiane to stay with her friends overnight. He didn't believe her; he didn't believe she was really staying with a friend. But spying on her — that was not my way. That was what my father used to do to me without my ever having done anything wrong.

One day Christiane told me that she had slept with Detlef. 'Mummy, darling,' she said, 'he was so sweet to me, you can't imagine.' Now I thought I knew why she always wanted to stay with her friends at the weekend.

But it had happened. And I couldn't really see anything wrong in it. From now on I occasionally gave her permission to stay overnight with Detlef.

How could I have prevented these two from going to bed together? On TV and in the papers psychologists keep emphasising that the young people of today mature earlier and that sexuality must not be repressed. I share this view.

At least Christiane had a steady boyfriend. Other girls in our neighbourhood just slept around. For this reason alone Christiane's steady relationship with Detlef reassured me.

On the other hand, if I am quite honest, I did at times feel uneasy. Above all on account of Christiane's new friends of both sexes whom she had met in the Sound. She told me that some of them were on drugs. She didn't mention heroin, but they smoked hash and went on trips. She described horrendous things to me, including that her friend Babsi was also a drug addict. But she talked of these things in so disgusted a tone, she found them so revolting — I should never have thought it possible that she was doing all this herself.

When I asked her: 'Why do you bother with these people?' she said: 'But, mummy, I feel so sorry for them. Nobody wants to have anything to do with them. And they're so pleased if I speak to them. They do need help.' And Christiane has always been ready to help. Today I know that she was talking about herself.

And one evening, half-way through the week, when she had not come home until eleven, she said: 'Don't be cross, mummy. I was at a release centre with the people.' And I asked: 'What goes on there?' 'Well, we talk and try to get them off drugs!' And then she added: 'If I should ever become an addict . . .' and giggled. I gave her a horrified look. Until she said: 'Well, I'm only saying that. I'm okay.'

'And Detlef?' I asked. Christiane was quite outraged. 'That's quite out of the question for Detlef. It would be the end.'

That was in the winter of '76. From then on I had a premonition, but I suppressed it. Nor did I listen to my boyfriend. By then he was willing to take any bet that Christiane was on drugs. But I wouldn't allow him to say anything against her. One isn't all that ready to admit to oneself that it has all been in vain, that one has failed as a mother. I persisted in believing that my daughter wouldn't do that.

I tried to put Christiane on a short rein. But when I told her: 'Be back by supper time,' she just didn't come back. And then there was nothing I could do. Where was I to look for her in this city? Even without my powers of self-deception I wouldn't have suspected her on Zoo station. I was glad when she phoned at half past eight saying: 'Mummy, I'll be home soon, don't worry.' I could simply no longer cope with Christiane.

There were times, though, when she did as she was told. Then she told her friends on the phone almost proudly: 'No, I'm not allowed to go out today. I'll have to stay in.' She did not seem to mind in the least. This was the contradictory aspect of Christiane. On the one hand, she was wayward, cheeky and wouldn't listen to a word one said to her. On the other hand, she seemed to respect me when I drew clear lines. However, it was already too late.

It was towards the end of January, 1977, on a Sunday, when my moment of truth came. It was terrible. I wanted to go to the bathroom. It was locked. This was not usual in our family. Christiane was in there and wouldn't open the door. At this moment I was certain. It was clear to me, for the first time, that all this while I had been fooling myself. Otherwise I couldn't have known all of a sudden what was happening in the bathroom.

I began to bang against the door. But she wouldn't open up. I nearly hit the roof. I scolded, I begged her to open the door. At last she dashed past me. In the bathroom I found a black spoon and splashes of blood on the wall. There was my confirmation. I knew it from reports in the papers. My

151

boyfriend said: 'Well, do you believe it now?' I ran after her into her room. I said: 'Christiane, what have you done?' I was completely at the end of my tether. I trembled all over. I didn't know whether to burst into tears or scream at her. But I had to talk to her first. She was sobbing her heart out and didn't want to look at me. I asked: 'Did you inject yourself with heroin?'

She did not answer. She was weeping so bitterly that she couldn't speak. I forced her arms straight and saw the mess. She had already got needle marks on both arms. However, it didn't look too bad. Not at all. There was nothing bruised, and all one could see were two or three màrks, one of them the fresh one. This one was still rather red.

And then she admitted it. Amid tears. At this moment I thought: 'I shall die.' I think I should have liked to die, too. I was so desperate that I simply couldn't think. I didn't know what to do. Then I said: 'What are we going to do?' That is what I actually asked Christiane. I myself was completely helpless.

So this was the blow I had tried to dodge. This was what I kept sweeping under the carpet. But then I didn't know how the symptoms would manifest themselves. So far I had not noticed anything languid about Christiane, nothing of the sort. Most of the time she was bright and cheerful. The only thing which had struck me during the past few weeks was that occasionally, when she came home a little late, she disappeared into her room rather quickly. I put it down to a bad conscience. On account of being late.

After I had calmed down a little we considered what we might do. And then Christiane admitted that Detlef was also a drug addict. Any withdrawal would be pointless, she said, unless Detlef would withdraw at the same time. Otherwise they would tempt each other again and again. This seemed to make sense to me. We decided that the two of them were to start withdrawing immediately at our house.

Christiane struck me as perfectly open and honest. She also confessed to me that Detlef was earning the money for heroin by working as a male prostitute on Zoo station. I was

152

horrified. That she solicited men herself for that very reason was never even mentioned. I did not suspect her either; after all, she loved Detlef. And he, she said, had always earned enough money for heroin. Over and over again Christiane declared solemnly: 'Mummy, believe me, I want to come off H. Really.'

That evening we started out in search of Detlef. And it was then that, for the first time consciously, I saw the emaciated pitiable creatures walking up and down between the tube trains. And Christiane said: 'I don't want to end up like them. Just look at these fucked-up guys.' She herself did still look comparatively decent. And I was almost reassured again.

We failed to find Detlef and therefore went to see his father. He knew all about Detlef's heroin addiction, but not that Christiane was an addict, too. I remonstrated with him. 'Why,' I asked him, 'didn't you tell me anything?' Because he was ashamed, he said.

Detlef's father seemed relieved. He wanted to help financially, he said. Up till now he had tried in vain to get help for his son. I must have seemed liked an angel. And I must say I felt quite strong myself. I had not the foggiest idea what was in store for me.

Next day I went off on my own looking for advice. At first I went to the youth welfare office and said: 'My 14-year-old daughter is a heroin addict. What am I to do?' They did not know. 'Put her in a home,' they suggested. I said that was quite out of the question. Christiane would have felt rejected. Besides they didn't know of a home. They would have to choose one; that would take quite a long time. In any case, good places for educationally subnormal children were few and far between. I said: 'It has nothing to do with that, she is not educationally subnormal. She's a drug addict.' They just kept looking at me and shrugging their shoulders. In the end they suggested that I should take Christiane to the child guidance clinic. When I suggested this to Christiane, she just said: 'Rubbish, what's the use, they haven't a clue. What I need is therapy.' But the

153

authorities had nothing of that sort to offer. I went from one drug advice bureau to the other, at the Polytechnic, at Caritas, and heaven only knows where else. I did not know how to handle the problem.

The various counsellors did not hold out much hope for the success of withdrawal at home. Without therapy, they said, withdrawal was rather pointless. But Christiane was still so young I might try my luck at home. They didn't have a therapy place available now, anyway. In three months' time, perhaps. They gave me advice on diet in case of deficiency symptoms.

The withdrawal took place during the first week. Neither of the two tried any tricks, nor did they want to clear out. My hopes rose again. After a week I was certain: Thank God, she's done it. Presently Christiane went back to regular attendance at school, where she is supposed to have taken an active part in the lessons.

But then Christiane began to hang out with the old crowd again. At least she told me every time where she was. She made unassailable statements. When she rang up at 8 pm, she said: 'Mummy, I'm in this or that café. I've met this or that person. I'll be home quite soon.'

By now I was warned. I checked her arms but could see no new punctures. She was no longer allowed to stay at Detlef's over the weekend. On the other hand, I wanted to show her that I trusted her. That's why I allowed her to stay out late on Saturday night. I was suspicious, but I simply didn't know how I was to act. I racked my brains.

I had the horror of once more being physically dependent on H. But when Detlef was high while I was not, then there was nothing going between us. We were like strangers to one another. For that reason I took the stuff Detlef had started to give me again. And while we were plunging in the spike we told each other that we would never become addicted again.

We still kidded ourselves that we were not physically addicted and that we could stop any day, at a time when we were already once again taking frantic care to see that we had enough stuff left for the following morning.

The whole shit started all over again. Except that we weren't all that aware of how deep in the shit we were once more, precisely because we imagined we had everything under control.

To begin with, Detlef went hustling for me. Naturally, this couldn't last, and before long I had to go back, too. But at first I was terribly lucky with regular customers, and then I didn't find it quite so repulsive.

On the first occasion when I had to go out on the game again, Detlef took me along to Jürgen's place. This Jürgen is a rather well known man in Berlin business circles. He is absolutely loaded and lunches with senators. Although he is over thirty he is in a way still a youthful guy. He uses the same slang as young people and understands their problems. He certainly isn't one of these old wankers who usually make pots of cash.

So this was my first visit to Jürgen's flat. There were about a dozen young people sitting round a huge wooden table. On the table stood silver candlesticks with lit candles and bottles of expensive wine. Everyone was talking and laid back. And I noticed that the chicks and guys round the table were really together, all of them. Jürgen led the discussion. And I thought that guy's got brains. In any case, I was impressed with this really fantastic flat which must have cost a bomb. And what impressed me also was the way in which he remained so laid back, really human.

He and the others treated us straightaway like old friends, although there were no fixers among them. After we had been chatting for a while, one couple asked whether they might go and have a shower. Jürgen said: 'Well, of course, what are the showers there for?'

The showers were next to the living room. The couple went in, and another couple of people followed them. And they returned naked and asked for towels. I thought this was quite a together group of people who must all somehow be fond of each other. And I felt really good because I imagined

155

that later Detlef and I would have just such a fantastic flat, and we should always invite friends who were totally okay.

By then a few people were running around naked or with only a towel round their middle, and now they started to touch each other up. One of the couples went into the bedroom where there was a huge bed which could be raised and lowered. A wide passageway led from the bedroom to the living room. In other words one could see what went on in the bedroom. The two were lying on the bed naked, cuddling and kissing and others joined them on the huge bed. Boys were feeling up girls and also other boys. Some did it straight at the table. I'd already sussed that a real orgy was getting under way. They invited Detlef and me to join in. But as far as I was concerned that wasn't on. I didn't fancy getting touched up by all and sundry. I wasn't by any means disgusted by what was going on there, though. I was even a bit turned on by the way they were having fun together so laid back. But that was precisely why I wanted to be alone with Detlef.

Detlef and I went into the next room. We cuddled and we got undressed. Suddenly Jürgen was sitting next to us, watching. It didn't bother me all that much because everything in this flat was relaxed and easy, and also because I remembered that Jürgen would give us money. I only hoped he wasn't going to touch us.

Jürgen just watched. While Detlef and I made love he jerked off. Later, when we left because I had to go home, he quite casually pressed a hundred-mark note into Detlef's hand.

Jürgen became a regular customer of ours. He was bisexual. As a rule we visited him together. Then I kept him busy up top and Detlef down below. He always gave us a hundred marks for that. Sometimes one of us went alone. For sixty marks. It's true, Jürgen was a customer, and, as customers go, almost as unpleasant as the others. But he was the only customer for whom I felt something like friendship. At least I respected him. I liked talking to him because he always had good ideas and was on the ball. He could

156

cope with this society. Most of all I admired the way he handled money. I think it was this I found almost the most fascinating aspect about him. When he told me how he invested his money and how, almost automatically, it kept growing. At the same time he was terribly generous. The others who took part in the orgies didn't actually get money, at least I don't think so. But once I was there when a young guy tried to touch him for a few thousand marks for a Mini Cooper. Without making a great palaver, Jürgen wrote out a cheque and said: 'There's your Mini Cooper.' Jürgen was the only customer I would visit, even if I didn't want anything from him nor him from me. Occasionally I watched TV at his place, and then I somehow thought the world quite a tolerable place.

Detlef and I now went regularly to the scene again. We were no longer interested in these normal teeny discos. When I wasn't on Zoo station, I hung around at Kurfürstendamm tube station. There were often up to a hundred customers on the narrow platform. Bargains were struck. But the customers who came here were those who specialised in fixers. Above all, Kurfürstendamm tube was our meeting place.

I went from group to group, chatting with my fellow fixers. At times, as I went about among the fixer crowd, I felt quite somebody. I was walking around this platform below the Kurfürstendamm like a star among stars. I saw the old grannies returning from their shopping, laden with parcels and plastic bags, looking at us, horrified and even frightened, and I thought: aren't we fixers vastly superior to them? True, we lead a tough life, we may die any day, and we are certainly going to die soon. But that's exactly how we want it. At least I like it that way. I thought of the money I was earning. I needed a hundred marks a day for stuff alone. With extras, my expenses came to four thousand marks a month which I had to raise. I thought: four thousand marks net, that's a director's salary. And I made those four thousand marks at the age of fourteen.

Going on the game was a grotty job, it's true. But on H, I

no longer minded all that much. And basically I did rip my customers off. What they paid me was out of all proportion to what I did in return. I still laid down all the conditions. Fucking was not on.

Among the others there were greater stars than me. There were some who said they needed four grammes of H a day. At that time this cost them five hundred to eight hundred marks a day. And they almost always managed to raise that much. In other words they made more money than any managing director, without the cops catching them. And these were the stars on Kurfürstendamm tube station, to whom I could talk at any time and who talked to me.

These were roughly my feelings and thoughts at this time, in February and March 1977, when I was doing okay. I wasn't particularly well, but I wasn't yet completely done in either. I was still able to lie to myself quite succesfully. I had once more got back totally into the role of a fixer. I thought I was the greatest. I was afraid of nothing. Before I got to be on H, I had been afraid of everything. Of my father, later of my mother's boyfriend, of my fucking school and my teachers, of caretakers, traffic policemen and tube train inspectors. I now felt unassailable. I wasn't even scared of the CID cops who sometimes crept around on the station. So far I had got away, cool as a cucumber, from every rumble.

During this time I was in contact with fixers whose handling of stuff I considered to be really together. For example, Atze and Lufo. Atze was my first boyfriend. The only boy with whom I had had a close relationship before Detlef, and on whom I had been really gone. Like Atze and Detlef, Lufo had belonged to our hash crowd in the Sound. Atze and Lufo had started on H shortly before me. Now they lived in a really great flat, complete with French bed, three-piece suite and wall-to-wall carpets. Lufo actually had a proper job as an unskilled labourer at Schwarzkopf's. Both of them said that they had never yet been physically dependent on heroin and sometimes managed without shooting for two months. I believed them, although they were almost always on it whenever I saw them.

For me Atze and Lufo were guys to model myself on. I did not want to get as low as I had been before my first withdrawal. And I thought that together with Detlef I, too, could achieve a flat complete with French bed, three-piece suite and wall-to-wall carpets, as long as we handled our stuff the way Atze and Lufo did.

Besides, those two were not as aggressive as other fixers. And Atze had a girlfriend, Simone, a really together woman, who didn't shoot at all. I thought it a terribly good thing that the two of them got on so well together in spite of it. I liked their company, and sometimes I slept on Lufo's divan when I had had a row with Detlef.

One evening when I returned home and was sitting in the living room with my mother because I was feeling okay, she fetched a paper. I thought I knew what was coming. She would hand me the paper whenever there was a report about another death from heroin. It got on my wick. I didn't want to read it.

I did read the paper although it got on my wick. I read: 'Glazier's apprentice Andreas W. (17) wanted to come off drugs. His sixteen-year-old girlfriend, a student nurse, wanted to help him: in vain. In the Tiergarten flat which his father had furnished for the young couple for several thousand marks, the young man died of an overdose . . .'

I didn't immediately catch on because I didn't want to believe it. But it all fitted neatly together: flat, glazier's apprentice, girlfriend, Andreas W. Or: Andreas Wiczorek, whom we had called Atze.

At first all I could think was: shit. My throat was quite dry and then I began to feel sick. This was really heavy. I thought it can't be true that Atze had died of an overdose. Atze of all people who handled stuff really beautifully. I didn't want to let my mother see how shattered I was by this piece in the paper. She had no idea that I was fixing again. I took the paper and went to my room.

I hadn't seen Atze for some time. Now I read in the paper

what had happened to him during his last days. He had already had a go at o.d.'ing a week earlier and was taken to hospital. Subsequently his girlfriend, Simone, had cut her wrists. Both had been saved. On the day before his death he had gone to the police and grassed on all the dealers he knew, including two girls who were known as 'the twins' and always had fine stuff. Then he had written a farewell letter which was also printed in the paper:

'*I intend ending my life because a fixer causes to his friends and relations nothing but anger, worries, bitterness and despair. He destroys not only himself but others too. Thank my parents and also my little granny. Physically I'm a wreck. To be a fixer is always the ultimate shit. But who drives people, who come into the world young and full of vitality, into disaster? This is meant to be a letter of warning for all who, one day, may be faced with the decision: Well, shall I try it? You stupid fools, take warning from my example. Now you'll have no more worries, Simone, good-bye.*'

I lay in my bed and thought: so that was your first boy-friend. In a coffin. I couldn't even cry. I wasn't capable of any real feelings.

When I went to the scene next afternoon no one was cry-ing for Atze. On the scene they don't cry. But some people were more than somewhat pissed off with Atze. On account of him having grassed on decent dealers who sold fine stuff and were now in prison, and also because he owed a lot of money to a lot of people.

The craziest thing about the whole Atze story was that a week after Atze's death his girlfriend, Simone, who had never before in her life taken H and had wanted to get Atze to kick the habit, chucked her job as a student nurse and went on the game.

Lufo died almost a year later, in January 1978, from an o.d.

With Atze's death the whole good feeling of being a fixer star who knows how to handle stuff had gone. In our crowd, with whom Atze had been in contact, fear and suspicion arose. Before when we had shot up together and there weren't enough syringes, everyone had always wanted to be first. Now suddenly everyone wanted to be second. Nobody said anything about being scared. But it was total fear that the stuff might be too pure, too strong, or else cut with strychnine or other poisons. You could die from an overdose, but you could also die from stuff that was too pure or too dirty.

So everything was a right fuck-up again. Basically it was as Atze had put it in his farewell letter. Meanwhile, I set about shattering my mother. Once again I took to coming home whenever I wanted. And whatever the time, my mother was still awake. And once I was at home she had to swallow a few valiums in order to get any sleep at all. I believe she could only carry on with the help of valium.

I felt sure that I would end up like Atze. Sometimes I had a mere glimmer of hope and clung to it. Even at school. There was a teacher, Herr Mücke, whom somehow I liked. In his class we acted out situations with which young people are faced. For instance, an interview for a job. One was the boss, the other the person looking for a job. I never allowed the boss person to tell me what's what. I quickly turned the tables on him, and the boy acting the boss would become subdued. Then I thought that perhaps I could assert myself like this in life.

Herr Mücke also took us to the careers advice centre. Before that we watched a military parade of the Allies. The boys were really interested, raving about tanks and their technology. I was sick to the back teeth of this technology, which made a diabolical din and was intended exclusively to kill people.

At the careers advice centre I was quite happy again. I read everything I could find on the job of animal keeper. On the very next afternoon Detlef and I went back to the centre and I had everything they had on animal keepers Xeroxed. Detlef also found several trades that interested him. He, too, was looking for something to do with animals and agriculture. We were really so much into this that we almost forgot that we still had to go and earn the cash for out next shot. As we stood on the station waiting for customers, with the Xerox copies from the careers advice centre in our plastic bags, it had all grown quite unreal again. If I carried on in this way, I wouldn't ever pass a single exam in any subject.

Next morning, on my way to school, I bought a copy of *Playboy*. I bought it for Detlef who was into *Playboy*, but I always read it before giving it to him. I don't quite know why we were so interested in *Playboy* of all magazines. Today I just can't understand it any more. But then *Playboy* was, for us, a clean world. Clean sex. Beautiful girls who had no problems. No queers, no customers. The guys smoked pipes and drove sports cars and had plenty of cash. And the girls had it off with them because they enjoyed it. Once Detlef had said that it was all a swindle, but he still wanted to go on reading *Playboy*.

This evening in the tube I was reading a short story in *Playboy*. I didn't quite get the contents because I was completely bombed out from my morning shot. But I liked the mood of the story. It was set somewhere far away under a blue sky and hot sun. When I came to where a pretty girl is waiting impatiently for her fantastic boyfriend to come home from work, I really began to cry. I couldn't stop myself until I had to get out at Wutzkyallee station.

At school I just sat dreaming about going a long way away with Detlef. When I met Detlef on the station in the afternoon, I told him about it. He said he had an uncle and aunt in Canada. They lived on the shores of a big lake with only forests and cornfields around them, and he was sure they would take us in. He said I must finish school because that was wiser in any case. He would go first and get a job, that was quite simple. And then, by the time I came out to join him, he would have bought or rented a wooden house for us.

I said I wanted to finish school anyway. In future I wouldn't shoot my big mouth off but concentrate on the lessons in order to get a good report when I left.

Detlef went away with a customer and I was still waiting. Suddenly two guys were standing behind me asking: 'What are you doing here?' I knew at once: plain-clothes cops. I had never been rumbled before and wasn't afraid of the cops either because up to now they'd left me in peace. After all, I had been hustling on Zoo station, off and on, for several months, as had other girls of my age. And police raids were a daily event. However, usually they were looking for wogs who'd brought a bottle of schnapps or a stack of cigarettes from East Berlin. They used to organise proper hunts for these wogs.

I said to these plain-clothes cops, quite calm-like: 'I'm waiting for my boyfriend.'

One of them asked: 'On the game, are you?'

I said: 'Do me a favour. Whatever gives you that idea. Do I look as if I am?'

They asked how old I was, and I said fourteen. They wanted to see my identity card, although you only get a proper identity card at sixteen. So I had to enlighten them on that.

The one who was in charge then said: 'Let's have a look in your plastic bag.' First he fished out my spoon. He asked what I used it for.

I said: 'To eat my yoghurt.'

Then he pulled out the loo paper and my works, and I had to go to the police station. I wasn't scared. I knew that they wouldn't lock up a fourteen-year-old. But I wasn't half pissed off with these two cops.

They locked me in a cell right next to the chief cop's desk. Somehow I was so self-assured that I never even tried to dispose of the stuff I still carried in the small pocket of my jeans. I couldn't do it, throwing away good stuff. Then a police-woman arrived. I had to take off everything, even my shirt and briefs, and she looked into every hole in my body before finally finding the H in my jeans pocket.

One of the cops typed everything terribly long-windedly on a sheet of paper. A copy of the statement went into a bulky file. So now I was a registered drug addict and no

163

longer just a mere statistic. The cops were really quite nice. Except that they were all giving me the same spiel: 'What are you doing, girl? You're only fourteen, so young and so pretty, and nearly dead.'

I had to give them the phone number of my mother's firm, and one of them went out of the room to ring her up.

My mother arrived at about half past five, after work, nearly sick with tension. And then she actually started a conversation with these cops. She said: 'Ah yes, these children. I'm at my wits' end what to do with her. And I did help her withdraw. But she doesn't really want to stop at all.'

I thought this was the end: *doesn't really want to stop*. My mother simply didn't have the slightest idea about me and H. Of course I wanted to. But how, that's what she might have told me. Outside she began interrogating me. Where had I been, for heaven's sake? I said: 'I was at the station, man.'

She: 'But I've told you not to go there.'

I said: 'I was waiting for Detlef, perhaps I might be permitted to do that at least.'

She thought I ought not to meet this 'unemployed asocial tramp' any more. And then she asked: 'Perhaps you're on the game, too, are you?'

I yelled at her: 'Are you crazy? Just say that again. Why should I go on the game, can you tell me that? So you think I'm a tart, do you?'

That shut her up. However, now I was really afraid for my freedom. And somwhere I was scared on account of my mother being so cold. I thought she'd dropped me too, given me up, wouldn't help me any more. But then I said to myself: what help is she, trotting out her 'Don't go to the station,' 'Stop seeing that tramp Detlef.'

I had to go home with my mother, and I had no stuff left for next day. In the morning my mother got me out of bed. She looked at my face: 'What eyes you have, child. They are quite blank. I see in them only fear and despair.'

When my mother had gone to work I looked in the mirror. For the first time I looked at my eyes while I was

164

doing cold turkey. They were all pupil. Quite black and quite dull. Really totally blank. I felt hot. I washed my face. I shivered, so I went and sat in a hot bath. Then I didn't dare get out of the bath because it was much too cold outside. I kept running the hot water. Somehow I had to bridge the time until midday. For in the morning I wouldn't find a customer at the station, nor anyone who'd stand me a shot. Nobody had any stuff in the morning. In any case it was difficult to find someone who'd stand you anything. Even Axel and Bernd made a huge fuss — they needed every quarter for themselves because they had a job making as much as they needed. Detlef, too, had grown very mean with his stuff. As for the others on the scene, they'd rather chuck their stuff down the drain than share it.

When my cold turkey got steadily worse, I forced myself to get out of the bath and went round the flat in search of money. For some time now the living room door had been locked. This was Klaus' doing because he maintained that I spoiled his records. But I had already found out how to open the lock with a bent piece of wire. There wasn't a pennypiece to be found in the living room. Then I remembered the beer can in the kitchen cupboard. My mother collected new five-mark pieces in this can.

My hand holding the heavy beer can shook because I was doing cold turkey, and perhaps also just a little because I was going to pinch from my mother. I had never done this before, honest. For me that had always been the end. In that respect I was different from other fixers. Bernd, for instance, Detlef's friend, had taken everything from his parents' flat, little by little. Television set, percolator, electric bread slicer, really anything for which he could get a few marks for stuff. All I had flogged was my own bits of jewellery and nearly all my records.

So now I tipped my mother's five-mark pieces out of the beer can. A quarter scene gramme had just dropped by five marks from forty to thirty-five marks. Therefore I needed seven fives. I worked it out: since as a rule I still charged customers forty marks, there would be five left every time. So I would easily be able to put back a five-mark piece every day. In only a week I would have paid back the money, and probably my mother wouldn't notice anything. I went with my seven fives to the scene which, in the morning, was in the refectory of the Technical College, scored my stuff and had my fix in the College toilet.

My mother had taken to checking my arms for fresh needle marks every night. I now shot into my hand. Always in the same spot. There I had a continuous scab. I told my mother that it was a wound which took a long time healing up. The time came when my mother tumbled to it that I had fresh needle marks. I said: 'Of course, man. Just one today. I only do it now and again, and that doesn't do any harm.'

My mother gave me a right walloping. I didn't resist. I didn't very much care any more. She treated me anyway like the ultimate dirt, getting on my nerves at every opportunity. Instinctively, she was doing exactly the right thing. For a fixer has to get to the point where he's in the shit up to his eyeballs and doesn't know which way to turn before he'll be ready to change anything at all seriously. Then he will either kill himself or use his slim chance to get away from H. However, in those days I was very far from possessing such insights.

My mother pinned her hopes on another thing. It had been arranged that at the start of the spring holidays I would go to the village in Hesse to stay with my gran and my cousins. Perhaps I would stay even longer. I no longer knew whether I ought to be glad or afraid of the separation from Detlef and the unavoidable withdrawal. By now I simply did what I was forced to do by others. I only insisted on Detlef spending the last night at my house.

On this last night I had yet another hope. After Detlef and I had made love, I said to him: 'Listen, strictly speaking we've always done everything together. During the next few weeks I really want to kick. I'll never get another chance like this. And I'd like you to kick, too. When I come back we'll both be off H and ready to start a new life.'

Detlef said, yes, of course, he would kick. He was going

to tell me anyway. He had already lined up a source of valeron. He'd also get work, he said, and starting tomorrow or the day after he would no longer go hustling either.

Next morning I had an extra large fix before starting off for my gran's and the new life. When I arrived I wasn't yet doing cold turkey properly. But in this idyll of the farmhouse kitchen I felt like the odd man out. Everything got on my wick. It got on my wick when my little cousin, with whom I had played when she was a baby, wanted to sit on my lap. The old-fashioned earth closet which last time I had thought so romantic, got on my wick as well.

Next morning withdrawal symptoms started with a vengeance. I crept out of the house into the woods. The twittering of birds got on my wick, and a rabbit made me nearly jump out of my skin. I climbed up on to a raised hide. I couldn't even finish my cigarette. I wanted to die on that hide. I crept back to the house and went to bed. I told my gran that I had 'flu or something. She was concerned but not really anxious about my piteous state.

Above my bed hung a poster. On it was the hand of a skeleton holding a syringe. And the message under it read: 'This is the end. It started with curiosity.' My cousin said she'd been given the poster at school some time or other. I had no idea that my mother had informed my gran that I was a drug addict. Now I was staring at this syringe. Only the syringe. I no longer saw the letters and this dead hand. I imagined that inside it was a quarter of fine stuff. The syringe was positively coming towards me out of the poster. For hours I stared at this fucking poster, it was nearly driving me round the bend. My cousin was often in the room and pretended not to notice what was the matter with me. She was continually droning out teeny bopper cassettes, probably imagining that this would amuse me. In retrospect it was, of course, quite touching, the things they got up to at my gran's just to help me.

My first day of kicking seemed to be never-ending. Once, when I dozed off, I dreamt of a guy who did actually haunt the Berlin scene. He was so fucked up with all the fixing that

167

he was bugged all over. He was rotting alive. His feet had already gone dead and quite black. He was hardly able to walk any longer. He stank to high heaven from several paces off. If anyone asked him why he didn't go to hospital, he grinned just like a death's head. He really was only waiting for death. It was this guy I had to think of when I wasn't staring at the syringe or half unconscious with pain. It was all exactly like the first time: the sweat, the stench, the puke.

Next morning I could stand it no more. I crawled to the telephone booth in the village and rang up my mother. I cried buckets down the receiver and grovelled to her to let me come back to Berlin.

My mother was quite unmoved. She said: 'I see, are you feeling poorly again then? I thought you took drugs only now and then. Well, in that case it can't be all that bad.'

In the end I just pleaded with her to send me some sleeping tablets by express letter. I knew that there was an H scene in the next little town. I had sussed that out during my last visit. But I hadn't the strength to get there. And then I didn't know anybody on this scene. When a fixer is away from his own scene he is totally alone and helpless.

Mercifully my cold turkey only lasted for four days, as before. When it was all over I felt empty and fagged out. It didn't even make me feel good any longer to know that the poison was out of my body. Once more I was overcome by revulsion for Berlin, but then I didn't feel at home in this village either. I thought I didn't belong anywhere any more, and tried not to think about it.

All I had to turn me on were the sleeping tablets my mother had sent me far too late, and cider, large quantities of which were stored in my gran's cellar. I got the chucks. In the morning I started with four or five rolls, and all during the day I went on eating twelve or fifteen crispbreads spread with jam. At night I raided my gran's shelves of bottled plums, peaches and strawberries. With whipped cream piled on top. I could never go to sleep before two or three in the morning anyway.

Within a very short period I put on ten kilos. My relations

168

were delighted at the sight of my stomach hanging over my trousers and my arse growing fatter and fatter. Only my arms and legs stayed thin. It was all the same to me. I had become a food addict, that was all. Very soon I could no longer get into my skin-tight jeans. My kind cousin gave me a pair of baggy check trousers like the ones I wore in Berlin when I was eleven. Gradually I was getting back into the community of village children. However, I didn't take all this for real. It was a trip, a rather pretty film, which would soon be over.

I didn't talk to the others about drugs, and presently I didn't any longer think about drugs either. I didn't want to spoil my pretty film. Only shortly after the cold turkey, I wrote a letter to Detlef and put twenty marks inside it for him to send me some H. That's what I wrote to the same Detlef whom I had asked to kick. Admittedly, I didn't post the letter because I thought that Detlef wouldn't send me any H anyway but use the money for his own shots.

My cousin took me to visit castles and country houses in the neighbourhood and I did some riding almost daily. Together with the other children we went to the quarry which once had belonged to my grandpa. He had drunk away the quarry before he drank himself into his grave. So my mother hadn't had an easy childhood.

My gran had told us that somewhere in the quarry there was supposed to be an iron door, behind which old family documents lay hidden. We searched for this door almost every night. Sometimes the workers forgot to pull out the key of the excavator. Then we would drive the excavator round and round the quarry. I seemed to get on very well with my cousin, who is my own age. I told her about my love for Detlef as if ours were just an ordinary teenage romance. I told her that Detlef and I slept together, and my cousin thought that was quite all right.

My cousin told me that there was a boy from Düsseldorf who came camping every year in the summer. She thought he was okay. But then he had started getting fresh and she'd told him to get lost. Did I think she'd been silly?

I said, no, I thought it a hundred per cent okay that she didn't allow this camper to mess her about. She ought to keep herself for the boy who she really wanted to go with. My cousin and all her friends came to me with their problems. I became a real agony column auntie. I told them what to do and particularly that they oughtn't to be so dead serious about everything. All their problems seemed ridiculous to me. But I was a good listener and I always had good advice ready. I was terribly strong when it was a question of other people's problems. It was only my own I couldn't cope with.

One night Detlef telephoned. I was terribly happy. He said he was with a customer and that was why he could telephone. We talked and talked because this customer was very generous. I told him about my beastly cold turkey. That this time I'd nearly gone crazy. He said he hadn't started kicking. It was bloody awful. I said I was looking forward to seeing him again. I asked him, wouldn't he like to write to me as he had promised. Detlef said, no, not really, he wasn't keen on writing. But he'd phone when he was at this customer's place again.

After this telephone conversation, I was once again quite certain that I was as good as married to Detlef. We belonged together, no matter what shit he got himself into. In bed at night I always had a proper minute's silence for Detlef. It was like praying. And I counted the days when I would be back with Detlef.

My grandma regularly gave me money. I saved resolutely. Actually I wasn't quite sure why. But when I had saved forty marks I knew why. I was really proud of my forty marks and hid them. Forty was my magic number: forty marks was normally the price of a shot. Forty marks was what, as a rule, I expected my customers to pay.

Once this had sunk in, I said to myself: 'It really can't be true that you've actually started saving for your first shot.' So I went out and bought a T-shirt for twenty marks only to get off this bloody figure forty again. Because after all I had come here so that I might never shoot again.

When the four weeks were up, my mother telephoned and asked whether I'd like to stay on. Without giving it much thought I said no. Perhaps if she'd asked, would you like to stay there for the rest of your life, I might have thought about it. But as it was, this had from the start been only a trip, with the horrors to begin with and then terribly gentle and beautiful. I was prepared for the trip to be over after four weeks. I wanted to get back to Detlef to whom I was as good as married.

On the day of my departure the first thing I did was to put on different clothes. My gran and my cousin tried in vain to talk me into keeping on those check trousers which fitted me very well now. I squeezed myself into my tight jeans. The seams creaked, the zip, with the best will in the world, wouldn't close. I put on my long black man's jacket and my boots with the highest heels. I was once again tarted up like a girl fixer even before I left my gran's. With gaping trousers I returned to Berlin.

On the very next afternoon I went to Zoo station. Detlef and his friend Bernd were there. Axel, the third of our group, was missing. I thought he was busy with a customer.

The boys gave me a great welcome. I really felt how glad they were that I had come back. Most of all Detlef, of course. I said to him: 'Well, and are you kicking, like a good boy, and have you got a good job, then?' All three of us laughed.

I asked: 'How's Axel?'

The boys looked funny, and after a while Detlef said: 'Don't you know that Axel is dead?'

It really knocked me sideways. At first I could hardly breathe. I said weakly: 'You're having me on.' But I knew it was true.

So now it was Axel. Axel, in whose flat I had spent most week-end nights with Detlef during the last few months. Axel with his stinking fixer flat, who had put clean bed-clothes on for me every week. Axel, for whom I used to bring that silly tuna fish of his and who always put out Danone yoghurt for me. The only one to whom I could go

171

with all my problems, whenever Detlef and I had another row. The only one who always had a shoulder for me to cry on. Because, at least within the crowd, he had never been aggressive, never hurtful to anyone.

I asked: 'But why?'

Detlef said: 'They found him in some toilet with the spike in his arm.' For the two boys Axel's death seemed to be yesterday's news. They seemed almost embarrassed to talk about it.

I kept thinking about the idiotic tuna fish again. And suddenly I thought about Detlef and that he might not have a place to sleep. I asked: 'Are you still sleeping in Axel's flat?'

Detlef replied: 'His mother sold the flat. I'm living with a customer now.'

I said: 'Bloody hell.' At that moment I thought that now I had finally lost Detlef to his customers. That Detlef had gone to live with a customer hit me almost as hard as Axel's death.

Detlef said: 'This customer's okay. He's still young, in his mid-twenties, and not a bit of a paunch. I've told him about you. You can sleep at his place too.'

We went to the scene where Detlef wanted to score. We met a few people we knew and I kept saying: 'Isn't it a right balls-up about Axel?' But the others wouldn't buy it. So I said: 'Isn't it a right balls-up about Axel?' to myself a few times.

From the scene we went to the Bülowbogen toilet. Detlef wanted to fix straightaway. I went along to help him. I waited for Detlef to offer me some of his stuff. Possibly because in that case I intended to say no, just to show him that I was strong enough to do it. But Detlef didn't offer me anything. The business with Axel hadn't half got under my skin and I thought I couldn't stand it. While Detlef cooked up his stuff I suddenly felt a craving for a shot. I thought a teensy-weensy shot won't get you hooked, but it'll put this shit with Axel and Detlef's customer out of your head. I asked Detlef.

Detlef said: 'Good God, you don't want to shoot again,

172

do you? I thought you'd stopped.'

I said: ' 'Course I'm stopping, old man. But you more than anyone should know how terribly simple it is to kick. You kicked so successfully yourself while I was away and stayed off it, haven't you? Listen, old man, honestly, now I've heard all this shit here, I need a little shot.'

Detlef said: 'Kicking isn't hard either. I could do it any day. Just didn't want to. But you, don't you start again.'

While he was still talking he had his fix and left a little for me in the syringe. After I had been off H for so long, this little bit was enough to turn me on a little and make me almost forget the business with Axel.

This time it didn't take very long at all before I was fully hooked again. My mother had no idea. She was pleased that I was so nice and fat, and I had one hell of a time getting all those kilos off.

Often, when I wanted to be with Detlef, I had to go to Rolf, his customer. There was no other place where we could share a bed. I didn't like this Rolf from the start. He was totally gone on Detlef. And naturally he was jealous of me. When I quarrelled with Detlef, Rolf was blissfully happy and on Detlef's side. It invariably made me go berserk. Detlef treated this Rolf like a totally submissive wife or girlfriend. He sent him out to do the shopping, made him do the cooking and the washing-up. This in turn annoyed me because I should have liked to shop and cook for Detlef.

I said to Detlef: 'Listen, we're a threesome that's simply not suited.' But Detlef said he had no other bed to go to. Besides, by and large, Rolf was okay. At any rate there was hardly another customer who wound him up as little as Rolf.

Detlef did what he liked with Rolf. He shouted at him and said: 'You can thank your lucky stars that I stay with you at all.' Detlef only shared his bed when he needed cash urgently. Our bed was in the same room as this Rolf's. When we made love, Rolf looked at the box or just turned round. He was totally queer and didn't want to watch Detlef and me making love. I must say, we were all three of us a pretty fucked-up lot.

I could never rid myself of the fear that through working as a bumboy Detlef might himself come to be queer. One night I really thought this was it. He had to go and sleep with Rolf because he was skint. I lay in the other bed. Detlef had switched off the light. He always did this when he had to gratify Rolf and I was there. The whole business seemed to me to take a suspiciously long time. And I believed I heard Detlef moan. I got up and lit a candle. The two of them were carrying on under the covers. I believed they were touching one another. That was against my deal with Detlef: no touching. I was terribly pissed off. So pissed off that I couldn't even ask Detlef to come back to bed with me. I said: 'Seems that someone's having a lovely time.'

Not a word out of Detlef; Rolf was hopping mad. He put out the candle. Detlef stayed in bed with Rolf all night. And I sobbed into the pillows. I wept silently because I didn't want the other two to hear how upset I was. Next morning I was so sad and pissed off that I seriously considered leaving Detlef. H was more and more undermining the substance of our love without our being fully aware of it. At any rate I realised that I would not have Detlef for myself as long as we were on H. That I would have to share him with his customers, in particular with Rolf. The other way round it was different, of course. I was back on the game at Zoo station every day, and since, as a rule, I was under pressure I could no longer afford to be quite so fussy about the person I would accept as a customer nor about the conditions I tried to lay down.

In order to avoid spending a lot of time at Rolf's, I began keeping company with the other members of our crowd, particularly Babsi and Stella. But even with them communication became increasingly difficult. All everyone wanted to do these days was to talk about themselves for hours on end and no one was prepared to listen for even a couple of minutes. Babsi, for instance, would go on and on about the meaning of a hyphen on a street sign, while Stella and I were bursting to relate how we had been ripped off by a dealer who'd sold us flour instead of stuff. We would shout: 'shut up' at Babsi. Then Stella and I talked all at once and yelled at each other because we both wanted to tell the story. So most attempts at having a conversation would end abruptly with a 'shut up.' Every one of us urgently needed somebody who would listen. But we no longer found that person in our crowd. There was no longer anything like real communication. One could only count on an audience if relating experiences with the cops. Then we were all united against those fucking cops. In this context I had an advantage over the others. In the early summer of 1977 I was arrested again.

It was on Kurfürstendamm tube station. We had just come from a customer. He had only wanted to watch — for a hundred and fifty marks. So we were quite happy, both had a quarter of stuff each in our pockets and ample cash left over. I was first to see the cops pouring on to the platform. A rumble. A train was just coming in, and in total panic I ran down the platform. Detlef, daft as he was at that moment, after me. As I ran into a carriage at the end of the train I bumped into a grandad. He said: 'Crikey, you half-dead old cow.' He really called me that. From the many reports in the papers, everybody knew what went on at Kurfürstendamm tube station. So the creeps in the tube cottoned on quite quickly that this was a raid on drug addicts.

Detlef followed me, and two plain-clothes cops followed him. After all, our behaviour had been conspicuous enough. However, they needn't have bothered streaking after us like this. For before they had reached us, the grannies and grandads in the tube carriage had rushed up to us, tugging at our things and screaming hysterically: 'Here they are. Police.' I felt like an outlaw in an old Western, about to be strung up from the nearest tree. I clung to Detlef. When the cops got to us, one of them said. 'You two don't have to come the old Romeo and Juliet with us. Get a move on.'

We were bundled into a Volkswagen bus and taken to the police station. The cops were very unpleasant to me, but

175

didn't ask any more questions. They just told me that because they'd caught me before there was already a file on me. One of them typed the usual statement which I had to sign. They didn't even bother informing my mother. For them I was one of many hopeless cases, about which they would file a few more statements before, finally, putting a cross after my name. Detlef and I were released after less than an hour. Since they had confiscated our stuff we had to go straight back to the scene to buy another two quarters. Luckily, we had some cash left.

By now almost all the plain-clothes cops on Zoo station knew me and as a rule left me alone. One of them was actually quite nice. A young one with a Southern German accent. Once he crept up on me from behind and suddenly thrust his badge under my nose. I nearly jumped out of my skin with fright. But he just laughed and asked whether I was on the game. I said, quite naively, as I usually did in reply to this question: 'No, do I look as if I am?'

I daresay he'd got my number. However, he didn't even want to take a look inside my plastic bag. He just said: 'Listen, kid, for the next few weeks, keep away from this place. Otherwise I'll have to run you in.' Perhaps he wasn't nice at all, only too lazy to take me to the police station. Besides, his colleagues at the station didn't much fancy having to write the same boring reports about a fourteen-year-old half-dead cow.

After our arrest on Kurfürstendamm tube station, Detlef and I were forced to score from a dealer we didn't know because we couldn't locate our regular dealer. We went to the toilet on Winterfeldplatz to fix. The toilet had been vandalised. The taps weren't working at all. I cleaned my syringe with water from the stinking loo. I did this frequently because in some toilets there were too many people to risk cleaning one's works outside in the wash basin.

Somehow this stuff from the strange dealer nearly knocked me out. I picked myself up immediately but I was still totally woozy. We hadn't been to the Sound for a long time, so we decided to pay it a visit. Detlef was cooling off on the dance floor while I stood next to an orange juice vending machine. There was a hole at the top. I leant against the machine, pushed two straws joined to each other through the hole and drank without paying a penny, until I had to go to the toilet to throw up.

When I returned I was got at by one of the manager guys. He called me a bloody fixer and demanded that I come with him. I was scared. He grabbed me by the arm and dragged me across the place. He opened a door which led into a storeroom. I saw that there was also a bar stool. I knew immediately what was up. At least I had often heard about it. They would strip fixers and other people they didn't want, and tie them to the bar stool. Then they'd flog them with whips and other things. I'd heard of guys who, after a session in the Sound's storeroom, had to stay in hospital for weeks with a fractured skull or broken bones. Afterwards they were so intimidated that they wouldn't go to the police. The manager guys did this because they were sadists but also in order to keep fixers away from the joint since the authorities were constantly threatening to close the Sound. However, girl fixers who slept with these manager guys were never molested. This Sound was a totally diabolical dump. If parents had known what really went on in 'Europe's most modern discotheque', they would never have allowed their children to go there. People were still being introduced to fixing and pimps were roping in teen-agers without the managers doing anything about it.

So I stood outside the open storeroom door and was seized by total panic. With a strength which I hadn't realised I still possessed, I tore myself free from this guy and ran like mad towards the exit. I got as far as the street before the guy caught up with me. He grabbed me and flung me full force against a car. I didn't feel my bruises. Suddenly I was panic-stricken because of Detlef. They knew that we were always together. And I hadn't seen Detlef after he went on to the dance floor, high as a kite.

I ran to the telephone booth and rang the police. I told the cops that my boyfriend was being beaten to a pulp in the

Sound. The cops seemed pleased to hear this, and a few minutes later they arrived in a police car. They were looking for evidence against the Sound which would enable them to close the place down. At least a dozen policemen scoured the place for Detlef. But of Detlef there was no trace. Then it occurred to me to ring up Rolf. Detlef was already in bed.

The cops said: 'On a trip, are you? Don't pull that again with us.' I went home and really did think that stuff had driven me round the bend.

The only consequence of my various arrests was a summons to the CID department. At three o'clock in the afternoon I was to be at room 314 of the Criminal Investigation Department in Gothaer Strasse. I've never forgotten the room number because later I had to go there repeatedly.

From school I went home first to give myself a decent fix. I thought if I'm really high the cops won't be able to get at me. However, I had no lemon left and the stuff looked rather cut. At this time it was getting steadily worse, anyway. Stuff went from hand to hand, from the big dealer via the middle dealer to the small dealer, and every one tipped in something to increase their profit.

Somehow I had to dissolve this totally cut H. I decided to use vinegar because it also contains acid. I poured the vinegar from the bottle on to the spoon which contained the stuff. But I poured out far too much vinegar. Therefore I had to bang this vinegar solution into my vein because otherwise I would have had to throw away the H.

No sooner had I shot up than I passed out. It took more than an hour for me to come round again. The syringe was still stuck in my arm. I had a beastly headache. At first I couldn't get up. I thought this was it, I was going to die. I lay on the floor and wept. I was afraid. I didn't want to die all alone. I crawled to the telephone on all fours. It must have taken me all of ten minutes before I managed to dial my mother's business number. All I said was: 'Please come, mummy, I'm dying.'

By the time my mother arrived I was already able to stand

up again. I pulled myself together, although my head still seemed to be bursting. I said: 'That was another attack of this daft circulation trouble of mine.'

I think my mother suspected that I'd had a fix. She had a look of desperation on her face. She said nothing at all. She just kept looking at me with those sad, despairing eyes. I couldn't bear this look. It pierced my head which seemed to be bursting.

At last my mother asked whether there was anything I wanted. I said: 'Yes, please. Strawberries.' She went out and brought me a large basket of strawberries.

That afternoon I really thought I'd had it. I hadn't shot a strong dose, only too much vinegar. My body simply had no resistance left. At least my body didn't want to go on like this. After all, I knew this from others who were already dead. They, too, had first passed out a few times after a fix. And then came the time when they didn't wake up at all: it was curtains. I no longer knew why I had been afraid of dying. Of dying alone. Fixers die alone. Mostly, alone in a stinking toilet. And I did want to die. Strictly speaking, that was all I was waiting for. I didn't know why I was in this world. Even in the old days that was something I hadn't been quite sure about. But why in the world does a fixer stay alive? Only in order to ruin others as well. That afternoon I thought I must die if only for my mother's sake. I no longer knew anyway whether I was or wasn't there.

Next morning I felt better. I thought, perhaps you'll last a little longer. I had to go to the police, if I didn't want them to come to me. But somehow I could no longer pluck up the courage to go to the police on my own. I telephoned round for Stella, and I was lucky to get hold of her at a mutual regular customer of ours. I asked whether she would come to the police with me. She said yes immediately. Her mother had just reported her to the police again as missing. But Stella was afraid of nothing, it was all the same to her. She was willing to come to the police with me, although she was dossing around.

And then I sat with Stella on a wooden bench in a long

corridor outside Room 314 and waited like a good little girl until I was called. When I was called I entered Room 314 so obediently, for two pins I'd have curtseyed. There was a Frau Schipke who shook my hand quite pleasantly and told me at once that she, too, had a daughter who was a year older than me, 15, but not on drugs. So this woman copper was coming over all motherly, like. She asked how I was and offered me cocoa, cake and apples.

And then this Frau Schipke talked in quite a motherly way about other people on the scene, asking me how they were. She showed me photos of fixers and dealers, and all I would say was, yes, I knew them by sight. Then she told me that certain people on the scene had said nasty things about me, and then she got me talking. I realised that this woman copper was pulling a fast one on me in the grottiest possible way, but still I said too much. Afterwards I signed a statement with all sorts of rubbish which she had more or less put into my mouth.

Finally, there was a copper who asked me about the Sound. And then I really spoke out. I told them how many people I knew who had been introduced to fixing and about the brutal floggers among the management. I asked them to call in Stella, who confirmed everything and said she was willing to take an oath on what she'd said in front of any judge.

All this time the Schipke woman was leafing through her files and before long she'd twigged who Stella was. She began to pump Stella, but Stella gave her plenty of lip. I thought they'd jug her there and then. But then it was the end of Frau Schipke's office hours and she said Stella was to come back next day. Of course Stella didn't go.

Before I left, this Frau Schipke said to me: 'Well, I'm sure we'll meet again.' She said that in as fucking pleasant a tone as she had said everything else. That was the rottenest thing of all. What she said was nothing but that I was a hopeless case, anyway.

GERHARD ULBER, DETECTIVE CHIEF
SUPERINTENDENT AND HEAD OF BERLIN
POLICE DRUG SQUAD

In our fight against drug abuse we of the police are making every effort to restrict the supply of illegal narcotics, in particular heroin, and thereby to support responsible authorities in their attempts to provide treatment.

In 1976 we impounded 2.9 kilograms of heroin; in 1977, 4.9 kilograms; and during the first eight months of 1978 no less than 8.4 kilograms. This does not mean, however, that we have increased the amount of confiscated drugs in relation to heroin on offer or actually consumed. In this respect I am personally inclined to be pessimistic. The quantities of heroin available have increased. Only a year ago the arrest of a German middleman with 100 grammes of heroin would have caused a minor sensation. Today it is recorded as an everyday occurrence.

We have to note that in view of the substantial profit margin, an increasing number of Germans are now involved in the heroin trade. Admittedly, smugglers and wholesalers are almost exclusively foreigners as are those middlemen with direct access to them. However, the next lower stage of middleman already consists predominantly of Germans. They pass on heroin in quantities of up to 100 grammes to the addicted small dealer who takes it to the final consumer.

As was to be expected, the success of our investigations has led to increased caution by smugglers and dealers, to which, in turn, we must reply by increasing our investigation activities. However, the more we undertake in public where drug addicts and their small dealers meet, the more we drive them into areas where it becomes almost impossible to detect them.

In principle, the police may do whatever they like. Whether they proceed by discreet surveillance of the so-called public scene or a police presence in the form of patrols, etc., the market will always find a way. More and more often heroin is sold in private flats where addicts evade police surveillance.

For instance, of the 84 who died of heroin in Berlin in the year 1977, 24 were completely unknown to us as consumers of heroin, and it can be safely assumed that they did not die as the result of their first injection. But the persistent drug consumer comes to the attention of the police only when he is admitted unconscious to a hospital where he is saved at the last moment with the help of medical care.

Otherwise a person may inject himself with heroin for years without the police getting to know about it. In a word: the police cannot solve the drug problem with its own resources. The Americans have experienced this during prohibition: where there is a strong demand, it will find a corresponding supply.

Of course I could employ another twenty officers, and in that case we could arrest more small heroin dealers. However, the problem would remain, the only effect being that it would be increasingly shifted to the prisons where it is already very strongly in evidence now. Prisoners who are addicts will do anything to lay their hands on stuff, and even imprisoned dealers do all they can to supply them. It must be said quite openly: the profit margins corrupt enormously.

Unless we succeed in concentrating delinquent drug addicts in a prison where they are isolated from other prisoners, the result will be — at least in Berlin — either chaos in the prisons or the end of modern prison methods. For it is not possible to grant to any prisoner either leave or parole, nor to allow generous visiting arrangements if, on the other hand, one wants to prevent drug abuse from being continued in prison and the creation of new addicts. Neither is it practically feasible to submit every prisoner on parole or on leave, or every visitor, to regular physical examinations, which would be necessary because women smuggle heroin into prison concealed in birth control devices in their vagina, while among men similar procedures are common and known as 'anal bombs'.

Continual arrests, sentences and imprisonment will not change anything. To the heroin addict it makes no differ-

ence, as long as he still has a possibility of satisfying his addiction. Preventive information would, in my view, be the only means by which the increase in the number of drug addicts might be tackled with some measure of success.

RENATE SCHIPKE, 35, SENIOR OFFICIAL IN THE DRUG ADDICTION DEPARTMENT

I met Christiane in the course of my work in connection with crimes against the drug law. On the first occasion she was on the basis of a routine police report and came to see me accompanied by her friend Stella. Altogether I saw her six or seven times.

At the time it was my task to interrogate addicts who had come to the notice of the police, with the aim of obtaining from them the names of the people from whom they purchase the illegal drug. There is a huge number of these police reports, and one has to do one's best to get through the workload. Thus one cannot spend a great deal of time pondering on the matter. Nevertheless, I try to get through personally to the summoned person and to make some sort of contact because otherwise a successful interrogation will not be possible.

At the beginning Christiane was very open and supplied information readily. I was struck by her modesty and she appeared to be a well brought up child. During the first few interrogations she still gave the impression of a little girl. At all times Christiane spoke well of her mother, and I must say that, unlike many other parents, the mother was very concerned for her daughter. I was in frequent contact with her on the telephone.

After several interrogations Christiane came to be impertinent and presumptuous in a way not commensurate with her age. I told her quite coldly that she would remain a fixer despite her withdrawals. We had a fierce argument. However, I do not want to say anything negative about Christiane.

Fixers simply cannot be helped. They always feel they have been tricked because they are unable to realise what

183

*they are to be punished for. In my view these young people
are far too irresponsible. Out of curiosity and boredom they
start fixing, and then they are surprised when they have to
bear the consequences. I consider it desirable that Christiane should receive the stiffest punishment possible, for the
shock of imprisonment might possibly bring about an impro-
vement in so young a person. At least I hope so.*

In the tube I could have cried with rage for having allowed a
woman copper to pull a fast one on me with cocoa and cake
and her disgusting fucking friendliness.

After I had attended to two customers on the station and
scored stuff at Kurfürstendamm, I went home. My cat lay in
the kitchen and could hardly get up. It had been ill for
several days. Now it looked so wasted and miaowed so pite-
ously that I thought it would die soon as well.

Now I was more concerned with my sick cat than with my
own state. The vet had given me some extract of ox blood
for the cat. But it no longer ate anything. It lay in front of the
bowl of ox blood extract and never even raised its head.

I intended having a fix immediately. I took out my works,
and then I had an idea. I drew some of the ox blood extract
into the syringe and squirted it into the mouth of the cat. It
tolerated this quite apathetically. It took me a long time to
clean the syringe and to have my fix. Things were no longer
the same. It was this daft fear of dying which was getting me
down. I wanted to die, but before every shot I had this daft
fear of dying. Perhaps it was my cat which made me realise
what a grotty thing it is to die if one hasn't yet lived properly.

Everything was hopeless. I had not exchanged a single
sensible word with my mother since she had found out that I
was shooting again. I shouted all over the place, and she just
kept looking at me with her despairing eyes. Now the police
were finally after me. The statement I had signed at the
Schipke's office was more than enough for me to be put on
trial and given a stiff young offender's sentence. I felt that
my mother would have been pleased if somehow she could
have got me off her hands. After all, she knew now that she

184

could no longer help me. She was constantly on the 'phone to authorities and drug advice places and was looking more and more desperate, for it dawned on her that nobody would or could help her and me. She threatened feebly to take me to her relatives in West Germany.

And it was some time in May 1977 that even I, with my brains gone to pieces, sussed that I had exactly two possibilities left: either I died of an overdose soon or I made a serious attempt to come off heroin. I could no longer count on Detlef. Above all, I could not let the decision depend on him.

I took myself to Gropiusstadt, and went to Centre House, the Protestant youth centre where my drugs career had begun. In the meantime the Club had been closed down because they couldn't cope any longer with the drug problem there. Instead they now had a drug counselling service. A proper counselling service exclusively for Gropiusstadt. That shows how many heroin addicts there were two years after the first H had appeared in Gropiusstadt. They told me what, actually, I knew already: that my only chance lay in a genuine therapy. They gave me the addresses of Drogeninfo and Synanon because they appeared to be the most successful with their therapies.

I was rather scared of these therapies, for they were terribly hard, so they said on the scene. Worse than prison, during the first few months. With Synanon one even had to have all one's hair cut off. Presumably to prove that one was resolved to start an entirely new life. I thought I couldn't possibly do it, having all my hair cut off and having to run around like Kojak. Somehow, for me my hair was the most important thing about me. I hid my face behind it. I thought if they cut off my hair I might as well kill myself.

The lady drug counsellor said herself that I would have little or no chance with Drogeninfo or Synanon because they very rarely had any vacancies. Conditions of admission were very hard, she said. One had to be still in good physical health and prove to them, in the first place, through voluntary self-discipline, that one actually had the strength

185

to get away from H. The lady drug counsellor said that after all, I was still very young — not even 15 — that was to say, still almost a child. Therefore I would find it difficult to succeed in doing what these people demanded. Strictly speaking, there was as yet no therapy for children.

I said that actually I wanted to go to Narkonon. Narkonon was the therapy centre of a sect, the Church of Scientology. There were a few fixers on the scene who had been to Narkonon. They said things were quite okay there. At Narkonon they had no conditions for admission as long as one paid in advance. One was allowed to wear one's fixer gear, bring one's records, and even pets.

The lady drug counsellor said I ought to think about why so many fixers reported that the Narkonon therapy had been great when they went on merrily shooting. At least she herself hadn't heard of a single case of a successful therapy at Narkonon.

At home I again squirted ox blood extract into my cat's mouth with my one and only syringe. When my mother came home, I told her: 'I'm definitely withdrawing with Narkonon. I'll have to stay there for a few months or even a year, and then I'll really be off H.'

My mother pretended that she no longer believed a word of what I said anyway. But straightaway she was hanging on the 'phone again, trying to gather information about Narkonon.

I was dead keen on the therapy trip. I felt newly born. That afternoon I hadn't had a customer and was totally without H. I wanted to withdraw before I went to Narkonon. I didn't want to have to start in their cold turkey room. I wanted to get there totally off H in order to have a lead on the others who had just arrived like me. I wanted to prove straightaway that I had the real will to get away from H.

I went to bed early. I laid the cat, who was getting steadily worse, on the pillow next to my head. I was a little proud of myself. I was withdrawing quite alone, totally of my own free will. Which fixer could do that? I had, in fact, told my mother that I would withdraw immediately, but she had only smiled incredulously. She didn't take time off either, this time. For her any withdrawal like this was by now almost something ordinary and altogether hopeless. So I really had to see this through alone.

Next morning I was doing cold turkey. It was as bad as my other withdrawals, perhaps even worse. But I never once thought, you won't be able to do it. When I thought the pains were going to kill me I told myself at once: Not a bit of it, that's only the poison coming out of your body. You will live because never again will any poison get into your body. Whenever I dozed off I didn't have horror dreams. The pictures I saw were of my splendid life after the therapy.

When on the third day the pains became more bearable I saw nothing but my paradise before me, like in a film. It was growing more and more concrete. I continued going to school, up to university entrance. I had a flat of my own. Outside stood a VW Convertible. Most of the time I drove it with the roof down.

The flat was in the country. In Rudow or perhaps in Grunewald. It was a flat in an old building. But not one of those upper middle-class flats that they have in the area round the Kurfürstendamm with terribly high ceilings and stucco. Not a house with a huge entrance hall and red carpet up the stairs, and marble and mirrors and people's names in gold letters on their front door. I mean, not a flat that somehow stank of wealth. For wealth, I imagined, meant ripping off, rushing around, stress.

I wanted a flat in an old working-class house, with two or three small rooms, low ceilings, small windows, a house with worn-down wooden stairs, where it always smelled a little of food and where the neighbours came out of their front door saying: 'Good morning, how are you?' The stairs were so narrow that you brushed against your neighbour when you met. Everyone in the house worked hard but they were very content. They did not want to grab more and more, they were not envious, they helped each other, they were quite different from the rich, but also quite different from the workers in the high-rise blocks of Gropiusstadt.

187

There simply was no stress and strain in the house.

The most important place in my flat was the bedroom. On the right-hand wall stood a wide divan covered in dark material. On either side was a night table. One for Detlef when he stayed with me. And then there was also a house-plant on either side of the divan. In any case, there were many plants and flowers in the room. Behind the bed was a wallpaper which wasn't on sale in shops. Depicted on the wallpaper was a desert, with huge sand dunes. And a few palm trees. An oasis. Bedouins with their white headcloths sat in a circle, totally relaxed, drinking tea. It was total peace on my wallpaper. On the left-hand side of the bedroom, in the niche where the dormer window is, was the corner where I would sit. It was furnished like in Arabia or India. Many cushions round a low round table. There I sat at night, I was in total peace, knowing no stress or strain, and had neither wishes nor problems.

Basically the living room was similar to the bedroom. The plants, the carpets. However, in the centre stood a large round table with wicker chairs. Sometimes my best friends sat round the table, eating what I had cooked and drinking tea. On the walls were shelves with many books. They were incredible books by people who had also found peace and who knew about nature and animals. I had made the shelves myself from planks and rope. I had made most things in the flat because there was nothing in the furniture shops that I liked. Because the furniture there was ostenta-tious and meant to show that it had cost a terrible lot of cash. There were no doors in the flat, only curtains. For when doors were opened and shut, it made a noise and caused stress.

At night I cooked the food in peace and quiet. Not all agitated, the way my mother used to cook. Then a key turned in the front door. Detlef was coming home from work. The dog jumped up at him. The cats arched their backs and rubbed against his legs. Then Detlef gave me a kiss and sat down at the supper table.

That was what I dreamt on cold turkey. Only I didn't

know it was a dream. For me it was the reality of the day after tomorrow. That's how it would be after the therapy, and I couldn't imagine that it might possibly be different. It was all so clear that on the evening of the third day doing cold turkey I told my mother that after the therapy I would move out into a flat of my own.

On the fourth day I felt well enough to get up. I still had twenty marks in my jeans pocket and these twenty marks make me restive. Because twenty marks are half of forty marks, that's why. And I thought if you had another twenty marks you could score one last fix before going to Narkonon tomorrow.

I talked to my sick cat. I said it wouldn't be too bad if I left it by itself for an hour or two. I used my syringe to feed it camomile tea and glucose, the only things it could still keep down, and said: 'You won't die either.'

I wanted to have just one last great stroll down the Kudamm. For I knew that at Narkonon we would not be allowed out, and if at all, then only escorted. And I also wanted to have a shot inside me because I felt sure that Kudamm without H wouldn't be all that great. All I needed was twenty marks. I had to do a customer. However, I didn't want to run into Detlef on the station, to have to tell him: 'Listen, I've done a fantastic kick, I've managed it terribly well. And now I'm out looking for a customer because I need twenty marks.' I'm positive Detlef wouldn't have understood me. He would have laughed at me, and then he would have said: 'You're an old fixer and you'll always be one.' I didn't want that under any circumstances.

The idea came to me only in the tube: kerb crawlers. It occurred to me on account of the twenty marks I needed. Kerb crawlers often paid only twenty marks. Babsi and Stella went to where the kerb crawlers picked up girls at the corner of Kurfürstenstrasse and Genthiner Strasse. But I was still terribly afraid of doing it. For starters I didn't like the idea that the customers didn't come to me, as they did on the station, so that I could give them the once-over in peace and quiet, but that I had to go up to the customer's car when he beckoned. It was all done in such a hurry, you couldn't quite make out what sort of a guy he was.

It was worst when you fell into the hands of a pimp. Pimps pretended to be customers. Once they got you in their car, that was your lot. Admittedly, pimps weren't keen on having a girl fixer working for them because too much of the money goes on stuff. But they wanted to get the girl fixers off Kurfürstenstrasse because fixing b.p.'s spoiled the market for professional tarts.

Once Babsi had got into a pimp's car. He'd locked her up for three days. She'd been properly tortured. And then they'd gang-banged her. Wogs and stoned tramps, and that. And of course Babsi was doing cold turkey all the time. She got a real crack during these three days. But afterwards she did go back to Kurfürstenstrasse. After all, she was the queen there with her angel face and no bum or boobs.

Professional tarts were almost as dangerous as pimps. Potsdamer Strasse, where the grottiest tarts of Berlin are on the game, was only about 200 metres from Kurfürstenstrasse where the b.p.'s went. Sometimes the tarts organised real hunts for girl fixers. If they caught one, they scratched her face to ribbons.

I got out of Kurfürstenstrasse tube station and was terribly scared. I thought of the advice both Stella and Babsi had given concerning kerb crawlers: no youngish guys with sports cars or similar crumpet catchers, no pimps. Older guys with paunch, tie and, if possible, hat are okay. Best of all are guys with a child's seat in the back of the car. Good family men who just want a quick change from mummy and are guaranteed to have the wind up worse than the girl.

From the tube station I went up the hundred metres to the crossing of Genthiner Strasse where the Sound was. I pretended that I wasn't on the game at all. I did not walk on the pavement near the kerb but close to the houses. Nevertheless a car stopped immediately. I thought the driver looked funny. Perhaps because he had a beard. He looked somehow aggressive. I put up two fingers and walked on.

There was no other girl to be seen. It was, after all, in the morning. From Stella and Babsi's stories I knew that customers were inclined to get all worked up when they had taken half an hour off and there wasn't a girl to be had. In Kurfürstenstrasse there were sometimes more customers than girls. Indeed, a few more stopped there and then. I pretended not to have seen them.

I peered into the window of a furniture shop and immediately I was back with the dream of my flat. I said to myself: Christiane, girl, pull yourself together. You've got to get it over with quickly, those ludicrous twenty marks. So, concentrate really hard now. With anything like that I always had to concentrate to get on with it quickly so that it was over as soon as possible.

Then a white Opel Commodore stopped. Although there wasn't a child's seat in the back, the guy didn't look nasty. I got in without thinking about it. We agreed on thirty-five marks.

We drove to Askanischer Platz. That's a piece of ground belonging to the GDR State Railway. That's where we went. It didn't take long. The guy was nice, and I got my good feeling back again immediately. I even forgot that the guy was a customer. He said he'd like to see me again. But not for the time being because in three days he was going on holiday to Norway with his wife and two children.

I asked him whether he could take me to the Polytechnic in Hardenbergstrasse, where the morning scene was. He took me there straightaway.

It was a beautiful warm day, 18th May, 1977. I remember the date exactly because my fifteenth birthday was two days later. I tore about on the scene, talking to a few guys. I spent a long time stroking a dog. I was totally happy. I thought it was a terribly great feeling not to be in a hurry and to wait before shooting for as long as I liked. After all, I wasn't any longer physically hooked, was I?

When a guy came past me and asked me whether I wanted to score, I said yes. He went ahead to Ernst Reuter Platz, where I scored half a half for forty marks. I went at once to the ladies' toilet at Ernst Reuter Platz. It's a fairly clean one. I only put half the stuff on my spoon because after a withdrawal one mustn't start with the full dose straightaway. I did the shot with something like a little ceremony. Because I thought this was my very last time on the scene.

I woke up almost two hours later. I was sitting on the loo, with my behind hanging well down into the loo pan. The spike still stuck in my arm. My things lay strewn all over the floor of the tiny cubicle. However, I was more or less okay again quite quickly. I thought that I had chosen just about the right moment, namely the very last, in order to finish once and for all with H. That great stroll down the Kudamm was off. The good feeling had gone. In the refectory I ate mashed potatoes and leeks but, of course, I threw up the lot immediately. I dragged myself to the station to say goodbye to Detlef, but he wasn't there. I had to go home because my sick cat needed me.

The cat still lay in the spot where I had put it. On my pillow. First I cleaned my syringe and then I fed it again with camomile tea and glucose. I must say I had visualised my last day as a fixer a little differently. I considered adding another day so that I might enjoy myself on the Kudamm before going to Narkonon.

My mother came in and enquired where I had been this afternoon. I said: 'On the Kudamm.' She remarked: 'I thought you wanted to drop in at Narkonon in order to find out about everything.'

Immediately I blew my top and began to yell: 'Leave me alone, for God's sake. I didn't have time. So bloody what?' Suddenly my mother yelled back: 'You'll go to Narkonon tonight. Pack your things this minute. And you'll stay at Narkonon from today.'

I had cooked myself a chop and mashed potatoes. I took the plate, went to the loo, locked myself in and ate on the loo. So that was my last evening at my mother's. I shouted because she'd sussed that I was back on H again, and also because I was sick of myself for having had another fix after all. And I decided myself it would be best to go to Narkonon.

I packed a few things in my wicker basket and slipped the syringe, a spoon and the rest of my stuff down the front of my panties. We took a taxi at Zehlendorf where Narkonon has a house. At first the Narkonon guys didn't ask me any questions. They really admitted anyone. They even had touts who went to the scene and accosted fixers, asking them whether they would like to come to Narkonon.

However, they did ask questions of my mother. They wanted to see the colour of our money before admitting me. One thousand five hundred marks in advance for the first month. Of course, my mother didn't have that much money. She promised to bring the money next morning without fail. She intended taking up a loan. She said her bank would give her a small loan without difficulties. She begged and implored them to keep me there. At last the guys agreed.

I asked whether I might go to the loo. They agreed. They didn't search you first of all, as they did in other therapy places, and send you home if you had your works on you. I went to the loo and quickly shot the remaining stuff. Of course they saw that I was bombed out when I came out of the loo, but they said nothing. I handed them my works. The guy to whom I handed them said quite surprised: 'We're very pleased to see that you're handing this in of your own free will.'

I had to go to the cold turkey room simply because they saw that I was bombed out. There were another two people in the cold turkey room. One of them beat it next morning.

Naturally this sort of thing was quite a nice profit for the Narkonon people, when they had been paid for a month for someone and he beat it at once.

I was given books about the teachings of the Church of Scientology. Quite fascinating tomes. I thought that this was quite some sect. At least they had rather fascinating stories which one might or might not believe. I was looking for something I could believe in.

After two days I was allowed out of the cold turkey room because after the two shots I had hardly any withdrawal symptoms. I shared a room with Christa. She was totally round the bend. She was immediately refused therapy because she kept laughing about therapy and therapists. Then she came into our room and searched the skirting boards for trips. She thought perhaps, at some time or other, someone might have hidden trips there. She took me into the loft and said: 'Listen, we ought to put up a couple of mattresses up here and then throw a terrific orgy with wine and hash, and that.' The woman really got me down. Because, although I thought her really fascinating, she kept taking my thoughts back to drugs and considered these Narkonon guys to be shitbags. And I intended to come off H in this place.

On the second day my mother rang me up and said that my cat had died. That was my 15th birthday. My mother wished me a happy birthday only after she'd told me about the cat. She was pretty put out, too. I spent the morning of my 15th birthday sitting on my bed crying. When the guys noticed that I was crying all the time they said what I needed was a session. I was locked in a room with one of the guys who used to be a fixer, and he gave me seemingly senseless commands. I was only allowed to say 'yes' and had to obey every command.

The guy said: 'Do you see the wall? Go to the wall. Touch the wall.' And then we started all over again. So there I was in this room nipping from wall to wall. At one point I'd really had enough and I said: 'Here, what's all this rubbish? Are you off your head? Leave me alone, will you. I want to pack this in.' But with his smile, which never changed, he somehow got me to carry on. Afterwards he made me touch other things too. Until I really couldn't go another step and flung myself on the floor screaming and howling.

He smiled, and I carried on after I'd simmered down. By now I was smiling this same smile. I was totally apathetic. I already touched the wall before he issued his command. All I could think about was: 'This has got to come to an end some time.'

194

After exactly five hours he said: 'Okay, that's enough for today.' I thought I felt really great. I had to go with him to another room. There was a peculiar, home-made instrument, some sort of pendulum between two tins. I was ordered to touch this. The guy said: 'Are you feeling well?'

I said: 'I'm feeling well. I believe that now I experience everything much more consciously.'

The guy stared at the pendulum and then he said: 'It hasn't moved. That means you didn't lie. The session has been successful.'

The peculiar thing was a lie detector. I suppose it was one of the ritual objects of this sect. Anyway I was quite happy that the pendulum hadn't moved. For me this was proof that I really felt well. I was ready to believe anything in order to get away from H.

In this place they did all sorts of strange things. When that same evening Christa got a fever, she was made to touch a bottle and to tell over and over again whether the bottle was hot or cold. Dopey with fever she did as she was told. After an hour her fever had gone, so they said.

I was so turned on by all this that next day I immediately went to the office and asked for another session. For a whole week I was on the sect trip and firmly believed that the therapies were really helping me. All day long, from morning to night, I was busy with my programme. Sessions, cleaning, kitchen duty. It went on up to 10 pm. There was no time to think.

The only thing which got up my nose was the food. Now I'm really not spoiled where food is concerned. But I could hardly swallow the muck they put before us. And I thought for the money they got they might provide better food — they hardly had any other expenses. Most of the time the sessions were conducted by former fixers who supposedly had been off H for a couple of months. They were told it was part of their therapy, and if they were lucky they were given pocket money occasionally. Nor did I consider it a good thing that Narkonon bosses always ate by themselves. Once I chanced to come in when they were having their lunch, feeding their faces with all sorts of lovely grub.

One Sunday I really had time to think. At first I thought of Detlef, and it made me rather sad. Then I considered, quite soberly, exactly what I might do after the therapy. I asked myself whether the sessions had actually helped me. I was bursting with questions to which I had no answers. I wanted to talk to somebody. But there was nobody. One of the first commandments of the house was that friendships were not allowed. And the Narkonon guys immediately gave you a session whenever you wanted to talk about problems. I realised that the whole time I had been in the house I had never yet really talked to anyone.

On Monday I went to the office and let fly. I did not let them interrupt me. I started with the food. Then I said that I had had almost all my panties stolen. You could never get into the laundry room because the girl who had the key kept going off to the scene. Anyway, there were a couple of people who popped out to get a shot and came back as they liked. I said that things like that got up my nose. And then these everlasting sessions and the housework. I was totally overtired because I simply didn't have enough time to sleep. I said: 'Okay, your therapies are quite fascinating, they're really good. But as for my basic problems, they don't solve them at all. Because basically the whole thing is nothing but drill. You're bloody well trying to drill us. But I need someone to whom I can sometimes talk about my problems. And anyway I need time to come to terms with my problems.'

They listened with their eternal smile. They never said anything at all. When I had finished, they gave me an extra session which went on all day until ten at night. This reduced me once again to a state of total apathy. And I thought perhaps they know what they're doing, after all.

During a visit my mother had told me that the Social Services Department was refunding her the money she'd paid for me to go to Narkonon. And it seemed to me that if the State was prepared to spend money on it, the thing ought to be okay.

Others had even more problems in the house than me.

196

This Gabi, for instance. She was gone on a guy and dead set on fucking him. Being a real dafty she told the Narkonon bosses about this and was straightaway given an extra session. When she did fuck the guy a couple of times, she was found out and the pair of them held to ridicule in front of everybody. The guy, who was supposed to have been off H for a couple of years and worked as an assistant, split shortly afterwards. He went back to being a total fixer.

Actually the Narkonon people weren't so much concerned with fucking. For them it was more important that there should be no friendships. But this guy had been there for a year, and how are you to survive for so long without friendship?

In the brief period late at night which was our free time, I always mixed with the younger ones. I was the youngest in the house. But in the crowd which slowly emerged no one was over sixteen. The first wave of those who had started fixing as children was arriving now. After only one or two years they had all been as finished as me because probably the poison takes it out of you even more during adolescence than later. Like me they'd no chance of getting into any of the other therapy places.

After some time most people were as unable as I to cope with these sessions. Whenever two of us were together the whole session turned into one big giggly riot. How was it possible in the long run to keep a straight face when you had to shout at a football or gaze into one another's eyes for hours on end? By now we no longer had to go to the lie detector because we told them straight out that the session had done absolutely nothing for us. There'd been nothing but giggling. The poor session leaders were growing more and more helpless when they had to work with us.

At night after work there was only one topic of conversation in our crowd: H. I also talked to a few people about splitting.

After two weeks at Narkonon I had worked out a plan of escape. Two boys and I disguised ourselves as the great cleaning squad. Armed with dustbin, scrubbing brush and bucket we managed to get through every door. We were wild with anticipation of a shot. At the tube station we parted company. I went to Zoo station to look for Detlef.

Detlef wasn't there. But Stella was. She was nearly doing her nut, she was so pleased to see me. She told me that lately no one had seen Detlef. I was afraid he might be in the nick. Stella said that there wasn't much doing on the station by way of customers. We went to Kurfürstenstrasse to try the kerb crawlers. But there was nothing doing there either. We trotted all the way from Kurfürstenstrasse tube station to Lützowplatz before someone stopped at last. We knew the car and the guy. He had followed us before. Even when we were going to a toilet to have a fix. We'd always taken him for a plain-clothes copper. But he was just a customer who totally specialised in very young girl fixers.

He only wanted me, but Stella was allowed to get into the car. I said: 'Thirty-five for a blow job. I only do blow jobs.'

He said: 'I'll give you a hundred marks.'

I was totally flummoxed. That had never happened to me before. Customers with the biggest Mercs were the ones who made the most fuss over a measly five marks. And this guy in a totally rusty Volkswagen freely offered me a hundred. Then he said he was an officer in the Federal Intelligence Service. In other words, a total nutcase. But these nutty Walter Mitty types were the best customers because they were doing a Walter Mitty with the money as well.

He did give me the hundred marks. Stella went to score, and we had a shot right there in the car. We went to a hotel. Stella stayed outside in the corridor. I took my time with the guy because I was completely high from my first shot after two weeks. And also because he paid a decent whack. I was so high that I didn't want to get up from the narrow divan in this grotty hotel room.

I stayed chatting a little to the guy. He was really a funny show-off. At last he said he had half a gramme of heroin at home. He'd give it to us if we'd be in Kurfürstenstrasse in three hours' time. Then I touched him for thirty marks. I said we needed them because we wanted to treat ourselves to a really good meal. And, I said, I knew he had pots of cash and only drove his old VW as a front because he was in Intelligence. So he couldn't but give me the money.

Stella and I went back to Zoo station because I wouldn't give up hope of finding Detlef. All at once a little black-and-white curly dog came running and jumped up at me. I suppose I reminded the dog of someone. I thought this dog was far out. He looked like a too-small husky. A rather dilapidated guy came behind the dog and actually asked whether I wanted to buy it. I did, straightaway. He asked seventy marks, but I got him down to forty. I was high and totally happy with the dog. Now I had a dog again. Stella said I ought to call it Lady Jane. So I called it Janie.

We ate, in a restaurant in Kurfürstenstrasse, chops and veg, and Janie got half. This guy from Intelligence really came punctually and gave me a real half a gramme. It was crazy. This half a gramme was worth a hundred marks.

Stella and I went back to Zoo station again on account of Detlef. We met Babsi. I was terribly pleased because, despite our squabblings, I liked Babsi better than Stella. The three of us went to the station café. Babsi didn't look at all well. She had legs like matchsticks and her last little bit of boob had gone too. She weighed 31 kilos [4st 10lbs]. Only her face was as beautiful as ever.

I reported that Narkonon was quite an okay place. Stella didn't want to know. Stella said she was born a fixer and wanted to die a fixer. But Babsi was dead keen on the idea of finally kicking at Narkonon with me. Both her parents and her grandmother had been vainly trying to find a therapy place for her. Babsi was crashing out again, but she really wanted to kick. She was in a very bad way.

When we had finished nattering I took my Janie to Metro, a bloody expensive shop in the station which is open late. I bought two plastic bags with dog food for Janie and stocks of instant puddings for myself. Then I rang up Narkonon and asked whether I could come back. They said yes. I said I was bringing a friend. I didn't tell them the friend was Janie.

I hadn't given it much thought but basically I had always

been certain that I would go back to Narkonon. Where else should I have gone? My mother would really have blown a gasket if I had suddenly turned up on her doorstep. Besides, in the meantime, my sister had moved out of my father's flat again and now lived with my mother in my room and my bed. Crashing out wasn't on either. For me it was the end to be dependent on a customer, who kept me in his place overnight. I'd never yet stayed overnight with any customer because that automatically meant fucking.

In the house — we always called Narkonon the house — they were unfriendly but didn't say anything. They didn't say anything about Janie either. There were already about twenty cats in the house, and now there was also a dog.

I fetched some old blankets from the loft and made up a bed for Janie next to my own bed. Next morning the dog had crapped and pee'd all over the room. Janie never became house-trained. She was really nutty. But then so was I. I loved Janie. I didn't mind having to clean up every-thing.

I was immediately given an extra session. I didn't mind that either. What did wind me up, though, was that I couldn't be with my dog for several hours. Other people were looking after her and that made me quite ill because Janie was my dog. Everybody played with her and she played with anybody. She was like a little tart in that respect. Everybody fed her and she was getting steadily fatter. But only I talked to her when we were alone. At least now I had somebody to talk to.

I split twice more. The last time I was away for four days. That is to say, I crashed out for the first time. I was able to stay with Stella because her alcoholic mother was away drying out in a clinic. The whole shit started all over again. Customer, fix, customer, fix. Then I learnt that Detlef had gone to Paris with Bernd. I did my nut.

That the guy to whom I was as good as married should skedaddle from Berlin without even telling me was the end. In our dreams we'd always wanted to go to Paris together. We were going to rent a small room in Montmartre or somewhere and kick because we'd never heard anything about a scene in Paris. We believed there was no scene in Paris. Only a lot of terrific artists who drank coffee and now and then some wine.

And now Detlef had gone to Paris with Bernd. I no longer had a boyfriend. I was all alone in the world, for with Babsi and Stella the old quarrels about fuck-all began immediately. I only had Janie.

I rang up Narkonon and they told me my mother had been to collect my things. So my mother had given me up too. Somehow that made me furious. Now I wanted to show all of them, I wanted to show that I could manage it all by myself.

I went to Narkonon and they did take me in again. I did therapy like mad. I did what I was told. I became a proper model patient and was allowed to go to this lie detector thing, and the pendulum never moved when I said I'd profited a terrific lot from a session. I thought now you're getting somewhere. Now, just to spite them, I didn't telephone my mother who had collected my things. I borrowed things. I wore boys' underpants. But I didn't mind at all. I didn't want to ask my mother to bring back my things.

One day my father rang up. 'Hello, Christiane. Listen, where have you got to, for heaven's sake? I've only just heard about it quite by accident.'

I said: 'Isn't it marvellous. Fancy you remembering you've got a daughter.'

He: 'Tell me, do you intend staying with these weirdos?'

Me: 'I do, come what may.'

There was a pause while my father was gasping for air, then he asked whether I would like to go out for a meal with him and a friend. I said: 'Yeah, you're on.'

Half an hour later I was called down to the office, and there was my father whom I hadn't seen for months. First he came up to the room which I shared with four others. He said: 'My God, what a mess.' He had always been fanatically tidy. And it really did look incredibly untidy in our room, as it did everywhere in the house. Filthy and dirty, with gear lying about everywhere.

We were just off to have our meal when one of the bosses said to my father: 'You'll have to sign a declaration that you'll bring Christiane back.'

My father was outraged. He shouted that he was the father and that it was up to him entirely to determine where his daughter went. He was taking me along now, and his daughter wasn't coming back either. I ran back towards the therapy room and shouted: 'I want to stay here, papa. I don't want to die, papa. Please leave me here, papa.'

The Narkonon people, who all came running, attracted by the noise, supported me. My father stormed out and screamed: 'I'm calling the police.'

I knew he was going to do just that. I ran up to the loft and climbed on to the roof. There was some sort of platform for the chimney sweep. I crouched on it and shivered with cold.

Two radio patrol cars turned up. Together with my father the cops searched the house from top to bottom. Meanwhile, the Narkonon bosses were calling for me because they'd got scared. But no one found me on the roof. The cops and my father went away.

Next morning I rang my mother at work. I started to cry and asked: 'What on earth's the matter?'

My mother's voice was quite cold. She said: 'What happens to you is a matter of complete indifference to me.'

I said: 'I don't want papa to fetch me away from here. You are my guardian. You can't just leave me in the lurch. I'm staying here. I'll never run away again. I swear it. Please do something to stop papa from taking me away. I've got to stay here, mummy, really. Otherwise I'll die, mummy, please believe me.'

My mother became really impatient and said: 'No, that's impossible.' Then she put down the receiver.

At first I was absolutely finished. Then my rage returned. I said to myself: 'They can get stuffed. All your life they've taken no notice of you. And now they do just as they please with you, these idiots, who've done it all wrong. These swine let you go to the dogs. Kessi's mother, now she took

202

care to see that her daughter didn't get herself into the shit. And these shitbags who call themselves your parents suddenly believe they know what's good for you.'

I asked for an extra session and threw myself into this session heart and soul. I wanted to stay with Narkonon and perhaps become a member of the Church of Scientology later. At any rate, I didn't want to be taken away from here. I didn't want my parents to ruin me still more. That's what I thought in my total hate.

Three days later my father returned. I had to go down to the office. My father was quite calm. He said he would have to take me to the Social Services Department on account of the money my mother had paid to Narkonon and which would be refunded.

I said: 'No, I'm not coming. I know you, papa. If I go with you now you won't let me come back here. And I don't want to die.'

My father showed the Narkonon bosses an authorisation which said that he was allowed to take me away. My mother had authorised him to do this. The Narkonon chief said there was nothing he could do, I would have to go with my father. They couldn't keep me against my father's wishes.

The boss said I wasn't to forget my exercises. Always confront. Confronting was some kind of magic word of theirs. Confront everything. I thought: what a lot of idiots you are. There's nothing to confront for me. I must die. I can't stand this. I know that by the end of two weeks I'll have another shot. I can't do it. I shall never do it on my own. This was one of the few moments when I saw my situation fairly clearly. Admittedly, in my despair I talked myself into believing that Narkonon really would have been my salvation. I sobbed with rage and despair. I couldn't stop myself for a long time.

CHRISTIANE'S MOTHER

I did not by any means consider it a happy solution for my former husband, after the fiasco at Narkonon, to take Christiane to live with him, in order, as he said, to get her to see sense. Apart from the fact that he could not watch her round the clock, leaving Christiane to him caused me, as it were, spiritual indigestion on account of the relationship between him and me. The more so since, shortly before, her sister had come back to me because her father was so strict.

However, I no longer knew what to do and hoped: Perhaps he will succeed with his methods where I have failed with mine. But I'm not ruling out the fact that I talked myself into believing this in order to rid myself, at least temporarily, of the responsibility for Christiane. Since her first withdrawal I constantly alternated between hope and despair. I was spiritually and physically at an end when I asked her father to take over.

Three weeks after the first agonising withdrawal which Christiane went through with Detlef, the first relapse was a severe blow. The police rang up at my office informing me that they had picked up Christiane at Zoo station. I was asked to come and collect her.

I sat at my desk shaking. Every two minutes I glanced at my watch to see whether it was four. I dared not go during working hours. There was no one I could have talked to. The two daughters of my boss would have been severely critical of me. All at once I understood Detlef's father. One is very much ashamed at the beginning.

When I saw her at the police station, Christiane's eyes were swollen from crying. The policeman showed me the fresh needle mark on her arm and told me she had been arrested on the station in an 'unequivocal position.'

At first I was puzzled as to what he meant by this. But then perhaps I did not want to be enlightened. Christiane was deeply unhappy about her relapse. We withdrew again without Detlef. She stayed at home and seemed wholly engrossed in getting on with her withdrawal. I plucked up the courage and told her tutor at school. He was shocked and thanked me for my openness. He said he was not used to openness from other parents. He suspected there were other heroin addicts in the school and he would have liked to help Christiane. But he didn't know how.

It was always the same. Anyone I approached — either they were as helpless as I or they had completely written off adolescents like Christiane. It was something I was to experience again and again.

Slowly I began to realise how easy it is for young people to get at heroin. The dealers lurked on Hermannplatz in Neukölln on her way to school. I couldn't believe my ears when one day, when we were out shopping together, one of these guys actually accosted Christiane in my presence. Some of these were foreigners, but there were also Germans among them. She told me where she knew these people from: 'He deals with this, and that one sells that, and the third one something else.'

I thought all this totally insane. I thought, for heaven's sake, where is it we're living?

I wanted to get Christiane into another school, a grammar school at Lausitzer Platz in order to avoid her having to face this temptation on her way to school. It was shortly before the Easter holidays, and at the start of term I wanted her to be at her new school. I hoped that in this way I might get her out of the whole atmosphere, out of the danger on the tube stations. Of course it was a naive idea, and, anyway, it came to nothing. The headmaster of the grammar school informed us straightaway that he was reluctant to take pupils from a comprehensive school. And Christiane's maths marks weren't good enough to make an exception. Merely out of interest he asked why she wanted to change schools. When Christiane said there seemed to be little or no form spirit, the headmaster chuckled: 'Form spirit? There is no form spirit in a comprehensive school.' He explained to me that due to the constant splitting up of pupils who attended different classes, it wasn't possible for any form spirit to be created in the first place.

I don't know who was more disappointed, Christiane or me. She only said: 'There's no point in any of this. I can only be helped by therapy.' But where was I to find a therapy place? I telephoned the authorities all over the place. The best thing they could come up with were drug advice centres. And the drug advice centres insisted that Christiane must come to them voluntarily. However much in-fighting there was between them — and they didn't seem to have a good word for each other — on this point they were agreed. The voluntary aspect was the precondition for any therapy. Without it recovery was impossible.

And when I went down on my bended knees to Christiane, begging her to go to a drug advice centre she immediately gave me lip: 'What's the use of my going there? They haven't got a place for me anyway. And I'll see them in hell first before I spend the next few weeks hanging around their place.'

What was I to do? If I had dragged her to the drug advice centre, it would have gone against their principles. In a way, today I can understand her attitude. Probably at that time Christiane wasn't actually ready for serious therapy. On the other hand, it is my opinion that children like Christiane who are heroin addicts have a right to be helped, even against their own will.

Later, when Christiane was yet again so low that she really would have gone voluntarily into a strict therapy centre, we were told: 'No place, there's a six to eight weeks' waiting list.' It left me speechless. All I could say was: 'And what if by then my child is dead?' 'Well, in the meantime, let her come here for counselling so that we can find out whether she seriously wants to withdraw.' Today I find it difficult to reproach those drug counsellors. I suppose, with so few therapy places available, they must choose carefully whom they will accept.

So I failed to get a therapy place. However, when Christiane came back from her Easter holidays I had the impression that she no longer needed one. She looked blooming. I thought that now she had really managed to get away.

She kept making derogatory remarks about her friend Babsi who, she said, sold herself to old men for heroin. She, Christiane, could never bring herself to do such a thing. She was so glad that she no longer had anything to do with the whole scene, with the whole mess of it. Of that she seemed

206

to be convinced. I could have sworn blind she really meant it.

Only a few days later, though, she was back in it. I could see it by her tiny pupils. I could no longer stand her excuses. 'I don't know why you're making such a bloody fuss, I've only had a little smoke,' she snapped at me. A very bad time began. She started telling me enormous lies. Mind you, I saw through them. I made her stay in. But she didn't keep to it. I considered locking her in. But she would have jumped out of the window from the first floor. And I didn't want to take the risk.

I was almost at the end of my tether. I couldn't stand these tiny pupils any longer. Three months had gone by since I had caught her in the bathroom. Every few days the papers reported another death from heroin. Mostly only in a couple of lines. By now they treated heroin victims as matter-of-factly as traffic deaths.

I was terribly frightened. Most of all, because Christiane was no longer open to me. Because she would no longer admit anything. This covering up made me quite hot under the collar. When she felt caught out she would become foul-mouthed and aggressive. Slowly her nature began to change.

I trembled for her life. I doled out her pocket money — twenty marks a month — in dribs and drabs. I constantly had this fear inside me: if I give her 20 marks, she'll go and buy a shot, and it may be a shot too many.

That she was an addict — was something I could just about resign myself to live with. It was this fear that the next shot might be the last which really finished me. I was glad that she still came home at all. Unlike Babsi, whose mother often rang me up in tears, wanting to know where Babsi was.

I constantly lived on my nerves. When the telephone rang, I was afraid it might be the police or the morgue or anything else dreadful. Today I still leap out of bed when the bell rings.

By now it had become quite impossible to talk to Christiane. When I tried to discuss her addiction she just said: 'Leave me alone!' I had the impression that Christiane was about to throw in the sponge. She kept insisting that she no longer injected heroin but only smoked hash; however, just as I had stopped pretending to myself, I did not allow her to pretend to me. I regularly turned her room upside down, and occasionally found addicts' utensils of some kind or another. Twice or three times even a syringe. I would confront her with them which resulted in her shouting at me in outrage. They were, she maintained, Detlef's. She'd taken the syringe away from him.

One day when I came home from work they were both sitting on the bed in Christiane's room and had just been heating the spoon. I was completely speechless about this impertinence. I could only scream: 'Get out of here, the pair of you.'

When they had gone I was in floods of tears. All at once I was seized with a tremendous rage with the police and with our government. I felt completely abandoned. In the paper there was yet another report about someone who had died from drugs. So far this year there had been more than thirty victims. And we were only in May. I simply could not grasp it all. On television we saw the huge sums the State spends in the fight against terrorism. Yet in Berlin the dealers were running around free and selling heroin openly in the streets like ice lollies.

I got completely worked up by these thoughts. Suddenly I heard myself say loudly, 'fucking State.' I don't know what else went through my mind. I sat in my living room, looking at my furniture, piece by piece. I think I'd very much have liked to smash up the whole caboodle. So this was what I had worked myself into the ground for. Then I wept again.

That evening I gave Christiane a terrible hiding. I sat up in bed waiting for her to come home. In my head things were going round and round. It was a mixture of fear, guilt feelings and self-reproach. I felt a failure, not only because I had made so many mistakes with my marriage and with working excessively hard. But also because for a long time I had been too cowardly to face facts where Christiane was concerned.

It was on that evening that I lost my last illusion.

Christiane did not come home until half past twelve. From the window I watched her getting out of a Mercedes. Right outside the front door. My God, I thought, this is the end. Now she has thrown aside all her self-respect. Now the catastrophe has happened. I was utterly shattered. I grabbed hold of her and thrashed her until my hands ached. In the end we both sat on the carpet crying. Christiane was completely dissolved. I told her to her face that she was a prostitute, that now I knew. She just shook her head and sobbed: 'But not the way you think, mummy.'

I didn't want to know more details. I told her to have a bath and then go to bed. How I felt is something no one can begin to imagine. That she sold herself to men threw me — I think — even more than her heroin addiction.

I never slept a wink all night. I reflected, what is there left for you to do? In my desperation I even thought of putting her into care. But that would only have made everything still worse. To begin with they would have placed Christiane in the central home in Ollenhauerstrasse. And I had been fore-warned about this place by a teacher, because the girls lure each other into prostitution.

I saw only one possibility: Christiane must be got out of Berlin at once. For ever. Whether she likes it or not. Out of this morass where she is being led astray again and again. Somewhere where she is safe from heroin.

My mother in Hesse was willing to have her at once. And so was my sister-in-law in Schleswig-Holstein. When I announced my decision to Christiane she suddenly grew quite subdued and distracted. I had already begun the necessary preparations. But then Christiane came to me, seemingly repentant, and said she was ready to go into therapy. She had actually found a therapy place. With 'Narkonon'.

It was a load off my mind. For I was not sure whether she would manage in West Germany without therapy and was *fearful that she might run away from my relatives.*

I didn't know any details about Narkonon, only that one had to pay. I took her to Narkonon there and then, two days before her fifteenth birthday. A young man talked to us politely about admitting Christiane. He congratulated us on our decision and assured us that now I no longer needed to worry. As a rule, the Narkonon therapy was a complete success. I could rest assured. I hadn't been so relieved for a long time.

Then he handed me the contract in which I undertook to pay for the therapy. Fifty-two marks a day and always four weeks in advance. That was more than my net earnings. But what did that matter? Besides, the young man indicated that the authorities might be willing to refund the therapy fees.

Next day I scraped together five hundred marks and took them to Narkonon. Then I took up a loan of one thousand marks and paid this in at the next parents' evening. In charge of these evenings was a young man who was supposed to be a former addict. One could not really tell his past from his appearance. Thanks to Narkonon, he said, he had become a new man. And this impressed us parents. He also assured me that Christiane was making good progress.

In reality they were putting on an act and were only after our money. Later I learnt from the papers that Narkonon is part of some dubious American sect and bent on making capital out of the fear of parents.

But as with everything else, once again I was only wise after the event. To begin with, I thought Christiane to be in very good hands. And I wanted to keep her there. So I needed money.

I went from one authority to the next. No one wanted to be responsible. No one opened my eyes about Narkonon. I felt discouraged and at a disadvantage. I felt as though I was stealing these people's time. Then someone told me that before I could make an application for the refund of therapy fees I needed a doctor's certificate concerning Christiane's drug addiction. I thought this must be a joke. Anyone who

210

knew about these things could see Christiane's state just by looking at her. But it was the official way — nothing I could do about it. Then, when after two weeks I had at long last managed to get an appointment with the medical officer, Christiane had once more run away from Narkonon. For the third time.

Again I cried buckets. I thought: Now the whole business is going to start all over again. Each time I had fervently hoped that perhaps she'll do it this time. With my boyfriend I went in search of her. In the afternoon we looked in Hasenheide; in the evening we went to the town centre and the discotheques; in between we visited the stations. All the places where the scene is. Every day, every night, we started out again. We even combed the toilets in the city. We had reported her as missing to the police. They just said they would put Christiane on their wanted persons list. She'd turn up, they said.

I should have liked to crawl under a stone somewhere. All I could feel was fear. Fear of that telephone call: your daughter is dead. I was a bundle of nerves. I no longer wanted to do anything. I was interested in nothing. I had to force myself to go to work. But I did not want to report sick. I started having heart trouble. I could scarcely move my left arm. At night it would go numb. My stomach rumbled. My kidneys hurt and my head felt as though it would burst. All that was left of me was a small heap of misery.

I went to see my doctor. He finished me off. It's your nerves, he said after the examination, and prescribed valium. When I told him why I was all mixed up he told me that a few days ago a young girl just like that had come to see him and had confessed that she was a drug addict. She had asked him what she was to do. 'And did you tell her?' I asked. 'I told her to go and buy a rope,' was his reply. There was no help. That's exactly how he said it.

When after a week Christiane reported back at Narkonon, I couldn't even be glad about it. It was as if something inside me had died. I was of the opinion that I had done everything humanly possible. But nothing *had helped. On the contrary.*

The whole mess had only grown worse. Narkonon, too, had done more to ruin Christiane than improve her. While she was there she changed abruptly. Now she made a vulgar impression — no longer girlish — repulsive, rather.

Even during my first few visits to Narkonon I had grown suspicious. Suddenly Christiane had become a stranger. Something had been destroyed. Up till then she had had an emotional link with me in spite of everything. Now it had gone. Blotted out as if after a brainwashing.

It was in this situation that I asked my former husband to take Christiane to West Germany. But he preferred to have her living with him. He would manage her, he said. With the help of a good hiding, if she didn't toe the line.

I did not object. I was at my wit's end. I had done so many wrong things that all at once I was afraid to continue this chain of mistakes by sending Christiane to West Germany.

Before going home from Narkonon my father dragged me to his favourite pub at Wutzkyallee tube station. He wanted to order something alcoholic for me, but I drank only a bottle of apple juice. He said that now I must once and for all finish with drugs if I didn't want to die, and I said: 'Yes, that was precisely why I wanted to stay with Narkonon.'

The jukebox was playing the same song over and over again. A few adolescents were playing pinball and others were at the billiard table. My father said they were all quite normal adolescents. Here I would find new friends quite quickly and realise for myself how daft I had been to take drugs.

I hardly listened. I was terribly pissed off and shattered, and all I longed for was to be alone. I hated the whole world, and Narkonon was the door to paradise which my father had slammed shut. I took Janie into bed with me and said: 'Do you know human beings, Janie?' I answered for her: 'You don't, that's your trouble.' Janie ran up to everybody wagging her tail. She thought all people were good. That was something I disliked about her. I'd have thought it better

212

if at first she'd have growled at everybody because she mistrusted them all.

When I awoke Janie hadn't yet pee'd on the floor and I wanted to take her downstairs. My father had already left for work. I wanted to open the front door. It was locked. I tore at the doorhandle, I flung myself against the door. It remained shut. I forced myself to stay calm, not to blow my top. I thought it couldn't possibly be true that my father had locked me up like a wild animal. After all, he did know that there was the dog.

I tore through the flat looking for a key. I thought he must have put the key somewhere. What if there was a fire? I looked under the bed, on the pelmets, and in the fridge. No key. I had no time to blow my top properly because I had to do something about Janie before she messed up the carpet. I took her out on to the balcony, and she seemed to understand.

Then I went on a tour of inspection of the flat inside which I was locked. Several things had been changed. The bedroom was empty because my mother had taken the beds when she moved out. There was a new divan in the living room on which my father slept. There was a new colour television. The rubber plant had gone and so had the bamboo stick in the rubber plant pot which my father had often used to wallop me. Instead there was a monkey-bread tree.

In the nursery there was still the old wardrobe where you could open only one door because otherwise it would have collapsed. The bed creaked every time you moved. I thought, so he's locking you up. That's supposed to make you into a normal teenager, and the old man can't even manage to get some decent furniture together.

I went back on to the balcony with Janie. She put her front legs on the balustrade and looked down eleven storeys and on to the desolate high-rise blocks of Gropiusstadt all around.

I had to talk to someone, so I rang up Narkonon. There was a huge surprise in store for me. Babsi had arrived. So she, too, was serious about withdrawing. She told me

213

they'd given her my bed. I was terribly sad because I wasn't at Narkonon with Babsi. We talked for a long time.

When my father returned I said nothing at all. But he talked all the more. He had already planned my whole life. I was given a proper timetable for every day. Housework, shopping, feeding his racing pigeons and cleaning them out.

He had a pigeon loft out in Rudow. In between times he intended to telephone to keep a check on me. For my free time he had organised a former schoolfriend of mine, Katharina, a real teeny-bopper. On top of all this the old man promised me a reward. He would take me to Thailand on one of his trips. For he had taken to flying to Thailand at least once a year. He was on a total Thailand trip. On account of the girls, of course, but also because of the cheap clothes one can buy there. He saved all his money for these trips to Thailand. That was his drug, in a way.

So I listened to these plans of my father's and thought I'd play along for the time being. There wasn't really much else I could do. At least he stopped locking me up.

Next day I had a full programme. I cleaned the flat, went shopping. And there was Katharina, come to take me for a walk. I nearly walked her off her feet, and when I told her I would have to go to Rudow to feed the pigeons she didn't fancy coming along.

So I was free for the afternoon. I had a terrible craving to get up to something because I was still pissed off. I didn't know exactly what, though. I thought I might go to Hasen-heide for an hour. That's a park in Neukölln. They had quite a good hash scene there. I fancied a joint.

However, I had no money. I knew where there was some. My father collected silver coins in a huge brandy bottle. The bottle already contained more than a hundred marks. A reserve for the next trip to Thailand. I shook fifty marks out of the bottle. I wanted to take a little more, just in case. The rest I would put back. I intended putting it all back from money I would save from my housekeeping. So I thought.

214

At Hasenheide I ran across Piet. Piet was the boy from Centre House with whom I had smoked hash for the first time. In the meantime, he, too, was fixing. That's why I asked him whether at Hasenheide they had any H.

He asked: 'Got any cash?'

I said: 'Yes.'

He said: 'Come with me.' He took me to a few wogs and I bought half a half. I had ten marks left over. We went to the toilet outside the park and Piet lent me his works. By now he had become a really mean old wanker. I had to give him half my stuff for the loan of his works. So we both had a little shot.

This was a bit more like it. The Hasenheide scene was not as fucked-up as the scene at the Kurfürstendamm. It was, after all, still mainly a hash scene. But there were fixers, too. Hash smokers and fixers lay peacefully side by side. At the Kudamm scene hash was a baby drug and hash smokers the end. No Kudamm fixer would bother with a hash smoker.

At Hasenheide it didn't matter which drug you were into. Or you could even be totally off drugs. It didn't matter. All you needed to bring along was a good feeling and turn on. There were groups making music playing the flute or bongos. And there were wogs lying around on the grass, too. They were all like one large peaceful community. The whole feeling here reminded me of Woodstock which must have been very much like this.

I was back home before my father returned at six. He never noticed that I was high. I had a bit of a bad conscience since the pigeons had gone unfed. I resolved to give them a double portion next day. I thought that in future I wouldn't take any more H because at Hasenheide I could get high on a little hash and still be fully accepted — even if only a hash smoker. I never wanted to get back to that grotty H scene on the Kurfürstendamm. I really believed I would be able to kick at Hasenheide.

From now on I took Janie to Hasenheide every afternoon at least for a brief period. She liked it very much because of the many other dogs there. Even the dogs were totally friendly here, and everybody liked Janie and stroked her.

As for the pigeons, I only fed them every two or three days. That was quite sufficient, if you allowed them to fill their crops to bursting and, in addition, scattered a supply for them.

I smoked shit whenever someone offered me some. There was always someone who did. For this is one of the big differences between the H scene and the hash scene, namely that hash smokers will share when they've got something.

I got to know the wog from whom I had bought stuff on my first day with Piet. One day I lay down next to the rug on which he was squatting with some other wogs. The guy invited me to come and sit on his rug. His name was Mustapha and he was a Turk. The others were Arabs. All of them between seventeen and twenty years old. They were eating pitta with cheese and melon and gave some to me and Janie.

I thought this Mustapha was somehow very together. He was a dealer. But I thought the way in which he dealt really together. With him there was nothing of the stress and fuss of German dealers. Mustapha pulled out tufts of grass and hid the bag of stuff under the tufts. He didn't mind if there was a rumble. The cops would never have found anything. If anyone wanted to score, Mustapha calmly poked about in the grass with his knife until he had found the stuff again.

He did not sell weighed-out papers like the dealers on the H scene. He always took about a quarter on the tip of his knife. The portions were okay. With two fingers he brushed off any remnants clinging to the knife, and I was allowed to snort this.

Mustapha said immediately that shooting was shit. If one didn't want to become hooked one should only snort H. He and the Arabs only snorted. And none of them was physically hooked. They only snorted occasionally when they fancied a little.

However, I wasn't always allowed to snort what clung to the knife because Mustapha didn't want me to get physically

216

hooked again. I realised that these wogs really knew how to handle drugs. Quite different from Europeans. For us Europeans, H was approximately the same as in the old days firewater had been for the Red Indians. The thought struck me that with H the Orientals could wipe out Europeans and Americans exactly as the Europeans had then wiped out the Red Indians with alcohol.

So now I got to know wogs from quite another side. Not as you-fuck customers who, for Babsi, Stella and me, had always been the end. Mustapha and the Arabs were very proud. They were easily offended. They accepted me because I gave them the impression of being very self-assured. I found out very quickly how things were with them. For instance, you must never ask for anything. For them hospitality was still something very important. If you wanted anything, you simply helped yourself. Whether it was sunflower seeds or H. On the other hand, you must never give them the feeling that their hospitality was being abused. Therefore I would never have considered asking them if I could take some H away with me. Whatever I took I snorted at once. The result was that they accepted me completely although, generally, they didn't have a very high opinion of German girls. It struck me that in some respects wogs have an advantage over Germans.

I thought all this really terrific. It never occurred to me that I was still a fixer until I noticed that I was once again physically hooked.

Meanwhile at night I played the reformed daughter for my father. Often I accompanied him to his favourite pub and, to please him, drank the occasional half of beer. Somehow I hated this beer society in the pub. On the other hand I was enjoying my double life. I also wanted to be accepted in my father's pub. I wanted to assert myself in my later life where there were to be no drugs.

I practised at the pin-ball machine and trained like mad at the billiards table. I wanted to learn to play skat.* I wanted to

*A three-handed card game using 32 cards, popular in Germany, particularly in public houses, and very much a man's game.

play all men's games. Better than men. If I must live in this pub society then at least I wanted really to assert myself. No one should be able to attack me. In this society I wanted to be a star. I wanted to be able to be proud. Like the Arabs. Never to have to ask anyone for anything. Never to feel inferior.

However, learning to play skat wasn't on any longer. I had other things to worry about when once again I had my first slight bout of cold turkey. Now I absolutely had to go to Hasenheide every afternoon, and what was more, I needed time because I couldn't just help myself to H from Mustapha and then beat it. So I had to sit there, negotiate for him and calmly chew sunflower seeds, while my father's pigeons went without food for the third day running. Every afternoon I had to shake off Katharina, my companion, then do the housework, go shopping, be there to answer the telephone at the times my father usually rang up and invent ever new stories when my father had found out that I wasn't at home. The whole good feeling was gone.

Then came the afternoon on Hasenheide when suddenly someone put his hands over my eyes from behind. I turned round. There was Detlef. We were in each other's arms while Janie jumped up at us. Detlef looked very well. He said he was off H. I looked into his eyes and said: 'Come off it, old man, pull the other one. Your pupils are like pinheads.' It turned out that Detlef had actually kicked in Paris, then he'd arrived back on Zoo station and had a shot.

We went home to my place. We still had time before my father's return. My bed was really too rickety. I put the eiderdown on the floor and we made love very happily. Then we talked about kicking. The very next week, that's when we were going to start. Not there and then, of course. And Detlef recounted how, together with his friend, he had ripped off a customer in order to get the cash for his kicking trip to Paris. They'd simply locked the guy in the kitchen, calmly nicked his Euro-cheque book and sold the cheques for 1000 marks to a fence at Zoo station. Bernd was already in the nick. Detlef thought the cops couldn't catch him

218

because the customer didn't know his name.

Now we met every day on Hasenheide and most times went home to my place afterwards. But we never talked very much about kicking because we were very happy together. The only trouble was that I was less and less able to get everything organised. My father stepped up his checks and kept me occupied with a large variety of new tasks. I needed time for the Arab crowd to swipe some stuff for Detlef, too. I wanted to have lots of time for Detlef. The whole stress business was starting all over again.

In the end I could see no way out but to go to Zoo station at lunchtime to look for a customer. I kept this a secret from Detlef. But the whole good feeling was going more and more up the spout, because the whole fixer routine was beginning again. After every withdrawal, the few holidays you always enjoy after kicking — without fear of cold turkey and thus without the necessity of always having to have stuff — became fewer.

About a week after Detlef's return, who should turn up on Hasenheide but Rolf, the queer guy with whom Detlef was living. He looked rather the worse for wear and said only: 'Detlef's been pinched.' It appeared that they'd picked up Detlef during a rumble and straightaway pinned the Euro-cheques number on him. The fence had grassed on him.

I went to the toilet at Hermannplatz, locked myself in and cried my eyes out. So once again there was nothing doing as far as our terrific future was concerned. Once more everything was totally realistic, namely totally hopeless. And then I was more than anything scared of cold turkey. In my present state I couldn't possibly sit calmly with my Arabs, chewing sunflower seeds and waiting for a snort to come my way. I took the tube to Zoo station. By the showcases of the Reichsbahn I sat on a ledge and waited for customers. However, there was absolutely nothing happening on the station because there was some fantastic football game on the box. There wasn't even a wog in sight.

Then a guy I knew came into the station, Heinz, Stella and Babsi's old regular customer. The guy who always paid with H, complete with syringe, but who insisted on fucking. I no longer cared, anyway, since I knew that Detlef would be in the nick for a long time. I went up to this Heinz, who didn't recognise me, and said: 'I'm Christiane, Stella and Babsi's friend.' This rang a bell and he asked at once whether I would like to go with him. He offered me two half halves. He did always pay in kind, and that was what was so welcome about this customer. Two half halves wasn't bad, eighty marks in money, after all. I negotiated some extra money for cigarettes, cokes and the like, and off we went.

On the scene at Lehhiner Platz Heinz scored because his stocks were used up. It was funny to see how this guy, who looked like some kind of bookkeeper, crept about among the fixers. But he knew what's what. He had his regular woman dealer who always sold him fine stuff.

I was in great need of a shot, with cold turkey coming on and would have liked to have a fix there and then in the car. But this Heinz fellow wouldn't cough up the stuff.

He insisted that first I must look at his stationer's shop. He pulled out a drawer and took out some pictures. He'd taken them himself. Dead stupid porn photos. Of at least a dozen girls. Sometimes they were on there full-length, in the nude, sometimes only their lower half, in detail. I only thought: You poor stupid pig. These photos would have been of more interest to a gynaecologist. But more than anything I thought of the stuff this daft customer still had in his pocket. I only looked more closely at a few of the photos when I recognised Stella and Babsi in full action with Heinz.

I said: 'Terrific photos. Now I really need a shot, so let's be having you, Heinz, old man.' We went upstairs to his flat. He gave me half a half and brought a tablespoon for cooking up. He apologised for having no teaspoon in the place. All his teaspoons had been swiped by different fixer chicks. I shot up the whole half a half, and he brought me a bottle of stout. Then he let me be for a quarter of an hour. He had sufficient experience with fixers to know that after a shot you need a quarter of an hour's rest.

His flat didn't look like a businessman's flat. Babsi and

Stella had always said that Heinz was a businessman. In his old living room cupboard he kept his ties. Trashy porcelain knick knacks and empty raffia-covered Chianti bottles were strewn all over the place. The curtains were quite yellow with dirt, and drawn so that no one could look inside the grubby flat. Two old sofas were pushed together against the wall, and it was on them that we finally bedded down. No sheets or anything, just an old check rug with a fringe.

Actually this Heinz wasn't too bad really, except that, unfortunately, his strong point was nagging. He really nagged at me, until I slept with him properly just for the sake of peace and quiet and because I wanted to go home. He was absolutely determined that I should enjoy it, and I pretended because he had paid quite well.

After Stella and Babsi I was now Heinz' regular chick. At first I simply thought him useful because he saved me no end of time. No longer did I have to hang around the Arabs for hours, just for a ludicrous snort; no longer need I wait for customers at Zoo station; I didn't even have to go to the scene to score. So now I could attend to housework, pigeons, shopping, and so on, before going to Heinz' flat.

I spent almost every afternoon with Heinz, and, to be perfectly honest, I no longer had anything against him. In a way he loved me. He told me constantly that he loved me and I had to say that I loved him. He was madly jealous. He was always scared that I might still go to the station. And somehow he was nice.

After all, he was the only one I could talk to. Detlef was in the nick. Bernd was in the nick. Babsi at Narkonon. And as for Stella, the earth seemed to have swallowed her up. My mother no longer wanted to have anything to do with me, I thought. And as for my father, I had to keep telling him lies. Every sentence I spoke to him was some sort of lie. There was only Heinz to whom I could talk about almost anything, from whom I needed to have no secrets. The only thing about which I couldn't speak openly was my relationship with him.

Sometimes when Heinz took me in his arms I felt really

221

good. I had the feeling that he respected me and that I meant something to him. Who else respected me? When we weren't on his scruffy couch I felt rather more like Heinz' daughter than his mistress. But he did nag pretty badly. And in time it got worse. He wanted me to be with him all the time. I had to help in his shop and was supposed to be on view to his so-called friends. He didn't have a single real friend.

The time I had to spend with Heinz once again upset my timetable. My father was getting more and more suspicious. He was always snooping around my things. I had to be careful to see that nothing suspicious was brought into his flat. I had to code all the telephone numbers and addresses which were connected with my role as a fixer and prostitute. Heinz, for instance, lived in Waldstrasse. In my address book I drew a few trees. House and telephone numbers were coded in the form of arithmetical problems. The telephone number 3954773 was noted down like this: 3.95 marks plus 47 pfennigs plus 73 pfennigs. And then I worked it all out neatly. So, occasionally, I still did my sums.

One day Heinz solved the mystery around Stella. Stella was in the nick. I hadn't got any of this because I had neither the time nor any reason to hang around the station or the scene. Heinz was rather shocked by the news. Not on account of Stella. But now he was suddenly scared of the cops. He was scared that Stella might grass on him. On this occasion I learnt that preliminary proceedings had been started against him some time ago. On the grounds of seducing minors and similar things. Up to now this had left him quite cold, although he had no previous convictions. He thought he had the best lawyer in Berlin. But he was worried in case Stella might say he paid girls with stuff.

I was shocked, too. But my first worries weren't about poor Stella either, only about myself. If they locked up Stella who was all of fourteen, then my turn was bound to come at the next opportunity. And I didn't fancy being in the nick at all.

I rang up Narkonon to tell Babsi the news. I telephoned Babsi nearly every day. So far she quite liked withdrawing at Narkonon. Admittedly, she had already skipped out twice in order to have a quick fix. When I rang Narkonon they told me that Babsi was at Westend hospital with jaundice.

Somehow Babsi seemed to have the same trouble as me. No sooner were we earnestly engaged in kicking than we would go down with jaundice. Babsi, too, had been trying umpteen times to kick. Last time she had even gone to Tübingen with a drug counsellor to start a therapy there. But at the last moment she got cold feet because this place in Tübingen was very strict. Babsi was physically in as poor a state as me. We always watched one another very carefully. From the state of each other we could deduce fairly accurately how far we had deteriorated. Because with the two of us things were very much the same.

Next morning I set out at once to visit Babsi at Westend hospital. Janie and I took the tube to Theodor-Heuss-Platz and then we walked across Westend. This is a rather terrific district. Crazy private houses and any amount of trees. I had no idea that this kind of thing existed in Berlin. I realised that I didn't know Berlin at all. All I had ever consciously seen in my life was Gropiusstadt and its surroundings, the little quarter of Kreuzberg where my mother lived, and the four places where the scene was. It was pouring with rain. Janie and I were soaked through. But we were both very happy. We were pleased about all those trees and I, most of all, was looking forward to seeing Babsi.

At the hospital there was a problem straightaway which I had not considered. Janie was not allowed to come in with me, of course. However, one of the doormen was really great. He looked after Janie for me in his little hut.

I asked my way to the ward where Babsi was supposed to be and questioned the first doctor I could get hold of about her. He said: 'Yes, we'd also like to know where Babette has got to.' He told me that Babsi had skipped on the previous day. He said it would be extremely dangerous if Babsi were to start taking drugs again because she was not completely cured of her jaundice and her liver couldn't stand much more.

Janie and I walked back to the tube. I thought that Babsi's liver was as ruined as mine. That everything ran parallel with the two of us. I longed to see Babsi. I had forgotten all our squabbles. I was going to let her finish what she wanted to say. And try to persuade her to return to the hospital. But then I sobered up. I knew that Babsi wouldn't go back anyway, after she'd been crashing out and on H for two days. I knew myself. I wouldn't have gone back either. Babsi and I were bloody well alike. Nor did I know where to look for her. She was either knocking around somewhere on the station or the scene, or she was with a regular customer. I had no time to look for her everywhere because my father made his telephone checks at home. I acted according to the old fixer motto: a fixer looks after number one. I went home. I had not the least desire for either the scene or the station because I still had stuff Heinz had given me.

Next morning I went downstairs to buy a paper. I bought a paper every morning. Actually, ever since my mother stopped showing me the pieces about heroin deaths in Berlin. It was rather unconsciously that I always first skimmed through the paper for reports about victims of heroin. They were growing shorter because there was an increasing number of deaths. But there were more and more people I knew among those who had been found somewhere with a spike still sticking in their arm.

So this morning I was making myself a jam sandwich and leafing through the paper. It was right in the front. A real big headline: 'She was only 14.' I knew at once. No need to read on. Babsi. I had suspected something like this. Quite frankly I was unable to feel any emotion whatever — I was totally dead. It was as if my own death was reported in that paper.

I went into the bathroom and had my shot. Only then was I able to cry a little. I wasn't clear whether I was crying for myself or for Babsi. I smoked a cigarette in bed before I could bring myself to read what they had written in the

224

paper. The whole thing had been written up as a minor sensation:

The disposable syringe of milky plastic material was still stuck in the vein of the young girl's left hand: Babette D. (14), schoolgirl, of Schöneberg, was dead. This was how the youngest drug victim so far was found by a friend in a flat in Brotteroder Strasse. Nadjy R. (30), explained to the CID that he had picked up the girl in the Sound discotheque in Ghenthiner Strasse. Since she had nowhere to go he had taken her to his flat. Babette is the 46th drug victim in Berlin this year.'

And so on. What a graphic description. So simple. Just as the papers always imagine the fixer scene to be. Even in the colour mag there was all this rubbish about Babsi, simply because she was the youngest person in Germany to have died from drugs.

Some time towards midday I had recovered and now I felt nothing but fierce rage. I was convinced that some fucking pig of a dealer had sold Babsi cut stuff, perhaps even stuff cut with strychnine, a hot shot. There was more and more stuff cut with strychnine on the scene. I took the tube straight to the police. I stormed into the room of the Schipke woman without knocking. And then I spoke my mind. I told her everything I knew about rip-off dealers and about pimps who were in the H business and about the Sound. Most of it didn't seem to interest her very much. And in the end she trotted out her usual: 'Well, see you again soon, Christiane.'

I thought these cops didn't give a damn if anyone sold cut stuff. They were only too glad if they could cross off another fixer. I swore to myself that I would find Babsi's murderer myself.

The guy at whose flat Babsi had been found was not suspect. He was relatively okay. I knew him quite well — a customer with pots of cash, and quite funny with it. He liked surrounding himself with very young girls. He had taken me for a drive through town in his sports car, had invited me for meals and given me money. But he would only go to bed with a girl if she really wanted to. With me he could have

225

waited until doomsday. He may have been a businessman, but he never grasped that hustling is strictly business too.

So I went to kerb crawlers' corner in Kurfürstenstrasse with the intention of making so much money that I would be able to test stuff from all sorts of rip-off dealers. Then I knocked around on the scene, bought stuff from a few guys and ended up completely stoned. In any case, no one knew where Babsi had bought her last shot. Or at least no one was willing to say they knew. I still kidded myself that I was hunting for Babsi's murderer when, in reality, all I was interested in doing was to get bombed out without qualms of conscience. So I could say to myself: 'You've got to find this con man dealer even if it kills you too.' And then I was no longer scared of getting bombed out.

BERNDT GEORG THAMM, HEAD OF THE PSYCHOSOCIAL ADVICE BUREAU OF THE CARITASVERBAND, BERLIN, AND HORST BRÖMER, PSYCHOLOGIST AND CARITAS DRUG COUNSELLOR

According to our estimate the percentage of twelve-to-sixteen-year-olds among drug addicts in the Federal Republic and in Berlin has risen from nought to twenty per cent within the last three years. Christiane is as typical a representative of this new target group of the heroin trade as her friend Babsi, who came to see us at the drug advice bureau in 1977 and died two months later from an overdose of heroin. We could not help this fourteen-year-old. In the meantime, Stella and other fixers from Christiane's crowd have turned to us. With, on the one hand, their obvious aggression potential and, on the other hand, their still infantile need for protection, affection and warmth, they display all the typical characteristics of the new child heroin consumer.

In May 1977, fourteen-year-old Babsi was brought to our drug advice bureau by her guardians. She behaved like a sad little girl, still clinging to her mother's apron strings. In actual fact she had already experienced all the heights and depths of two years as a fixer.

There comes a time when any fixer wants to free himself from the compulsions of heroin — from prostitution and delinquency to physical ruin. The old fixer, who became addicted at seventeen, eighteen or nineteen, will, after several failed attempts to undertake this step by himself, turn to the drug advice bureaux. So far their entire programme — advice, treatment, therapy — has been geared to these more adult drug addicts. The basic idea is to encourage self-help based on complete voluntariness.

The approximately 50,000 German fixers have at their disposal about 180 State or municipal and 1100 private therapy places in communes, hospitals, etc., where ex-fixers live together, following an extremely strict programme. There are no authenticated figures about the success rates of these therapies. At least eighty per cent of all who are willing to undertake therapy relapse, one of the reasons being that after withdrawal they are faced with the same conditions which led to their becoming addicted in the first place.

The drastically increasing number of twelve-to-sixteen-year-old fixers does not even get this chance of rehabilitation. Although under pressure from their guardians, the youth welfare office, or other institutions, these children come to the advice bureaux — as, indeed, did Babsi — then totally reject the strict rules of existing therapy establishments and thus fail to fulfil the essential precondition for their admission: namely that of voluntariness.

On the scene they hear from relapsed fixers 'horror stories' about therapy establishments. Babsi, too, had a distinct mistrust of drug advice bureaux which never left her, not even in the course of our talks. There remained her fear that she might be taken somewhere against her will. In fact, for every addict the decision to enter a therapy is a very difficult one. His addiction with all its after-effects does cause him suffering, but he becomes used to this suffering. In a therapeutic commune, not only will he have to do without his familiar surroundings and familiar people, but he will also have to allow others to tell him what he must and must not do, to the point of interfering with his personal freedom. As a symbol of his separation from the drug scene, for example, he will have to allow his hair to be cut short, he will have to discard the clothes he has worn as a member of the scene and he will have to do without the 'progressive' music which up till then served to stimulate him.

But for a fourteen-year-old, hairstyle, fashion and music are of far greater importance than for a twenty-year-old fixer. For two years he may have argued with his parents about his long hair, his skin-tight jeans and his music. And now he is asked to sacrifice all these attributes with which he had gained the acceptance of friends and acquaintances in his crowd, as entrance fee into a therapy which, in any case, he regards as dreadful. In our opinion, such a sacrifice asks too much of these children.

The emotional make-up of child fixers is not consolidated. They oscillate between childish dreams of a secure world and the behavioural patterns of the adult engaged in the competitive struggle. The disruption of the adolescent in puberty is 'counterbalanced' by his emotional and physical bond with drugs. Child fixers do not experience a gradual detachment from the home leading to eventual independence. All they have learnt is constantly to withdraw from reality during a critical phase in their lives.

Despite the harsh living conditions which twelve-to-sixteen-year-olds manage to withstand on the scene, and also the techniques they develop in this connection, they remain on the emotional level of a child, and therefore they are obstinate and defiant when asked to submit to existing forms of therapy which are simply not suited to children.

Babsi, too, was not prepared to submit to all the conditions of long-term therapy, although we tried, in couselling sessions lasting many hours, to prepare her for this step. After her physical withdrawal we took Babsi to Drogenhilfe Tübingen, one of the few institutions which, in exceptional cases, accepts patients of her age group. Incidentally, all we can do is to find therapy places; the actual admission is *up to the institution in question.*

On the journey to Tübingen, Babsi seemed excited and full of eager anticipation. We talked incessantly about everything and anything. Her physical withdrawal had led to her feeling cheerful and self-confident. Only when Tübingen began to draw closer and closer did she grow nervous and agitated.

On arrival Babsi was welcomed by a former addict and led into the waiting-room for newcomers. But even before the interview, prior to admission taking place, Babsi wanted to return to Berlin. She was brought face to face with the consequences of her decision to undertake therapy: her luggage, her clothing and her body were searched for drugs. Additionally, she was to have her long hair cut short. When she saw the hairdresser approaching with his scissors she could not stand it any longer. A female assistant at the therapy institution tried intensively once more to persuade Babsi, but could not make her alter her decision. It would have been pointless to keep Babsi in Tübingen against her will, because she would have resisted the therapy and in so doing would have become a danger to others willing to withdraw. Moreover, she would presumably have used the first opportunity to run away.

Babsi died 44 days later from an overdose of heroin and became the youngest of the 84 official heroin victims in Berlin in 1977.

Babsi's death stresses the urgent need for an extension and modification of the existing welfare network for older heroin addicts to include twelve-to-sixteen-year-olds, or, alternatively, for a new one to be set up.

Without wishing to dramatise the issue, it is on account of these children that drug work in Germany is at the crossroads. If everything remains as it is at present, this age group will continue to slip through all the loopholes. A therapy concept will have to be developed which is geared especially to the situation of these children and which limits the principle of voluntariness. If we fail in this, deaths from heroin at an early age will, before long, cease to be the exception in Germany, as is the case already in the USA.

However, neither drug counsellors nor drug therapists can solve the drug problem, nor, for that matter, can the police. Neither can it be reduced to a pathological process in the individual, in the sense of an infectious disease of the emotions or a fracture of the mind, in connection with which all the treatment required is correct splinting and nailing.

Even the best therapy cannot perform miracles and will be able to help only few of the young addicts.

We reckon with a further drastic age lowering of the fixer scene which has already extended disastrously into schools, discotheques and places of recreation. Meanwhile, it is no longer only a minority of young people between the ages of twelve and eighteen who are potential drug addicts. Whether, for example, a thirteen-year-old girl will get through her puberty comparatively unscathed or end up addicted to alcohol, a sect, heroin, or some apostle of anarchy and violence, is often determined by accident. Today the adolescent is open to drugs just as the adult is to the offerings of the pharmaceutical industry. Almost every adolescent has among his friends and acquaintances somebody who has taken drugs, is taking them or intends to take them. Today's drug addicts differ significantly in their motivation from the trippers and pot smokers of the sixties. It is no longer, as it once was with the hippies, a question of the extension of consciousness, but primarily of its exclusion. This applies also to alcohol and soft drugs. That is why today it is no longer possible to categorise endangered adolescents into alcohol users, pot smokers and fixers. Transitions are fluid and the goals aimed at through drug abuse identical.

Regretfully, we have discovered that the public are insufficiently informed about the true extent of the drug problem, qualitatively as well as quantitatively. The majority of responsible politicians still believes in a so-called drug wave which is supposed to have passed its peak and is poised for the downward journey. This attitude determines the choice of words, when parliamentarians speak of 'getting a grip' on

230

the situation as if it were merely a question of a tap which needs to be turned off.

In fact, society produces an increasing number of people who opt out. It is particularly young people, finding no satisfaction at school, recreation or work, who take refuge in drugs. Analogous to this constantly accelerating development and in addition to the socially sanctioned drugs of the pharmaceutical and drinks industries, the illegal drugs — marijuana, LSD and heroin — have become consumer commodities on an outstanding scale which, obviously, are also outstandingly well managed. In West Berlin alone a relatively small target of 5000 people, representing the hardcore of heroin users, raises by means of theft, robbery and prostitution, about half a million marks daily. If one applies this figure to the whole of the Federal Republic one will arrive at awe-inspiring sums. In the face of this volume of money the criminal profiteers of addiction will not allow such a profitable source of income to be snatched from under their noses, most certainly not by the police and the Criminal Investigation Departments of the Länder. The quantities of heroin and soft drugs confiscated by the police are, at most, a minute fraction of the drugs actually consumed.

In the meantime, the drugs black market is active throughout the Federal Republic and West Berlin with a Social distributing network, so that today, in addition to soft drugs, heroin is now available anywhere at any time. There exists practically no area free from drugs, only areas with a differing degree of acute danger of infection.

Every large town already possesses its 'scene', while in rural areas the bases of the distribution system will be found in the places of recreation used by adolescents; such as discotheques.

Almost every place with a postal code has been included in the heroin trade organisation. The omnipresence of the drug is doubtless a decisive factor in its increasing comsumption. Today the young person who is forced into compensatory behaviour will find it simply everywhere. In town

231

and country many adolescents suffer from endless boredom and a vague feeling of the futility of their existence. The only change and diversion is offered at week-ends by local discotheques.

This constantly growing minority of adolescents seeks amusement in whatever discotheque is popular at the time. What takes place in these establishments which, to a large extent, are devoid of verbal communication, is, in the last analysis, only an anaesthetising with music and the subsequent disappointment of once again having experienced nothing.

These children and adolescents see no satisfaction in their present; they see no rewarding perspectives for their future; and they can draw no strength from their past. For what was supposed to be their childhood, with its many years of free, relatively unmanipulated and thus stabilising possibilities of development and experience, has now shrunk, in favour of early achievement orientation and in favour, too, of passive consumption, to the period up to the beginning of school.

Thus cheated of his childhood, the young person possesses only the rudiments of imagination, independence and self-confidence; he chases from one attraction to the next, unable, for this reason, to muster resistance to the massive stimulation of demand on the part of commodity producers, to which he has been exposed from at least nursery school age onwards.

Today, as a result of intensified selection procedures in schools, more and more young people realise already during puberty that, however hard they might try, their future financial potential is unlikely to afford them access to the attractive world of shop windows and advertising which has fascinated them from their early days. A realisation to which they may pay lip service by occasional quick demands for an alternative lifestyle, but which basically does nothing but embitter many adolescents because they are deprived of the blessings of consumerdom.

In personal relationships among young people, too, money has increasingly become the main criterion. In order

232

To get to know a girl a youth will first have to spend ten, twenty or thirty marks in the discotheque. To say nothing of fashionable clothing, records, pop concerts, and so on. For an apprentice or a schoolboy these are considerable burdens. It is in these small areas that the big problems arise, it is here that things begin to be in turmoil, and the young people have to realise their wishes in a different way.

Their parents are unable to show them a path they may tread. The majority of parents are themselves stuck in insoluble contradictions: with what they have achieved in their life and still hope to achieve they will never be able to afford what they really want, or rather what they have learnt to want. Nevertheless, in contrast to their children, they do not abandon the race and carry out their Sisyphean talk with all their strength. What perishes in this struggle are values like friendship, neighbourliness, trust, confidence, helpfulness and understanding for the troubles of others.

The destruction of family life has advanced disastrously. Today in Berlin the authorities despatch so-called family helpers (social workers, psychologists, students) into families. There they find unimaginable wretchedness of mute coexistence or hostility. Increasing divorce figures, constant abuse of television during leisure time, suicide statistics, alcohol, pharmaceutical 'crutches' — that is the surrounding field with which the adolescent will have to cope in addition to the problems of his puberty. An adolescent such as this stands in a labyrinth with several exits and interlocking sliding walls which are called, among others, family home, leisure time opportunities, work expectation, achievement pressure at school, sexuality and dreams. The question is, how is he to get through? The exit may well lead him to a crowd of alcoholics, to sectarians or simply to fixers. There is no more dangerous drug, but also none that is more effective, than heroin for quickly 'solving' all problems.

The decisive barrier for drug-endangered adolescents is the high price of the drug. For this reason the drug trade concentrates increasingly on girls; in the last few years the

233

share of female twelve-to-sixteen-year-old heroin consumers has shot up in comparison to young male fixers.
Because they can raise the necessary money through prostitution, girls find it easier to finance their drug requirements. They are deliberately being made dependent by
dealers.

This often begins in the discotheques, with quite simple
techniques. A good-looking young man, dressed in the
prevailing fashion of the discotheque in question, accosts
young girls. They think him terrific because he is so
'together'; after which he purposefuly distributes the first
heroin snorts among them free. He needs to do this only a
few times, and a new heroin-dependent person is created
who, in her turn, may well introduce the drug into the circle
of her friends. This is the usual method of canvassing for
new customers, used by small and agency dealers, who,
unlike middlemen and wholesalers, are themselves dependent and make just enough profit for their living, or often
merely to pay for their own heroin requirements. They need
no special powers of persuasion for their activity. The readi-
ness of adolescents to take risks is great. In their understand-
able desire to wrest from an environment, where the
chances of genuine experiences grow steadily poorer,
experiences 'exclusively theirs', adolescents and, in an
increasing measure, also children, grasp the 'helping' hand
of the dealer and, thanks to his gift of heroin, actually
experience, to begin with, a general feeling of happiness
and of carefreeness. Because this stands in sharp and seemingly positive contrast to their real situation, they are all the
more reluctant to do without this 'high feeling'. After they
have consumed heroin on three occasions they will be emotionally dependent. Now it depends only on the frequency
of repetition before, after a few weeks, physical dependence will have been reached. From this point the addict
can no longer do without heroin without extremely painful
withdrawal symptoms, and he becomes a regular customer
for the dealer. By then the majority of addicts can no longer
be saved. The place of a small dealer who has been arrested

234

will be taken by a new one on the following day. To be a dealer himself becomes a desirable goal for every heroin addict, because it enables him to finance his addiction in a more agreeable way than by theft and prostitution. This means: with every buyer the heroin trade gains a potential seller. In Berlin we are faced with fourteen and sixteen-year-old small dealers.

In rural areas the problems of drug addiction are, to a large extent, underestimated, one of the reasons being that their exponents are not as clearly seen as in the conurbations. Sooner or later many rural youngsters turned fixers move to the large cities because in the long run they have no possibility of acquiring the necessary means in their home town.

Girls and women are almost exclusively driven into prostitution by their addiction. The majority of male fixers specialise in offences against property; some in breaking into storerooms, training establishments or motorcars, others in handbag thefts or thefts in department stores. And each one has a regular fence, or at least contacts with the black market in pocket calculators, portable radios, electrical goods, cameras, liquor, and so on. Irrespective of the value of the stolen goods, the profits will only rarely exceed the sum required for the addicts' daily ration of heroin, unless the fixer did his pinching to order.

With a requirement of forty to two hundred marks daily, the structures of the scene are determined by a permanent lack of money. The daily pressure of having once again to acquire the necessary means leads to coarsening, brutalisation, aggression and isolation among heroin addicts. Despite a continuous increase of the dose the euphoric effect of heroin decreases slowly and finally fails to appear. By then the addict fixes only in order to escape from the cruel pains of withdrawal symptoms.

I didn't bother trying to pull the wool over my father's eyes. He had been suspecting it for a long time, anyway. I believe he was only waiting for the final proof. And he got it. One evening when I had no stuff left for next morning and was unable to go out because my father was at home, I surreptitiously rang up Heinz and arranged to meet him in Gropiusstadt. My father caught Heinz and me outside the pub. Heinz only just managed to beat it in time. But my father found the stuff Heinz had given me.

I immediately confessed everything. Above all he made me tell him all about Heinz. I no longer had the strength to tell lies. My father ordered me to arrange a meeting with Heinz for the following day at Hasenheide where he was again to give me stuff. Then my father rang the cops, telling them everything and demanding that they arrest Heinz at the meeting. The cops told him that at Hasenheide they would need to arrange a proper raid and that wasn't something that could be done at the drop of a hat. In other words, they weren't mad keen to arrest this 'child seducer' — as my father called him — because it was far too much trouble. Naturally I was glad that I didn't have to play the grotty part of a stool pigeon.

I always thought my father would beat the living daylights out of me when he found out how I had hoodwinked him. But my father reacted quite differently. He was rather desperate. Almost like my mother. He kept talking to me very sweetly. Somehow he had sussed that it isn't possible to stop taking H just like that, even if one really wants to. But he still had some hopes of succeeding with me somehow.

Next day he locked me in the flat again. As for my dog Janie, he took her away with him. I never saw Janie again. I was doing an absolutely diabolical cold turkey. By midday I thought I couldn't stand it any longer. Then Heinz telephoned. I implored him to bring me some stuff. Since he couldn't even get inside the house without a key, I would let a rope down from the 11th floor. In the end I talked Heinz into it. In return he demanded that I should write him a love letter, and send the letter, together with a pair of my panties, down the rope. He never gave away stuff without getting something in return. He was simply a businessman.

So I gathered together whatever I could find in the flat by

way of rope, some string, a plastic washing line, a dressing gown cord, and so on. I had to make many knots and try again and again until this knotted rope was long enough to reach from the eleventh floor to the ground. Then I scribbled this letter. All on cold turkey.

Heinz actually announced himself by the prearranged ring on the bell. I took a pair of panties I had embroidered myself out of the cupboard, put them inside the cover of my hairdrier, together with the letter, and lowered this air mail out of the nursery window. It worked. Down at the other end Heinz put in the stuff. Meanwhile a few people stood watching our strange game. However, this didn't seem to bother Heinz, and it certainly didn't bother me. All I wanted was the stuff. It was only when a little boy on the ninth floor leant out of the window trying to grab the rope that I totally blew my top. I screamed and tried to keep the rope away from him. I was terribly scared about my stuff.

At last I got it up, and I was just about to cook up when the phone rang. Heinz. There was a misunderstanding. He wanted a pair of panties I had actually worn. I had my stuff and, really, I didn't care tuppence. Simply to stop the guy from nagging me I fished the dirtiest pair of knickers out of the laundry basket and threw them out of the window. They landed in some bushes. At first Heinz ran away, but then he crept back and collected his precious knickers.

This Heinz was a totally cracked and crazy guy. As I learnt later, at the time we had the hooha with the rope, a warrant for his arrest had been out for about three weeks. The cops just hadn't had the time to pick him up. And his solicitor had already told him that he was in a tight spot. But if it was a question of girls, Heinz would do his little nut.

I was called as a witness at his trial. I told the truth. In some respect I cared as little about Heinz as about any other customer. Still, I didn't find it easy to be a witness against him because I felt sorry for him. At any rate, he was no worse than other customers who give girl fixers money knowing full well that they would use it to score. Only he was worse off, poor sod, because he was positively addicted to young girls. I believe they should have put him on a psychiatrist's couch rather than in the nick*.

Heinz' stuff just about lasted for the couple of days my father kept me locked up. But the withdrawal wasn't on. On the first day my father didn't lock the front door I beat it. I had been crashing out for a week before my father found me and took me back home with him. Once again I waited, expecting him to give me a hiding. But he was just a bit more desperate.

Then I told him that I couldn't manage it by myself. I couldn't, I said, if I was completely alone all day. Babsi dead. Detlef in the nick. Stella in the nick. I told him about Stella. That Stella, aged fourteen, was being destroyed in the nick. I had heard this from a girl who shared a cell with Stella and who had been released. Stella was constantly wanting to kill herself. Her only support were the women terrorists who were in the same nick. Stella had talked a couple of times to Monika Berberich of the RAF (Rote Arme Faktion, a terrorist organisation) and was totally gone on the woman. Many fixers thought the terrorists absolutely fantastic. There were fixers who tried to get into a terrorist group before they turned on to H. And when the Schleyer kidnap took place it somehow turned me on, too. Strictly speaking, I was against any kind of violence. But then again I thought perhaps the RAF people might know what it was all about. Perhaps one could only change this fucking society through violence.

My father was really put out by this business with Stella. In the end he wanted to get her out of the nick and adopt her. I talked him into believing that, together with Stella, I would manage to kick. That was a last hope. An idiotic hope. But how could he have known any better? I'm sure my father didn't do the right things while I stayed with him. But he just did what he could. Like my mother.

My father kept pestering the youth welfare office and

*On 10th February, 1978, Heinz G. was sentenced to three years' imprisonment for passing heroin to Christiane and Babsi, as well as for the sexual abuse of another child.

managed to prise Stella out of the nick. She really was physically and mentally finished. She was much, much worse than in the time before the nick. When she came to us I had still not kicked, although I had been firmly determined, and on the first day I got her back on H. She would have started to fix anyway. During the first few days we still talked seriously about kicking. But we quickly found out that together we could pull a fast one on my father almost perfectly. We shared all the tasks. Hustling, too, we often did in shifts. Now we only used Kurfürstenstrasse where the kerb crawlers went.

I cared so little about anything that even the kerb crawlers no longer gave me the horrors. We were a group of four girls: in addition to Stella and me, there were the two Tinas. They just both happened to be called Tina. One of them was a year younger even than me. That is to say, just fourteen.

We always worked in twos, at least. When one of us drove off with a customer the other noted down the car number in such a way that the guy was bound to see it, which stopped him from trying any funny business. We weren't scared of the cops. The patrol cars would drive past and often the cops waved to us. One of them was actually a regular customer of mine. A queer bird. He always wanted love. And it was always hard to make him understand that going on the game is work and not love.

There were other customers who needed to have this explained to them. Most of them also wanted to talk to me. At first we always had the same spiel. Why was a pretty girl like me on the streets? I really didn't need to do it, and so on. Those were the sort of phrases which got up my nose most of all. And then they wanted to save me. I received real proposals of marraige. And all the time they knew quite well that they were simply taking advantage of the fixer's wretchedness for their own gratification. Terrible liars they were, these customers. They thought they could help us and yet they had enough problems of their own, and they couldn't even cope with those.

Generally they were guys who didn't have the guts to go

to professional tarts. Who, in any case, had difficulties with women and therefore preferred b.p.'s. They told us how totally frustrated they were with their wives, their family and their whole life in which nothing ever changed. Sometimes they even seemed to envy us a little, at least the fact that we were still so young. They wanted to know what the young people were into, what music, what clothes, what slang.

One guy, almost fifty he was, was dead keen to smoke pot, because he thought all the young people smoked pot. So, for extra money, I traipsed across half Berlin with him in an attempt to raise a dealer who held pot. Up till then it had never really struck me, but it was really crazy, at every corner there was H, but nowhere any shit. It took us nearly three hours to score a bit of pot. The customer smoked a joint in the car, and afterwards he was quite thrilled to have smoked.

There were queer and nasty birds among the kerb crawlers. There was one who wanted me to knock on the steel splint in his leg. He'd had the splint since he'd had a motor accident. One came with a sheet of paper which looked like an official certificate complete with stamp. It certified that the guy was infertile. He only wanted to do it without a French letter. The nastiest guy asserted he was from a model agency and wanted to take trial pictures. Once you were in the car he drew out a gun and demanded service without pay.

In the end the ones I liked best were the students who arrived on foot. They were rather inhibited guys. But I enjoyed talking to them. About this fucking society. They were the only ones whose pads I'd go to. With the others I did it in the car or in a hotel. The room would cost the customer at least another ten marks. And then we weren't allowed to use the freshly made up bed. For us they put up a special divan. These hotels were really the dreariest.

Stella and I would communicate through coded messages which we wrote on advertising stands or empty poster walls. In this way we always knew when we were changing shifts what the other one was doing just then, and what new

240

idea my father had thought up to keep a check on us. When I felt like crying and throwing up while doing my shift, I sometimes went into a shop which called itself 'Teen Challenge'. They had set up in business right next to the Sound, where the b.p.'s were hanging out, in order to convert the likes of us. In this shop they gave you brochures and books about little b.p.'s and girl fixers in America whom Teen Challenge had shown the way to God. I had a good natter there, drinking tea and eating bread and drippping. When they started talking about Our Dear Lord I beat it. Basically they also exploited girl fixers in this shop by trying to rope us in for their sect when we were feeling really down.

Right next door to the sect's cellar in Kurfürstenstrasse a Communist group had their shop. Sometimes I read their posters in the shop window. So they wanted to change society completely. I liked it. But their slogans didn't do anything to help me in my situation.

Then I used to stare at the windows of the large furniture shops. The dream of a flat of my own with Detlef came back. That made me feel even more pissed off.

At that stage I had just about arrived at the very bottom of a fixer's career. When there was nothing doing with the kerb crawlers I committed crimes. Small crimes: I'm not really born for a life of crime because I never quite had the nerve. Once when fixer guys wanted to take me along on a break-in, I chickened out. The worst thing I ever did, after a whole bottle of vermouth, was smashing a car window with a knuckle duster and swiping a portable radio. Apart from that, I helped fixers to sell the things they'd knocked off to a fence. I transported hot merchandise, even from ordinary criminals. I put loot into the lockers at Zoo station and took it out again. For that the most I ever got was twenty marks. And yet it was more dangerous than nicking. But then I no longer had a clue, anyway.

At home I lied to my father and quarrelled with Stella. I had agreed with Stella that we were to share the jobs and also the stuff. That's what we had most of our quarrels about. Because each of us believed the other was ripping her off. There was absolutely nothing lower than the life I led then.

Of course, my father had long since realised what was up with me. However, by now he was completely helpless. Me too. I did know, though, that my parents could no longer help me.

I couldn't any longer cope with school. Even if I was just sitting around. I couldn't stand sitting around. I couldn't stand anything any more. I couldn't mess around with a customer. I couldn't even leap about on the scene in a laid back way. I couldn't stand my father any longer.

So, once again, things had got to a fine pass. End-of-the world gloom and despondency. Thoughts of suicide. I already knew it, this situation when you just can't go on. But I was still too chicken to o.d. I was still looking for some way out.

And then I thought that I might go into a lunatic asylum as a voluntary patient. Into the *Bonhoeffer Heilanstalten*, or Bonnies' Ranch, as it was called. That was just about the very last thing a fixer could do. Bonnies' Ranch was the total horror for any fixer. They always said: better in the nick for years than four weeks in Bonnies' Ranch. Some fixers had been forcibly taken to Bonnies' Ranch after a breakdown, and afterwards they told horrendous horror stories.

But I thought, ever so naively, if I were to surrender voluntarily to this horror, someone's attention might be drawn to me. Then the Youth Welfare Office, or whoever, would have to notice that here was an adolescent who urgently needed help. And that her parents were totally incapable of helping this adolescent. The decision to go to Bonnies' Ranch voluntarily was like a suicide attempt where secretly you hope to wake up again so that afterwards everybody will say: 'Ah, poor thing, if only we'd cared more about her, but from now on we'll never be so nasty to her again.'

Once I had made the decision, I went to see my mother. At first she treated me very coolly because somehow she had written me off. I immediately began to cry, really to cry.

Then I tried to tell her my story, rather truthfully. And then she cried, too, and took me in her arms and didn't let me go. We both really cried ourselves happy. My sister was very happy, too, that I had come back again. We slept together in my old bed. Soon I was doing cold turkey.

A new withdrawal began. I no longer knew how many withdrawals there had been before this one. But now, I daresay, I held the world record in withdrawing. At least I knew nobody who withdrew voluntarily as often as I. And always without any chance of success, too. It was almost exactly like my first withdrawal. Once again my mother took time off and brought me whatever I fancied: valium, wine, blancmange, fruit. On the fourth day my mother took me to Bonnies' Ranch. I really wanted this because by now I knew that otherwise I would have shot up again on the very next day.

I had to strip naked and was shoved into a bathroom. Like the worst leper. Two rather mad grannies were being bathed in two bathtubs. I was put in the third and made to scrub under supervision. I didn't get my own clothes back. Instead I got a pair of knickers reaching up to my armpits which I had to keep clutching to stop them from slipping. And a rather old granny nightie. I was taken to the observation ward. I was the only one under sixty there. The grannies were all pretty well round the bend. Except for one. They called her Dolly.

All day long Dolly was busy with some kind of work for the ward. She really made herself useful and relieved the nurses of quite a lot of work. Dolly and I talked together. She didn't seem mad, but somehow she thought very slowly. She had been in the observation ward for fifteen years. Fifteen years ago her brothers and sisters had her admitted to Bonnies' Ranch. Apparently she'd never gone through any therapy. She'd simply always remained in the observation ward. Possibly because she made herself so useful there. I thought there must be something not quite right if someone stays in the observation ward for fifteen years just because they're slow thinkers.

243

On my first day I was inspected by a whole team of doctors. That is to say, most of these white-coats were probably students and they eyed me rather impertinently in my granny nightie. The boss of the white-coats asked a few questions, and I told him quite naively that I wanted to go into a therapy in a few days and afterwards into a boarding school in West Germany to do my university entrance exams. He kept saying 'yes, yes,' the way you say yes, yes to lunatics.

As soon as I was back in bed I remembered a few lunatic jokes. I wondered if I'd said something wrong because somehow they'd treated me like someone who says he's Napoleon. Suddenly I was afraid that, like Dolly, I would never get out of the observation ward and would spend my life dozing.

After two days I was transferred to B ward because I no longer had withdrawal symptoms. I got my clothes back and was even allowed to eat with a knife and fork and not with a child's spoon like in the observation ward. In this ward there were another three women fixers whom I knew from the scene. The four of us sat at a table which the grannies immediately called the terrorists' table.

One of the girls, Liane, had had a lot of experience in the nick. She, too, said that Bonnies' Ranch was much worse than being in the nick. Especially because in the nick you could get H any time, whereas in Bonnies' Ranch it was difficult.

So far it was quite fun on Bonnies' Ranch because there were four of us. Nevertheless, gradually I got panicky again. The doctors would never give me a sensible answer whenever I asked when I was going to be put into a drug therapy. They just said 'we'll see,' and whatever else they were in the habit of trotting out daily to the poor lunatics.

My arrangement with my mother and the Youth Welfare Office had been that I was to stay in Bonnies' Ranch for four days so that they could be quite sure I was off H. And then I was to get a therapy place. But I had already kicked by myself and was almost off when I got there. And nobody

244

said another word about a therapy place.

The biggest blow came after a couple of days. They brought me a document which I was supposed to sign saying that I agreed voluntarily to remain in the institution for three months. Of course I refused and said I wanted to get out at once. I had, I said, come of my own free will and could therefore go when I wanted. Then the senior doctor came and said if I didn't sign on for three months he would arrange for compulsory hospitalisation for six months.

Now I felt completely conned. I really got the horrors. Suddenly it became as clear as day to me that now I was completely dependent on these idiotic doctors. How did I know what sort of a diagnosis they'd make about me? They might lumber me with a severe neurosis or schizophrenia or God knows what. As the inmate of a lunatic asylum you no longer had even the slightest right. I really thought, now you've had it, just like Dolly.

The worst thing was that suddenly I no longer knew myself how mad I was. I certainly did have a neurosis. That much I had taken in during talks with drug counsellors — that an addiction is a neurosis, a compulsive action. I thought about all the things I had done already. All those withdrawals, and then straight back on stuff again, although I knew very well that I would kill myself with it at some time. This whole fuck-up I'd made of my little bit of life, what I had done to my mother, how I had treated other people. It was certainly not normal. I was quite a nutcase all right. And all I thought about now was how I could conceal from doctors and nurses that I was really not normal.

These nurses treated me like an idiot, that is to say, like all the other idiots. I pulled myself together terribly in order not to react more aggressively. When the doctors came and asked questions I tried to give them only answers which normally I wouldn't have dreamt of giving. I tried desperately not to be myself but some other person who was quite normal. And when the doctors had gone again I thought that I'd said exactly the wrong thing. That now they would think me totally barmy.

245

The only thing they offered me by way of therapy was knitting. And I really didn't fancy that at all. Nor did I think it would help me.

Naturally the windows were barred. But these were no ordinary bars like in the nick, because it wasn't a nick, but beautifully ornamental bars. I found out by twisting my head a certain way I could stick it through and look out of the window properly. Sometimes I stood there for absolutely hours, the iron bars round my neck, peering out. Autumn was coming, the leaves were turning yellow and red, the sun was already rather low and shone for about an hour every day between two trees, straight into the window.

Sometimes I tied one of the tin cups to a woollen cord, let it hang out of the window and banged it against the house wall. Or I tried vainly all afternoon to pull a branch close to the window with my woollen cord so that I could pick a leaf. At night I thought: 'If you weren't mad before, you've certainly gone mad in here.'

I wasn't even allowed into the garden where the grannies used to walk round and round. Even a terrorist has the right to get into the fresh air once a day, but not me. With me there was the risk of an attempt to escape. They were dead right.

In a cupboard I found an old football. I kept kicking it against a locked glass door, hoping the glass would break. Until they took away the football. I ran my head against glass panes. But of course they were all made of reinforced glass. I felt like a wild animal in a tiny cage. For hours I prowled along the walls. Once I thought I couldn't stand it. I simply must run. And then I started running. Always up and down the corridor. Until I couldn't go on any more and collapsed.

I got a knife, and at night Liane and I scraped the putty out of a window that was locked but not barred. The pane never moved at all. On the following night we took a bed to pieces and tried to force out the bars of an open window. Previously we had so intimidated the grannies in our room that they didn't dare make a peep. Some of them really did

246

think we were terrorists. Our undertaking was, needless to say, completely senseless, and we made so much noise that the night watchman caught us.

The way I behaved in this loony bin I didn't have a hope that they would ever release me. I went further and further downhill. Only my body seemed to recover without drugs. I got a fat paunch. My face was pasty, haggard and at the same time bloated, and in the mirror it seemed to me like the face of someone who had already done her fifteen years in Bonnies' Ranch. I hardly slept any more. Besides, almost every night there was some sort of commotion in the ward. And I always thought I might miss a chance of escaping. Although everything was quite hopeless, I got myself ready every morning as if I was about to go to the scene. I brushed my hair with incredible patience, put on my make-up and slipped my jacket across my shoulders.

Once somebody from the Youth Welfare Office came to see me. Like everybody else all he said was: 'We'll see.' But at least through him I found out which nick Detlef was in and his reference number. I sat down at once and wrote pages and pages. As soon as I'd handed in one letter I started another one. At least I was able to chatter away. Although I had to watch what I said because the letters were being read. Probably already at Bonnies', but certainly in the nick. So once again I had to lie my head off. That I had no desire for drugs whatever, and so on.

From Detlef I received a whole pile of letters all at once. He wrote that he'd produced a right fuck-up when he'd pinched the customer's Eurocheques. That he'd only done it so that he could go to Paris to kick. He'd wanted to surprise me because together we'd never have done it. Detlef wrote that he was coming out soon and would go into a therapy. I wrote that I'd be going into a therapy as well. And both of us wrote that after the therapy we would move into a flat together. In these letters, then, we once again talked a lot of nonsense about our joint paradise after the therapy. And yet whenever I was not thinking about Detlef, I thought that I would never ever get out of Bonnies' Ranch.

247

I had one more real chance. My fungus infection had returned and every day I told the woman doctor in the ward that I must go into hospital for an operation because I simply couldn't stand the pain any longer. One morning they did take me to the Rudolf Virchow hospital, closely guarded, of course. After they'd examined me, they took me in at once because it was really rather bad. I'd already heard from other fixers how to get out of the hospital. I got myself a park ticket. That allows you to use the hospital park. Of course, as a fixer, it wasn't all that easy to get one of these tickets. But there was a fantastic trick. I went to a rather sweet, slant-eyed nurse and told her I wanted to push old grannies who couldn't walk round the park. She wasn't a bit suspicious and thought it was terribly sweet of me.

I got hold of an old granny who said I was a very sweet child. I pushed her into the park and said: 'Wait a moment, granny, I'll be back in a second.' And quick as a flash I was over the fence.

I ran to Amrumer Strasse tube station and went to the Zoo. I never felt so free in my life. I went straight to the scene at the TU refectory. I knocked around a bit and then sat down on a bench with three young fixers. I told them that I'd just cleared out of Bonnies'. Needless to say they were greatly impressed.

I had a terrible craving for a shot. One of the boys was a dealer. I asked whether I could have some on tick. He said if I helped him get customers he would give me some. I said okay. He gave me some. And I immediately shot it in the refectory toilet.

I only shot barely half a quarter, and the stuff wasn't particularly good either. Although I felt good, I still had my wits about me. I had to, anyway, because I was supposed to get customers for this guy. He was quite a young guy whom I knew slightly from the hash scene on Hasenheide. He was still going to school, about sixteen. I realised at once that he hadn't much experience with dealing. Otherwise he wouldn't have stood me the shot, but would have waited until I had got him a few customers first.

Then I sussed that outside the refectory the place was lousy with plain clothes cops. The guy didn't notice anything. I actually had to go up to him and whisper 'cops' before he tumbled. I walked slowly in the direction of Zoo station and he crept after me. When a fixer came towards me from the station I said: 'Stay here, old man. There's a rumble on at the refectory. But I can get you some fine stuff.' This young dealer came up at once and actually got all his stuff out of his pocket and said the guy could try some. I thought, well, fuck me. There's a rumble three hundred metres back and this idiot pulls H out of his pocket.

Then two plain clothes cops who'd been lurking there came up to us. Running was out. This young kid threw his papers all over the place. There was purple foil paper absolutely everywhere. He seemed to think he could pin it on the fixer or on me and kept repeating he'd nothing to do with it.

We were made to lean against a VW, hands up, and were searched for arms, although none of us was older than sixteen. This cunt of a cop had a feel of my tits while he was about it. But I was totally calm. I'd had my shot, and after Bonnies' nothing could shake me any more. I immediately came the well brought-up child. They were quite friendly while taking down our particulars. One of them said to me: 'Listen, girl, you're barely fifteen, what on earth are you doing here?' I said: 'Strolling,' and lit a fag. He got quite cross: 'Come on, throw that fag away. That's pure poison at your age.' He made me throw away the cigarette.

We were taken to the police station at Ernst Reuter Platz and locked in a cell. The would-be dealer immediately did his nut and screamed: 'Let me out, let me out!' I took off my jacket, rolled it up into a pillow, lay on the bunk and dozed off. An arrest like this was the last thing to frighten me. It never occurred to me that the cops might find out that I'd hopped it from Bonnies'. I was sure that I hadn't yet been reported as missing.

After two hours they let me go. I went back to the refectory. On the way I didn't half get remorseful. I began to blub. So once again I had fixed at the first opportunity after a withdrawal. And besides I didn't know where to go. I couldn't possibly turn up at my mother's, pin-head pupils and all, and say: 'Here I am, mummy. Hopped it. Now how about some supper.'

I went to the drugs advice centre in the old refectory of the Technical College. The guys there were very together and managed to straighten me out sufficiently for me to ring my mother. My mother was fairly reassured when she heard I was phoning from the college. On the way home I developed a temperature. By the time I got into bed it was over forty degrees [104°F]. My mother fetched the emergency doctor because I was beginning to get delirious. He wanted to give me an injection, and suddenly I was absolutely terrified because he wanted to inject into my behind. I injected myself in the arm two or three times daily. But when he put the needle in my behind I nearly went crazy.

The temperature dropped immediately. But I was totally finished. Bonnies' Ranch had been the last straw, physically and mentally. When I was able to get up again three days later I went immediately to the drugs advice centre. On the way there I had to walk through the scene in the refectory. I ran through without looking either left or right.

For a week I went to the drugs advice centre every day. At last here was a place where I could let my hair down and talk. So far I had always been talked at. My mother was always getting at me, my father, the Narkonon guys, everybody. In the TU refectory they wanted me to talk and suss for myself what was the matter with me. I was still going to see the counsellors when my face turned yellow as a lemon. When I ran into a few people I knew outside the refectory, they literally ran away from me shouting: 'Fuck off, you with your fucking jaundice.'

I didn't want to admit to myself that I had got another bout of jaundice. It really was enough to drive you up the wall. Whenever I had really kept off stuff for quite a long time and my hopes were rising, I promptly got this fixer disease. When my bellyache became unbearable, my mother took me to the medical centre in Steglitz. I wanted to go to

Steglitz because they have a really great canteen there. So there I was, sitting in reception for two hours, doubled up with pain on my chair. Any nurse coming in could see from my yellow face what was up with me. But they did damn all about it. The waiting room was full of people, including children. If my jaundice had been infectious again I could have infected the lot of them.

After two hours I started to walk. Always along the wall because I was very weak and in great pain. I wanted to ask my way to the isolation ward, and when a doctor came past me I said to him: 'I want a bed. I don't want to infect all the people here. You can see I've got jaundice.' He said that might well be so, but there was nothing he could do about it. I would have to go to admission. So back I went.

When at long last I did get to see a woman doctor and thought I'd better tell her straightaway that my jaundice was probably the result of fixing she, believe it or not, said coldly: 'I'm sorry, but we're not responsible for cases like this.'

That's just it: nobody wants to be responsible for fixers. So, back my mother and I got into the taxi. My mother got terribly worked up about the doctors, because they did nothing for me. Next morning she took me to Rudolf Virchow hospital. Naturally, I was rather pissed off about it, on account of my having skipped from there once before.

A youngish houseman came to take a blood sample. I immediately showed him my veins and the places where it would be useless to put in the needle. 'I've got a thrombosis there. This vein is fucked anyway. You'll have to take one below it. Don't stick the spike in straight but at a slant, otherwise you won't get through anyway.'

The guy was unsure, and then he did inject into a totally fucked vein. Because of the vacuum in the syringe the needle literally flew out of my arm again. The next few times he came, he asked me first where to inject.

I slept for two days. The jaundice wasn't infectious. And on the fourth day the liver tests were quite good, the urine hardly red at all, and my face was slowly becoming clear again.

Every day I had to ring up the drugs consultants, and I did. And then, whaddya know: Detlef was released from the nick. My mother brought him along on the next visiting day, a Sunday.

Well, you can imagine, great love, hugs, kisses, bliss. We wanted to be alone for a moment and went outside into the hospital grounds. It was as if we'd never been separated. No sooner were we outside than we were sitting in the tube, heading for the scene. Chance played a part. We met an acquaintance, Wilhelm, who'd had a stroke of luck. He was living with a queer, a very eminent doctor and writer. This doctor gave Wilhelm not only plenty of cash but he also sent him to a private grammar school.

So Wilhelm stood us both a shot. I was punctually back in hospital for supper. Next afternoon Detlef came again. This time we really had a job getting hold of stuff and I didn't return to the hospital until half past ten at night. My father had been to visit me because he was off on one of his trips to Thailand next day.

When my mother came she wore that desperate look on her face again. I thought I was the ultimate shit. And then my drugs counsellor came and said that probably it was no use going on with me. I swore to myself and to everyone else that I was serious about kicking. Detlef cried too and said it was all his fault. Then he went to the drugs advice centre too. And when he came back next Sunday he'd already got a therapy place for the following day.

I said: 'I think it's a hundred per cent okay that you've got it together. Now everything will really be okay. I'm sure I'll get a place myself. I'll make it, you'll see. We'll never get ourselves in a fucking mess again.'

We went into the park and I said: 'Let's just quickly go to the Zoo. I need to buy a thriller, it's called *Return from the Death's Head Moon*. Part three. I've read the first two books and my mother can't get the third part anywhere.'

Detlef said: 'That's great, old girl. So you've got to go to the Zoo of all places to buy a thriller. Why don't you say straight out you want a fix?'

It didn't half get on my nerves that Detlef was suddenly coming the superior one, the one who was kicking for good and all. I really hadn't been thinking of stuff. I really wanted part three of *Return from the Death's Head Moon*. I said: 'Don't talk so far back. Me, shoot, whatever gives you that idea? Don't have to come if you don't want to.' Of course Detlef came. In the tube an old game of ours began. I immediately started to wind up a couple of old grannies. This always embarrassed Detlef no end and he went to the other side of the carriage. I yelled across the whole carriage: 'Hey, old man, don't you pretend you don't know me. Anyone can see you ain't no better than me.' Then my nose started to bleed. For a few weeks now I'd been having these nose bleeds in the tube. It got on my wick something cruel and I kept wiping the fucking blood from my face.

Luckily I got my thriller at the Zoo. By now I felt a lot better and said to Detlef: 'Let's scoot around a bit, shall we? Today's your last day of freedom.' Of course we scooted automatically to the scene. Stella was there and the two Tinas. The two Tinas were really in a bad way. Cold turkey. They'd been to kerb crawlers' corner in Kurfürstenstrasse, forgetting that it was Sunday. And on Sunday afternoon it's dragsville up there. That's the time when customers are with mummy and the kids, they haven't time for you know what.

Somehow I was glad to be out of the bleeding mess. That needn't any longer be scared of cold turkey and didn't have to find customers. It'd been weeks since I last picked up a customer. I felt superior to the others and was really happy, really high-spirited. And I thought: This is the first time, old lady, that you're scooting around the scene without having a craving for a shot.

We were standing at the bus stop by Kurfürstenstrasse tube station. Next to us were two wogs who kept winking at me. I suppose that, in spite of my jaundice, I still looked the freshest of the four of us because I had been off stuff for a relatively long time. I didn't wear fixer gear either, but real teeny clothes which I had borrowed from my sister because I wanted to distance myself from the fixer crowd outwardly as

253

well. At the hospital I had even cut my hair rather short.

The wogs never stopped winking. I asked the two Tinas 'Shall I line up these two for you? Once you've got forty marks, you can at least share half a half.' The two Tinas were doing cold turkey so badly, they no longer cared anyway. So, full of the joys of spring I went up to the wogs and said: 'You want the two girls? Me ask for you. Fifty marks Capito?' I pointed at the Tinas.

They grinned like two twits and said: 'No, you. You fuck you hotel.' I was totally laid back and no longer the least bit aggressive, and I said: 'Not a hope, that's not on, for a start. But girls really fantastic. Fourteen years. Only fifty marks. The younger Tina was in fact only just fourteen.

The wogs wouldn't wear it. And when I looked at the two Tinas I could understand the wogs up to a point. The Tinas doing cold turkey really weren't a pretty sight. I went back to the girls and told them that it wasn't on. And then somehow the devil got into me. I took Stella to one side and said to her: 'Listen, the state they're in, the Tinas won't be able to cope with customers. To say nothing about wogs. Let's go along with them. We'll work them up and the Tinas will bring them off quickly. They fuck customers anyway. We'll ask for a hundred marks and buy half a gramme.'

Stella was all for it. And yet for both of us wogs were the end. At least neither would have admitted to the other ever to have slept with a wog.

So I went up to these two Turks and put the proposition to them, they were immediately raring to go into action. Only Detlef was totally pissed off and said: 'So now you're going on the game again?' I said: 'Why don't you shut up. I'm not going to do anything . There are four of us.' I imagined I was doing the whole thing out of pity for the Tinas. Pity may have been in it. But unconsciously I was probably looking for devious ways and means of getting at stuff.

I told the others we would have to go to the Norma Hotel in Nürnberger Strasse because they had larger rooms. In the other hotels they wouldn't allow the six of us into one room. Then we were on our way. And suddenly there was a third wog following us. The other two explained: 'He friend. He come hotel.'

For the moment we didn't say a word and just took the hundred marks off them. Stella went off to score with one of the wogs. She knew a dealer who sold the biggest half grammes on the scene. When she returned with the stuff the eight of us marched down the Tauentzienstrasse. We four girls and Detlef in front, all arm in arm. We cleared the pavement. The three wogs bringing up the rear.

However, there was tension in the air. The two Tinas wanted the H. Stella wouldn't hand it over. She was afraid, naturally, that the two Tinas might beat it. Besides, we wanted to get rid of the third wog who wasn't included in our deal.

Stella turned round, pointed at the third wog and declared firmly: 'If wog there comes along, we no do nothing.' She actually had the bleeding nerve to address a Turk as wog.

Meanwhile the three wogs were holding hands and not budging. Stella said in that case we ought to rip them off and run for it. At first I was all for it because I was wearing flat-heeled shoes. For the first time in at least three years I was walking about in flat heels. I borrowed them, too, from my sister. But then I began to have doubts. I said: 'We're sure to run cross them again at some time or other and then we'll be in the soup.' I really had forgotten that this was to be my last afternoon on the scene and at the station.

Stella was pissed off. She stayed behind and once more talked insistently to the wogs. We were just walking along under the stairs at the Europa Centre. I turned round because it had grown quiet behind us: Stella was gone. As if swallowed up by the earth. With all the stuff. The wogs noticed it too and pretended to be agitated.

I just thought: 'Typical Stella.' I was absolutely livid. I felt she could only have beat it into the Europa Centre, and so raced up the stairs of the pedestrian flyover after her. Detlef after me. The two Tinas couldn't get away. The wogs were holding on to them. I ran like mad through the Europa

255

Centre. Me to the left and Detlef to the right. Not a trace of Stella. I didn't find her either and, on top of it, I had a bad conscience on account of the Tinas. I saw the Turks dragging them into an hotel and waited outside for hours until they had finished with their dirty work. At least I wanted them to have the shot they were dying for. I guessed where we might find Stella. The Tinas and I went down to Kurfürstendamm tube station. Things were rather quiet there because about this time the scene moved to the Treibhaus. However, it was Stella we were looking for, and therefore we went straight to the toilets. We had hardly stepped through the doors when we heard Stella. She was well away, chatting to someone. In this toilet there are a large number of doors, but I sussed at once which loo Stella was inside. I banged my fists against the loo door and screamed: 'Stella, open the door this minute. Or there'll be trouble.'

The door burst open immediately. Out came Stella. To start with Little Tina fetched Stella a belt. Stella, completely stoned: 'There you are, there's the whole fucking stuff. I don't want any of it.' And swept out.

A thumping great lie, of course. Stella had quickly shot a good half of the half gramme, to stop us from getting at it. The two Tinas and I pooled the rest of the half gramme as well as the stuff we had just scored and divided it fairly among ourselves.

For me it was more than enough after my withdrawal. I had quite a job getting up from the loo again. We went to the Treibhaus. There was Stella again, carrying on. She was helping a dealer to get customers. We got at her immediately: 'Come along, you still owe us half a half.' She coughed up at once, I'll grant her that. She still managed to have a little bit of a bad conscience.

I said: 'You are the bleeding end. I never want to have anything to do with you ever again.'

I went to the Treibhaus, shot my share of Stella's stuff and bought a coke. I sat alone in a corner. This was the first time since this afternoon that I had time to simmer down a bit. For one moment I hoped Detlef would turn up. Then it was

256

too late, anyway. I had begun to do some thinking.

It started quite harmlessly. I thought: this is a right fuck-up. First your only boyfriend rips you off and then your best friend. Friendship among fixers simply doesn't exist. You're completely alone. You're always alone. Anything else is just imagination. The whole terror this afternoon over a shot. It wasn't anything special, was it? This terror is there every day.

I had a lucid moment. I did have lucid moments — sometimes. But only on H. When I was sober I was not responsible for my actions. Something this day had proved more than adequately.

So I went on thinking. It was not at all dramatic. I was quite calm because I had shot sufficient H. Didn't return to the hospital, though. It was already past eleven.

They'd have given me the boot anyway, and no other hospital would have admitted me. The lady doctor had told my mother that I was on the point of having cirrhosis of the liver. If I carried on in the same way, she'd give me no more than another two years. As for Drogeninfo, that had now gone up the spout. I needn't bother ringing them up because they were in touch with the hospital. They did quite right not to accept people like me. After all there were plenty of fixers in Berlin who'd give their eye teeth to get into a therapy, but hardly any therapy places. It went without saying that only those people who still had enough will power were given therapy places, people who still had a chance to come off the drug. And I was most certainly not one of those. I suppose the long and the short of it was that I had started a little too early to get out of it again.

I was quite lucid. Soberly I drew up a balance sheet while drinking my coke. I thought quite practically. Where was I to go tonight? My mother would have slammed the door in my face. Or she would have got on to the police next morning and have them put me in a home. At least that's what I should have done in her place. My father was in Thailand. Stella wasn't on anyway. As for Detlef, I didn't even know which customer's pad he was dossing down in tonight. Or if he really meant it with the withdrawal, in which case he was with his father. Then he would be gone anyway from tomorrow. So I didn't have a bed. Not tonight and not tomorrow night either.

The last time I had done some sober thinking I had discovered the two possibilities I had then: either to stop using H once and for all or o.d.'ing. The first possibility was gone, unfortunately. After all, five or six withdrawals without the least success were enough, surely. I was neither better nor worse than the other fixers. Why should I of all people belong to the few per cent who manage to come off the drug? I was nothing special. I went to the Kudamm and travelled to Kurfürstenstrasse. I'd never yet done any hustling in Kurfürstenstrasse at night . Girl fixers didn't go there at night because there were too many professional tarts. Quite quickly I did two customers and went back to the Treibhaus. I had a hundred marks and bought half a gramme.

I didn't want to use the toilet at the Treibhaus nor the toilet on the Kurfürstendamm. There was too much hustle and bustle there at night. I bought another coke and considered which toilet to use. I remembered the toilet at Bundesplatz. There wasn't a soul there at night. Even in the mornings it was usually perfectly quiet there.

I walked to Bundesplatz. I felt no panic. I was totally calm. At night there really is something eerie about an empty toilet like that. But somehow I felt safe and secure in this toilet. It was clean and light. I had it all to myself. The Bundesplatz toilet was the best in Berlin. The loos are huge. Once there were six of us in these loos. The doors aren't open at the bottom, they reach right down to the floor. And there are no holes anywhere in the walls. Because the Bundesplatz toilets are the best, quite a few fixers have already killed themselves there.

No old grannies, no voyeurs, no cops. There was no need to hurry. I took my time. I washed my face and brushed my hair before I cleaned the works I had borrowed from Tina. I was sure that the half gramme would be enough. After my last few withdrawals a quarter of a gramme had always been enough to knock me out. Now I had already more than a quarter inside me. And my body was bound to be weakened by jaundice. I would rather have had a whole gramme. Atze had done it with a whole gramme. But I couldn't have done another two customers.

Calmly I selected the cleanest loo. I really was totally calm. I wasn't scared. I would never have thought that suicide is so undramatic. I didn't think of my past life. I didn't think of my mother. I only thought of my shot.

As always I scattered all my bits and pieces around the loo. I put the stuff on the spoon, another thing Tina had lent me. For a moment the thought flashed through my mind that now I, too, had ripped off Tina. For she was at that moment waiting at the Treibhaus. Then I realised that I had forgotten to bring some lemon. However, it was good stuff and dissolved without it.

I looked for a vein in my left arm. Basically it was just like any other shot. Except that this was really meant to be my last. At the second attempt I hit the vein. Blood spurted out. I shot the half gramme. I didn't have a chance to pull up the plunger and shoot the last remnant. What I felt was that first it tore apart my heart and then it literally exploded my skull.

When I woke up it was light outside. The cars were making a terrible din. I was lying next to the loo. I pulled the pump and spike out of my arm. I wanted to get up when I noticed that somehow my right leg was paralysed. I could move it a little, but when I did, my joints ached like hell. Especially the hip joint. Somehow I managed to open the door. At first I crawled, then I pulled myself up. I managed to hop along the wall on one leg.

Outside the toilet were two boys, about fifteen years old they were. Satin jackets, skin-tight jeans. Two little queers. I was glad they were queers. They really caught me when I came hopping out of the toilet like an apparition.

They immediately sussed something, and one of them said: 'Well, what have you been doing to yourself?' I didn't know them, but they had seen me on the station. The boys led me to a bench. It was a terribly cold October morning. One of them gave me a Marlboro. I thought: 'Funny how queers always smoke Marlboro or Camels. Must have something to do with the butch guys in their advertisements.' Somehow I was quite happy that it hadn't worked with the half gramme.

I told the boys how Stella had ripped me off and that I had shot the half gramme. They were very sweet. They asked where they should take me. The question got on my wick because I didn't want to think. I said they should leave me sitting on this bench. But I was trembling with the cold and they thought I ought to see a doctor because I couldn't even walk.

I didn't want to see any doctor. They said they knew quite a together guy, a doctor, who was queer, who they could take me to. I was reassured by the fact that the guy was queer. In a situation like this I had more confidence in queers. The boys fetched a taxi and took me to the queer doctor. The guy really was together. He immediately let me lie in his bed and examined me. He wanted to talk to me about shooting, and that, but I no longer wanted to talk to anyone. I asked him for some sleeping tablets. He gave me a sleeping tablet and some other medicine.

Presently I got my temperature and my nosebleeds. I slept through most of the next two days. When on the third day my brain started to work properly again I couldn't stand it any longer. I didn't want to think. I really had to force myself not to think and go round the bend. I concentrated on two thoughts: 'God did not want you to give up the spoon,' and: 'Next time you'll be sure to take a whole gramme.'

I wanted to get out, to the scene, score a shot, bomb around, and not think until the real o.d. I still couldn't walk properly. The queer doctor was really concerned about me. When he realised he could no longer stop me, he even got me a pair of crutches. I started limping with my crutches but on my way I threw them away. I didn't want to turn up on the scene on crutches. If I pulled myself together I could hobble without them.

I hobbled to Zoo station and started looking for customers. Straightaway a wog came up to me. Not a Turk, though, but a Greek. Strictly speaking, I had nothing against wogs. And I couldn't care less about this funny gentlemen's agreement Babsi, Stella and I once made that we would never do it with a wog. I didn't care about anything.

Perhaps somewhere I still hoped against hope that my mother might come to the station looking for me. If she had been looking for me she would have come to the station. That was probably why I didn't go to Kurfürstenstrasse. But in my heart of hearts I felt that no one was looking for me any more now. And for a moment I thought how lovely it was when my mother was still waiting for me.

I scored, shot and went back to the station. I needed cash in case I didn't get a customer for the night and would have to go to a hotel.

On the station I met Rolf, Detlef's former regular customer, in whose pad I'd spent many week-ends. During the last few weeks Detlef had slept at Rolf's. But Rolf was no longer a customer. He had been on H for some time and went to the station looking for customers himself. Being twenty-six he had quite a job getting customers. I asked Rolf about Detlef. And Rolf burst into tears. Yes, Detlef was in therapy. Everything was a right fuck-up without Detlef. Rolf thought life was meaningless; he wanted to kick, too; he loved Detlef; he wanted to do away with himself. In other words, the usual fixer rigmarole. All this yapping about Detlef rather pissed me off. I didn't understand what claims this grotty queer had on Detlef. He suggested in all seriousness that Detlef ought to pack in this therapy and come back to him, Rolf. He'd even given Detlef a key to his flat. When I heard that, I blew my top: 'What a bleeding shit you are. Give Detlef the keys to make quite sure he knows where to go when he gets hung up with his therapy. If you were really fond of him, you'd do everything to see Detlef gets off H. But then you really are only a grotty old queer.'

261

Rolf was doing cold turkey so it was easy for me to shatter him. Presently I decided to be a little nicer to him because I suddenly had the idea that I might be able to stay in Rolf's flat. I told him if he'd let me doss down in his pad, I'd do a customer and score for him. Rolf was thrilled that I wanted to stay with him. He only knew two people: Detlef and me.

I shared his French bed with him. On the whole I got on very well with Rolf because Detlef wasn't there. Basically he was a poor old sod, really. Even if I thought him repulsive. So there were Detlef's two lovers, in this French bed, and every night Rolf started the same old story: how he loved Detlef. Regularly, before he went to sleep, he started to cry. It didn't half get on my wick but I kept my mouth shut because I needed my place in Rolf's bed. I didn't even say anything when he started blathering about wanting to furnish a nice flat for Detlef once they were both off H. I didn't care a shit about anything, anyway. Besides, at some stage I told myself that we had Rolf on our conscience. He would have remained a poor crane-driving queer who'd occasionally get stoned to drown his sorrows, if he hadn't met us.

This went on for a week. Customers, shot, customers, shot, and at night Rolf's yapp, yapp, yapping. Then one morning I woke up rather early, just as someone was opening the front door and banging about in the hall. I thought it was Rolf and yelled: 'Stop making that row, man, I want to sleep.' And then Detlef stood in the room.

Huge hug, great joy. Until it struck me: 'My God, they've kicked you out of the therapy.' He nodded, and then explained why.

Like anyone who has been newly admitted, Detlef had to do three weeks' early morning duty. For any fixer it is almost impossible to be punctual. Waking up at the same time every morning and then having to spring into action to rouse the others, that's about the most difficult thing to ask of a fixer. That's precisely why they ask it in the therapy so as to fill the few places available with people who still had willpower.

Detlef, any rate, couldn't make it: he'd overslept three

262

times and was sent packing.

Detlef told me that basically he'd enjoyed the therapy. It had been bloody hard, but next time he'd do it for sure. Now he wanted to stay off H as best he could and then try for another place in a therapy. He said he'd met some guys there whom we knew well from the scene. Frank, for instance, whose friend Ingo had just died, aged fourteen. Like Babsi.

I asked Detlef what he wanted to do now and he said: 'First of all, get a shot.' I asked him to bring me some stuff. Two hours later Detlef was back. He'd brought a former customer whose name was Piko. From out of his pocket Piko produced a plastic bag and put it on the table. I thought my eyes were deceiving me. A plastic bag full of stuff. Ten grammes. I'd never seen so much H in my life. After I'd finished gawping I asked Detlef: 'Have you gone daft, ten grammes here in the flat?'

He said: 'Certainly not. For your information, I've become a dealer.'

I asked: 'Have you by any chance thought of the cops? If they catch you once more, you've had it. Then you'll be out of circulation for a few years.'

Detlef said: 'I haven't the time to think about the cops now. First of all I've got to see how I'm going to make it. And stop getting at me.'

He began at once to divide up portions with his pocket knife, heaping them on small pieces of foil paper. I noticed that the pieces of foil were much too small. I said: 'Listen, old man. People want to be ripped off. You'll have to use bigger pieces of foil, put in the same amount of stuff you've got there and roll them out flat. Then it'll look bigger than it really is. People go by what they see. Think of washing powders. Giant packets but only two-thirds full.'

Detlef said: 'Stop getting at me. I'm putting an extra lot of stuff in, so's people will notice. And word will get round that there's an extra lot of stuff in my papers.' Only then did it occur to me to ask: 'Tell me, whose stuff is this?' It belonged to Piko, of course, the bloody little crook. He used to keep his head above water by breaking into offices. Now he had just come out of the nick, on probation. And intended making a quick buck with goodnatured, daft Detlef. He got the stuff from some pimps in Potsdamer Strasse. Acquaintances from the nick. Piko had bought it at dealer rates. Except that he didn't mean to deal himself, but left it to Detlef. Piko had no idea about H and the scene. He only drank.

When Detlef had finished his packing we added together the halfhalves, the halves and the grammes he had done. I was never very good at maths. But I sussed even before Detlef that all together it came to eight grammes. Instead of not quite enough he had put far too much into his papers. If he had dealt it like this he'd have to pay for two grammes out of his own money.

So, back with the whole lot into the plastic bag. Some of the powder always clung to the foil paper. I scraped it off for my own use. Then Detlef prepared larger papers and rolled the stuff flat with a beer bottle like mad so that it would look bigger. He prepared only halves, and in the end he actually had twenty-five.

We shot two papers to try it out. It was really fine stuff.

That very evening we took the papers to the Treibhaus. Most of it we stashed. We buried it in the refuse containers behind the Treibhaus. We never carried more than three papers. In case of a rumble they couldn't have pulled us in as dealers. It went quite well. On the first evening we sold five grammes. Word got round that the stuff was good and the portions decent. Only Stella ran our stuff down, naturally. But then she came crawling and wanted to find customers for us. And I let her, stupid tit that I was. For five halves she got a half herself. Which meant there wasn't anything in it for us at all, because we didn't get a pennypiece from Piko for dealing. If we sold ten grammes we were allowed to keep one and a half. But out of that we still had to pay our own agents. In other words, our dealing activities only just paid for our daily requirements of H.

Piko came every morning to cash up. As a rule we had

taken about 2000 marks. For Piko it was 1000 marks net profit, for the profit margin from middleman to dealer is 100 per cent. And Piko took almost no risk unless we were to grass on him. And, in order to prevent this from happening, Piko had taken precautions: he threatened that if we were ever arrested and told the police a single word, we might as well order our coffins. His mates from Potsdamer Strasse would take care of that. Nobody got away from them, not even in the nick. They had their boys everywhere, Piko said. He also threatened us with his pimps if we didn't settle the accounts correctly. We believed every word. As it was, I was really terrified of pimps. Ever since they tortured Babsi.

Detlef didn't want to see that his Piko was ripping us off something cruel. He said: 'What do you want? The main thing is that you don't have to go looking for customers any longer. I don't want you to start on the game again. And I don't want to see any grotty customers either. So, what do you want?'

The majority of small street dealers were in the same boat as us. They never had enough money to buy ten grammes from the middleman. Moreover, they didn't have the connection. How could we have approached the pimps of Potsdamer Strasse? As a rule the small street dealers, who were themselves addicts, needed a middleman who paid them only with stuff. The addicted small dealers were the poor sods, who at some time or other went in the nick. Guys like Piko were out of reach of the cops. And these guys had never any difficulties in finding new street dealers when the cops had picked up the previous lot. Almost every fixer was prepared to deal for two shots a day.

Already after a few days of dealing, the Treibhaus was growing too hot for us because plain clothes cops were continually hanging about there. I could hardly stand the stress any longer. So we organised it differently. I went on looking for buyers at the Treibhaus while Detlef hung around at Steglitz station. When I had a buyer I sent him to Steglitz station.

When a week later Detlef was once more at the Treibhaus

with stuff in his pocket, a car stopped suddenly and a guy asked the way to Zoo station. Detlef completely lost his nerve and ran off. He threw the stuff into some bushes.

When we met again Detlef was sure the guy who asked for Zoo station had been a cop. Everyone knew where the station was.

It was bad. We really got the copper jitters. Any car, any guy hanging about the Kudamm was a cop, we thought. We didn't even dare look for the stuff Detlef had thrown away. We thought the cops were only waiting for us to come looking for it to catch us redhanded.

We went into a snackbar to talk about it. We couldn't settle up with Piko next morning because the stuff was gone. He wouldn't have believed our story anyway. Then I had the idea that we ought to tell him we'd been ripped off by wogs. That wogs had taken away all the stuff and all the money. I said: 'There's bound to be a right ding-dong with Piko, anyway. So we might as well spend the money we've got already. I think it's a rotten trick that we never get a pennypiece while this pouffy swine makes a cool thousand out of us every day. I'll have to buy some gear, I've nothing warm to wear. I can't run around all winter in what I wore when I skipped from the hospital.'

We weren't cut out to be dealers. Detlef still refused to admit it. But in the end he did admit that it was all the same whether we handed in a mere two hundred marks or nothing at all.

Very early next morning we went to the flea market. If I liked something Detlef would try it on first, then me. We only wanted to buy things both of us could wear, so that occasionally we could swap round. At last I bought a second-hand black rabbit-skin jacket in which Detlef looked very sweet. Then we bought some perfume, a musical box and other grot. However, we didn't manage to spend all the cash because we couldn't buy some expensive junk just for the hell of it. We stashed the money.

No sooner had we got back to Rolf's flat than Piko turned up. Detlef said that he hadn't had a shot and he must have a shot before cashing up. That wasn't true, of course, for, as always, we'd had a shot immediately after getting up. Detlef was afraid of the ding-dong with Piko. Piko said: 'Okay' and read one of my thrillers. Detlef shot another half a half. He dozed off immediately and didn't even pull out the spike first.

I thought it wasn't surprising that he should nod off like that, seeing that he'd already got half a half inside him. I pulled the spike out of his arm because I thought it bloody disgusting that he left it in just like that when the blood would clot in the needle and we'd never get it out again. This was our last works, after all. As I wiped the puncture in Detlef's arm with cotton wool and alcohol, I noticed that there was no resistance whatever. I lifted his arm and it flopped down, completely limp. I shook Detlef to get him to wake up. He slid from the armchair. His face was grey, his lips blue. I tore open his shirt and tried to feel his heartbeat. But I couldn't feel any heartbeat at all.

Wearing only panties and a shirt I ran out of the flat. Piko was after me: 'Don't do anything silly.' I rang the doorbell of a neighbour who had a telephone and told her I must ring the police at once. I dialled the emergency number and said: 'My boyfriend has stopped breathing. He's taken an overdose.' I was just giving the address to the cops when Piko burst in, shouting: 'Stop, stop, he's come round.' I told the copper: 'You needn't come, after all. Thanks anyway. False alarm.' And put down the receiver.

Detlef lay on his back, his eyes were open again. Piko asked whether I'd said anything on the phone about drugs and had I given them the address. I said: 'No, not exactly. I think they didn't take it in, it all went so fast.'

Piko said: 'You're a stupid, hysterical cow.' He busied himself frantically with Detlef, slapping his face and demanding that Detlef should get up. I told him to leave Detlef alone. He screamed: 'Shut up, stupid cow, and get me some water.' When I returned from the kitchen, Detlef was already standing up and Piko was talking to him insistently. I was terribly happy that Detlef was standing up again and wanted to put my arms round him. Detlef actually pushed me away. Piko flung the water in his face and said: 'Come on, boy, we've got to split.'

Detlef's face was still quite grey and he could scarcely keep on his feet. I told him to lie down. Piko screamed: 'Shut up' to me again. And Detlef said: 'I haven't got the time.' Piko supported Detlef and they left the flat.

I no longer knew whether I was coming or going. I was shaking like a leaf. I really had thought for a moment that Detlef was dead. I lay on the bed and tried to concentrate on my thriller. Then the doorbell rang. I looked through the peephole. The cops were standing outside.

My mind went completely blank. Instead of beating it through the window I opened the door. I said I had telephoned. The flat belonged to a queer who was away. And this morning two young guys had arrived and injected something in their arm, and one of them had collapsed, and that's why I had phoned the police.

The cops wanted to know the guys' names and what they looked like and I told them some lies. They took down my particulars. It didn't take long for a reply to come through from the police station, and one of the cops said: 'Well, you'd better come along with us. You've been reported as missing.'

The cops were quite nice. They allowed me to put two thrillers in my plastic bag and to write a letter to Detlef. I wrote: *'Dear Detlef, no doubt you'll have guessed they've picked me up. Further news before long. Lots of love and kisses, Christiane.'*

I stuck it on the flat door with sticky tape.

First they took me to Friedrichstrasse Police Station and then to a collecting point. There they put me in a cell which was straight out of a Western. With real bars instead of a wall. The barred door slammed shut with the same clang as the one at the sheriff of Dodge City's, and the key creaked in the lock as it was turned to lock me in. There I was, my hands clutching two of the bars, and it wasn't half depressing. I didn't want to think how depressing it was, so I lay on

268

the bunk and fell asleep because I was rather high. At some time they brought me the receptacle for the urine sample and a bucket to put underneath in case I missed the bottle when I pee'd. Anyone happening to come past could watch me piss. All day I was given nothing to eat or drink.

Towards evening my mother arrived. Once she went past the bars without looking at me properly. I suppose she had to sort out things with the cops first. Then the door was unlocked, and my mother said: 'Good evening' as though to a stranger and took me very firmly by the arm. Outside, Klaus, my mother's boyfriend, was waiting with the car. My mother shoved me into the back of the car and sat down beside me. No one spoke. Klaus lost his way, and we were careering all over Berlin. I thought: 'Now they're even too daft to find the way to Kreuzberg.'

When we stopped at a petrol station, I told my mother I was hungry and asked if she could buy me three Bounties. She got out and bought me three Bounties.

After the second Bounty I felt sick. Klaus had to stop so that I could throw up. We got on to the Autobahn, and then I knew that we were going somewhere else. I thought it might be a home, and that I would clear out from there soon. Then I saw the sign 'Tegel Airport' and thought: 'Well, this really is the fucking end. They want to get you out of Berlin.' We got out at the airport. My mother got a firm hold of me at once. And then I spoke for the second time since we had met again: 'Would you please let go of me now.' I said it very slowly and emphasised every word. She did leave go of me, but kept very close to my side. Klaus brought up the rear, watching me all the time. I was rather limp. Let them do whatever they want. There was nothing that could be done about me anyway. That was how I felt. When my mother took me to a terminal, above which it said Hamburg, I did look round to see whether there might be a chance of getting away. But what the hell, I was too apathetic to get away.

Hamburg: that was a real blow. In a village, about fifty kilometres from Hamburg lived one of my grannies, an aunt

269

and uncle and a cousin of mine. The ultimate creepy squares in my eyes. A house so tidy, it was real hell. Not a grain of dust. Once I went barefoot all day long in that house and at night my feet were still so clean I didn't need to wash them.

In the plane I pretended to be reading my thriller. I actually managed a couple of pages. My mother was still not speaking. She hadn't even told me where we were going.

As the stewardess reeled off her little speech about how she hoped we'd had a pleasant flight, I realised that my mother was crying. Then she began to talk terribly fast: She still wanted only what was best for me, she said. And the other day she'd dreamt that I was lying dead in a loo, my legs all twisted and blood everywhere. A dealer had killed me and she, she said, had been asked to identify me.

I always thought my mother had parapsychological powers. There had been evenings when she said: 'Stay at home, child, I've got an uncomfortable feeling.' And then I would promptly either get into a rumble or be ripped off, or there would be some other disaster. Now I had to think of Piko, of the fact that we had ripped him off, and of his pimp friends. I thought perhaps my mother had actually saved my life. I didn't think any further. I didn't want to think any further. Ever since my failed o.d. I didn't want to think at all.

At Hamburg airport, my mother, my aunt who'd come to meet us, and I went to the restaurant. My mother was flying back almost at once. I ordered a Florida Boy. They didn't stock it in this bleeding posh establishment. I thought what a dump this Hamburg is, where they don't even stock Florida Boy. I didn't have anything to drink, although I was absolutely parched.

Then my mother and my aunt got at me together. In half an hour flat they planned my entire future life. I would go to school like a good girl, make new friends and later train for something and, when I'd learnt a trade, return to Berlin. It was all dead simple — for them. My mother was crying again when we said good-bye. I fought back all emotion. That was on 13th November, 1977.

CHRISTIANE'S MOTHER

All day I had had to make a tremendous effort to control myself. On the return flight to Berlin I cried the tension of the last few weeks out of my system. I was sad and relieved at the same time. Sad, because I had to give Christiane away; relieved because I had finally snatched her away from heroin.

At last I was certain I had done the right thing. It was after the failure of the Narkonon therapy that I realised: in the long run Christiane will have a chance of survival only if she is taken to a place where there is no heroin. While Christiane was living with her father I had time to gain a little distance and calm, and I felt increasingly that remaining in Berlin would be the end for her. Although my former husband assured me that while she was staying with him Christiane had stopped taking heroin, I didn't set much store by that. I wouldn't have thought that my fear for Christiane's life could have grown worse. But after the death of her friend Babsi, I no longer had a quiet minute.

I wanted to take Christiane immediately to her relatives in Western Germany, but her father wouldn't allow it. Because Christiane was living with him he had obtained an interim injunction giving him Aufenthaltsbestimmungs-recht*. My pleadings were of no avail. He was adamant. Possibly because he hadn't yet had my experience. Possibly because he couldn't admit defeat.

During this period I received the indictment against Christiane. She was to be put on trial on account of offences against the drugs law. Frau Schipke of the Narcotics Department rang me up to warn me beforehand. By way of comforting me she told me I was not by any means to blame myself on account of Christiane. 'Anyone who wants to fix will fix,' she said, 'that's something every fixer decides for himself.' She said she knew many fixers who came from respectable homes. They would be put on trial too. I needn't torture myself.

---

* *Aufenthaltsbestimmungsrecht*: literally, the right to determine where a person should reside. Equivalent to legal guardianship.

I considered it insidious that, as part of the evidence against Christiane in the indictment, there was mention of a small packet of heroin which on one occasion I had found in her room. In my agitation I rang up Frau Schipke at the time. I had no idea that my find would one day be used against Christiane, when Frau Schipke asked me hypocritically to send her this small packet for inspection. She said: 'Don't put your address on the letter, then they won't be able to prove anything.'

I do not think it right that young people like Christiane are sentenced because of their addiction to drugs. Christiane has not harmed anyone. She has destroyed no one but herself. Who is to sit in judgement on that? To say nothing of the fact that so far no fixer has yet been cured in prison, as everyone knows.

The indictment was one more reason for me to take Christiane to Western Germany. Suddenly I was determined. I went to the office dealing with guardianship and explained the situation to them in great detail. For the first time I was actually listened to attentively in a government department. Herr Tillmann, the social worker responsible, shared my opinion that Christiane would be best looked after in Western Germany. He said he would try to secure a place in a therapy institution because it was difficult to say how quickly he would be able to restore Aufenthaltsbestimmungsrecht for Christiane to me. On the other hand, it would be difficult for him to gain consent from my ex-husband for Christiane to go into therapy. This seemed reasonable to me. These were no empty promises. I felt determinedly Herr Tillmann worked on Christiane's behalf.

Suddenly, one afternoon, shortly after my interview with Herr Tillmann, Christiane appeared on my doorstep. She had just come from the drugs advice centre. She was completely shattered, full of heroin and talking about suicide and o.d.'ing. I calmed her down and put her to bed. Then I immediately rang up Herr Tillmann. He came at once. Together with Christiane, we made a practical plan. Christiane was to withdraw physically in the psychiatric hospital.

Subsequently, she would be given a place in a therapeutic commune. This she had been promised by the drugs advice centre. In addition, Herr Tillmann was himself in touch with the therapy place concerning Christiane.

Christiane readily allowed everything to be done for her. Herr Tillmann made the necessary arrangements with commendable speed. We were given an appointment with the child psychiatrist and also with the public health officer who ordered Christiane's admission. After that Herr Tillmann went to see Christiane's father and leant on him heavily until he consented, and then I could take Christiane to the hospital.

Two weeks later Christiane was transferred to Rudolf Virchow hospital, where she was to have an operation for a fungus infection. I took it for granted that a child who is a heroin addict would be taken from Bonnie's Ranch under supervision to Virchow Hospital where she would continue to be looked after and closely watched. Instead they just dumped Christiane there. What happened afterwards was a matter of indifference to them. Nobody stopped Christiane from absconding.

I was very bitter about this unforgivable carelessness which now threatened to ruin all our plans.

After this experience I lost what little faith I still had in institutions. Only you alone can help your child and yourself. Herr Tillmann tried to give me new courage. He was the only one in whom I had confidence.

Fortunately, Christiane did not stay away long. On the following evening she cried her eyes out in my flat. She was so very sorry about everything. But she had shot heroin again. I did not scold her. I no longer felt aggressive towards her. How often, in the early days, I had vented all my rage on Christiane out of sheer despair about my own inability to help her. Now that she had come back to me I put my arm round her and we talked calmly to one another.

Christiane was determined to pursue the plan we had drawn up with Herr Tillmann. And I said, very well, that's what we'll do. But I also made it perfectly clear to her that

273

she would be taken to Western Germany once and for all, if she made a mess of things one more time. She took this very much to heart and gave me her word of honour on it.

During these days she went regularly to the drugs advice centre. She really hung all her hopes on this chance of a therapy. Sometimes she waited for hours for her turn at the drugs advice centre. At home she sat down and wrote out her curriculum vitae for the admissions procedure.

Everything looked very hopeful. Her place in the therapy seemed as good as certain. The commune in which she was to live was already fixed. We were talking about how it might not be possible for her to spend Christmas at home, since it was already early November.

Meanwhile her father had come to realise the failure of his attempts and had stopped being obstructive. We really thought we were out of the woods. But just at that point Christiane went down with her second bout of jaundice. Suddenly her temperature rose to 41 degrees [105.8°F]. Next morning I took her to Steglitz Medical Centre. Christiane was as yellow as a lemon. She could no longer stand up and crawled along the corridor. After examining her, the lady doctor said Christiane had congestion of the liver as the result of her drug abuse. Unfortunately they could not keep her there because Steglitz Medical Centre had no isolation ward. That was not true. I made enquiries afterwards. Steglitz Medical Centre does have an isolation ward with 25 beds. The truth was that they did not want to have a fixer in their smart medical centre. At least the doctor arranged a firm date for admission at Rudolf Virchow hospital next morning.

Within a few days Christiane's yellow colour began to disappear. Before long she was again quite chirpy and looking forward to her therapy. Her counsellor from the TU's drugs advice centre even came to visit her. We all joined forces to get her to stick to her guns. I was more confident than I had been for a long time. Until the day when Christiane's friend, Stella, visited her. Although I'd asked the sister most emphatically not to allow anyone, except the drugs counsellor, to see Christiane unless I was present.

Admittedly, on one occasion I had made the unforgivable mistake of bringing Detlef. Christiane had so wanted it. Detlef had been released on parole from the prison where he had undergone withdrawal. He had managed to secure a place in a therapy. I did not begrudge the two of them their reunion. They were fond of each other. And I thought perhaps it might encourage them mutually to know they were both going into therapy. Just how naive can you get?

Very soon Christiane ran away for an afternoon. When I visited her that evening after work she had just come back. I could see that she had injected herself. That alone wouldn't have knocked me sideways, not any more. But when she tried to tell me all she'd intended to do was to have a meal of spaghetti at a restaurant by the Gedächtniskirche, when she lied to me yet again, I thought I'd die.

I asked the ward sister whether I might stay with Christiane. I would pay for the bed. She said that, unfortunately that was not possible. She would keep an eye on Christiane herself. Three days later, when once again I wanted to visit her after work, the sister came to meet me saying: 'Your daughter is not here.'

'Well, might I ask where she is?' I said.

'We don't know. She was given permission to walk in the park and failed to return.'

I cannot describe how I felt. At home I lay down in the living room by the telephone. That night the hospital telephoned at twenty past eleven to say that Christiane was back. The indifference of the nurse was shattering. Their attitude is: 'If she clears out, she clears out. It's her affair. We've had enough drug addicts here. They all clear out.' That was exactly what I was told next day when I reproached the nurses.

Similarly, the lady doctor seemed rather unmoved by it all. She merely explained to me that she had no influence in the matter. If Christiane contravened hospital regulations once more she would have to leave the hospital due to lack of discipline. She informed me that liver tests had shown that if she continued her present way of life Christiane would, at most, live to the age of twenty. She would have a heart to heart talk with her. There was nothing else she had to say.

Next evening there was another telephone call from the hospital. Christiane had disappeared again. I spent all night on the sofa next to the telephone. And Christiane never came back at all. She disappeared for two weeks without a sign of life to anyone.

During the first two or three days my boyfriend and I went out looking for her. The usual round of the discotheques and tube stations. Then I had to collect her things from the hospital. And when I returned home with her bag and unpacked her books and all the bits and pieces I'd brought her in the hospital, I had, for the first time, reached the point where I told myself: Now you'll let her fall flat on her face.

I told myself: Very well, if that's how she wants it, let her get on with it. I stopped looking for her. I was unspeakably hurt. I wanted her to feel that my patience was exhausted. I wouldn't like to say how long I should have been able to keep this up.

I reported her as missing at the nearest police station and left a photograph of Christiane with the officers. I felt sure that they would catch her at some raid or other. And then I intended to get on the next plane with her and take her to Western Germany.

A fortnight later, on a Monday morning, I received the telephone call from Friedrichstrasse police station. The officer on the phone was exceptionally nice. Although Christiane was raging about at the station. I asked the officer to hold Christiane there. I would collect her in the early afternoon and take her straightaway by plane to Western Germany.

I ordered the tickets. A return flight for myself. A single ticket for Christiane. As I said this, I felt a pang. Then I rang up my relatives.

By the afternoon everything was settled. On the way to the police I called for my boyfriend. I thought if we had her

276

sitting between us she would not be able to jump out of the car.

Christiane did not say a word. Neither did I. I just couldn't. At the airport my knees were shaking, my heart was beating wildly. Christiane was still not talking. She ignored me completely. While we were waiting for our plane to depart she sat silently in her chair, chewing her nails and reading a novel she had brought. At no time did she try to run away.

I heaved a sigh of relief when we had boarded the plane. During take-off she looked out of the window. By now it was dark. I said to her: 'All right, this is the end. The drug business is over and done with. You're going to your aunt Evelyn's. I hope that you'll finally start a new life there.'

To begin with, at my auntie and granny's, I did four days' cold turkey. As soon as I was able to get up again, I got myself all tarted up. From my rabbit-skin jacket to my boots with the highest heels, I was a fixer chick. I put on my make-up and took my aunt's dog for a walk in the woods. Every morning I made up as if I was going to the scene, only to go walking in the woods instead. I got stuck in the sand with my high heels. Every few metres I stumbled and fell, giving myself some nasty bruises on my knees. But when my granny suggested taking me shopping to buy me a pair of 'walking shoes', the mere words walking shoes gave me the creeps.

After a while I discovered that I could actually talk to my aunt who was only just thirty. Not about the problems I really had, because I didn't want to talk about them, I didn't want to think about them at all. My real problem was H. Stuff and everything connected with it. Detlef, the scene, Kudamm, being high, not having to think, being free. I tried not to think too much, even without H. All I ever thought, to be truthful, was that I would beat it quite soon. But, in contrast to the old days, I never made a proper plan towards beating it. I kept putting it off. I thought: one day you'll beat it. Probably I didn't really want to beat it because I was afraid of what, during the last two years, I had come to regard as freedom.

My aunt totally hemmed me in with don'ts. If I was allowed out at all, I had to be back at half past nine sharp, and me all of fifteen. I hadn't known anything like it since I was twelve. These don'ts got on my wick something cruel. But, funnily enough, I almost always observed them.

Before Christmas we went to Hamburg to do our Christmas shopping. It started in the morning. Off to the department stores. It was total horror. Forcing your way through these wretched crowds of creeps who were grabbing things and fumbling with their bulging wallets. My granny, my aunt, my uncle and my cousin tried on grotty clothes and took them off again. For Auntie Hedwig and Auntie Ida and for Jochen and for Mr and Mrs Thingummy, they couldn't find anything anyway. And then my uncle needed a pair of stick-on soles for his shoes and something for the car which is cheaper in department stores.

My granny is so tiny and she whizzes around in department stores so fast that she constantly got lost in the crowds. Then we had to go in search of her. At times I'd lost the lot of them and then, naturally, I thought about beating it. I had sussed at once that in Hamburg there was a scene in Mönckebergstrasse. All I needed to do was to run out of the store and talk to a few fixers and everything would have run smoothly from there. But somehow I couldn't do it. Because I didn't really quite know what I wanted. Although I told myself: rather than becoming like them and thinking only about shops and shopping, it'd be better to peg out in some toilet. I think if a fixer had come along and talked to me then, I'd have been a goner.

But in my heart of hearts I didn't really want to go. And that's why I told my family a few times: 'I just can't stand any more. Please can we go home now, and then you go shopping another time without me.' They looked at me as if I had gone round the bend. I daresay for them Christmas shopping is the highlight of their year.

In the evening they couldn't find the car again. We ran

around from one parking place to the other without finding
it. Somehow I thought this quite a good situation. Because,
suddenly, we were a family community. We were all talking
at once, everybody offering their own good advice, and at
last we all had a joint goal: we wanted to find the bleeding
car. I differed from the others only in that I thought it all a
hoot and had to keep laughing while they were getting more
and more into a panic. Meanwhile, it had got rather cold
and everyone's teeth were chattering. I was the only one not
affected by the cold because my body was used to much
worse things.

In the end my aunt was standing under the hot-air blower
in the entrance of a big store and declared she didn't intend
walking another step. My uncle had to use force to get her
out from under the hot air. And then at long last we did find
the car again after all, and everybody was laughing. On the
way home I felt really good. I felt like being in a family to
whom I belonged somehow.

I adapted myself a little. At least I tried. It was difficult.
With every sentence I spoke I had to watch terribly carefully
what I said. With every word. If the word 'shit' slipped out,
my granny would say: 'Such a pretty child and such an ugly
word.' And then there might possibly ensue a long discussion because I felt pissed off and was sulking. And in the end
I would lose my temper.

Christmas came. The first Christmas for two years that I
celebrated under a Christmas tree. I didn't know whether to
look forward to it. But I resolved to pull myself together and
show some pleasure over my presents. And then I really
was pleased about my presents. I'd never had so many
Christmas presents before. However, at some stage I
caught myself calculating how much it must all have cost
and converting it into half halves.

My father came to stay over Christmas. As usual, he
didn't stay at home long. On both evenings of the holiday
he took me to a teeny bopper discotheque. Each time I
knocked back six or seven rum and cokes, after which I fell
asleep on my bar stool. My father was delighted that now I

drank alcohol. And I kept telling myself: at some stage you'l
get used to the village teenagers and to the disco sound.

Next day my father flew back to Berlin because of an ice
hockey game that evening. In the meantime he had become
an ice hockey fan.

After the Christmas holidays I had to go to school. I was in
the fourth form at a grammar school. At first I was scared of
school. After all, for practically three years I hadn't taken
part in lessons. During the last year I had only been at school
a few months because for the rest of the time I was ill, or
withdrawing again, or playing truant. But from the first day
liked being at this school. The class was busy painting a
picture on an empty white wall in the classroom. I was
immediately invited to join in. We painted beautiful old
houses. Exactly the sort of houses in which one day my
dream flat would be. In front of the houses all the people
were cheerful. In the street was a palm tree with a camel tied
to it. This picture was really it. We entitled it: 'Under the
asphalt is the beach.'

I realised quickly that the young people in the country
and in the little town not far from our village, were not very
satisfied either. Even though outwardly many things were
different from the way they had been in Berlin. There wasn't
nearly so much rowdiness in school. Most teachers stil
managed to assert themselves. Most young people stil
dressed very conservatively.

I wanted to make it at school, although there were great
gaps in my education. I absolutely wanted to do it, at least
my school certificate. For the first time since my early
schooldays, I actually did homework. After three weeks I
had settled down quite well in my form and felt that I really
could get a grip on it.

We were doing cookery when I was called to the headmaster. He sat behind his desk, nervously fumbling with
some folder. I twigged quite quickly that this folder was my
file which presumably they had just sent him from Berlin.
And I knew that this file contained everything about me. At
some time the youth welfare office had sent a full report

280

to my school in Berlin.

At first the headmaster hummed and hawed a bit and then he said that, much to his regret, he was unable to keep me at his school. I was, he said, unable to cope with the demands of a grammar school. He must have got so worked up over my file that he had to have me fetched straight out of a lesson. He couldn't even wait until school was out before kicking me out of his grammar school.

I said nothing because I couldn't speak. The headmaster wanted me to go at once. During the next break I was to report to the headmaster of the secondary modern school. I was totally shattered. I went across to the secondary modern in a daze. And when I sat facing the headmaster I burst into tears. He said things weren't all that bad, really. I was to pull my socks up and finish the secondary modern with a good final report.

When I had got outside I did a long, overdue review of my situation. I wasn't really sorry for myself. I told myself: 'It was only to be expected that now you're being handed the bills for what you did.' All at once I sussed that all my dreams about an entirely new life without H were rubbish. That others didn't see me the way I believed I was at this moment, but that they judged me by my past. My mother, my aunt, and now the headmaster.

I also realised that I wouldn't be able to become a different person from one day to the next. My body and my psyche kept handing me more bills all the time. My ruined liver reminded me constantly of what I had done to it. And it wasn't as if I managed to cope with life at my aunt's just like that. At the least disagreement I'd go berserk. There were constant rows. I couldn't stand stress or strain. And if I had once again got into a real low it would occur to me that drugs would have got me out of it quite easily.

After I got booted out of grammar school, I no longer had any confidence in myself. Once again I was rather apathetic. I could not fight against having been booted out, although after only three weeks this headmaster couldn't possibly know whether or not I might have made it. I no longer had any plans for the future. I could have gone into a comprehensive. There was one I could have got to by bus. At the comprehensive I could have proved that I had brains. But I was far too afraid of being a failure there, too.

What my being relegated to the secondary modern meant was something that only struck me gradually. We have two discos here, sort of youth clubs. One was the meeting place of mostly people from the grammar school, the other of secondary modern pupils and apprentices. At first I went to the club with the grammar school lot. But once I'd been thrown out of the grammar school I felt they were giving me funny looks. So I went to the other disco.

It was quite a new experience for me. This separation didn't exist in Berlin. Not at the comprehensive and certainly not on the scene. In my new school the separation started in the playground. Right across the playground went a white line. One side was reserved for grammar school pupils, the other for pupils from the secondary modern. You weren't allowed to step across the white line. Consequently, I could only talk to my former classmates across the line. I really thought that was absolutely the worst aspect of this division into young people who might achieve something in life and young people who, being at a secondary modern school, were the dregs anyway.

So this was the society to which I was to adapt myself. 'Adapt' was my granny's every other word. At the same time she thought that outside school hours I ought not to waste time with pupils from the secondary modern, but choose my friends from among grammar school pupils. I told her: 'You'll just have to resign yourself to your granddaughter being at a secondary modern school. And I'll adapt myself and choose my friends from the secondary modern school.' And then we had a huge row.

At first I decided to do damn all at this school. But then I realised that our form master was a bit of all right. He was an older guy. Totally old-fashioned in his views, that is to say really conservative. Sometimes I actually had the impression that he could find something good even in the Nazis.

But he had authority without shouting all over the place. He was the only one for whom we would voluntarily get up when he entered the classroom. He was never under pressure and really took an interest in each individual pupil. Including me. Many of the younger teachers certainly had quite a lot of idealism. But somehow they couldn't cope with their job. They knew as little about life as their pupils. Sometimes they let everything go and then, when chaos resulted, they shouted their heads off. Above all, they had no clear answers to the problems with which we were preoccupied. They kept trotting out their ifs and buts because they were totally disconcerted, and just didn't know themselves what it was all about.

Our form master didn't mince his words when he told us what we could expect as secondary modern pupils. He told us that we would have a tough time. But if we applied ourselves, there were some subjects in which we might do better even than grammar school pupils. Spelling for instance. Today no one taking his university entrance exams could spell perfectly any more. Therefore we stood a better chance if we could write our applications in perfect German. He tried to teach us how to deal with people who think they're superior. And he always had some apt saying up his sleeve. Mostly wordly wisdoms from the last century. You could laugh at them. And most of my classmates did. But I often thought that there was always a grain of truth in them. I often held a different view from his. But what I liked about him was that he still knew what it was all about.

Most people in the class didn't particularly like the form master. Probably they found him too strenuous, his everlasting moral standards got on their nerves. Most of them were totally uninterested anyway. A couple saw to it that they got a good final report, hoping that, although they were secondary modern pupils, they might manage to get hold of an apprenticeship. They did their homework conscientiously, exactly what they'd been told to do. But reading a book or taking an interest in something not set as homework just wasn't on as far as they were concerned.

Whenever our form master or any of the younger teachers tried to start a discussion, they all just sat there looking stupid. None of my classmates had any plans for the future any more than me. What plans can a secondary modern pupil make? If he's lucky, he'll get hold of an apprenticeship. It isn't a question of what he would actually like to do, but of what is being offered.

Many didn't really care what they did after they left school. Perhaps an apprenticeship earning money as an unskilled labourer, or drawing unemployment benefit. The general opinion was: here in Germany no one starves, as secondary modern pupils we haven't a chance anyway, so why make an effort? Some guys already had the makings of criminals, a few were on the bottle. The girls never gave much thought to the future anyway. They had made up their minds that one day a guy would look after them, and until then they could work as salesgirls or do a job on a production line or hang around at home.

Not all were like this, but it was the basic mood at the secondary modern school. Totally sober, no illusions, and certainly no ideals. It didn't half get me down. I had imagined my life without drugs quite differently.

I often thought about why the young people were so pissed off. They weren't satisfied with anything any more. A moped at sixteen, a car at eighteen: somehow that was a matter of course. And if you had to do without, you were inferior. In my own dreams, hadn't it always been a matter of course that first of all I would have a flat and a car? Working your fingers to the bone for a flat or a new settee, like my mother, simply wasn't on. Those were the boring ideals of our parents: to live in order to acquire things. For me, and I believe for many others too, these few material things were the minimum expectation of life. But then there must be something else, too. That thing, precisely, which makes life meaningful. And that was nowhere in sight. But a few, including myself, were still seeking for what is meaningful in life.

Whenever we spoke about National Socialism at school,

284

my feelings were mixed. On the one hand my stomach turned over when I remembered the fearful brutality of which human beings are capable. On the other hand, I approved the fact that in former days there was something in which people believed. Once I expressed this in class: 'Somehow I should have liked to have been a youngster during the Nazi period. At least young people then still knew what it was all about, they still had ideals. I believe for a young person it is better to have false ideals than none at all.' I didn't mean it all that seriously. But there is somethng in it.

Even in the country the young people were into all sorts of trips because life, as offered to them by their elders, didn't satisfy them. Even the brutality trip had got to our small village. Dealing out blows rather than getting them. Just as in Berlin two years earlier, a couple of boys and girls were really turned on by the punk movement. It has always appalled me that people who otherwise were quite okay should regard punk as the fantastic trip. It's basically nothing but sheer brutality. Even the music is simply without any imagination and just dead brutal rhythm.

I knew one of our punk rockers quite well. You could really talk to him as long as he didn't stick a safety pin through his cheek or the knuckleduster in his pocket. Later he got done over in our village inn. They smashed two chairs over his head and rammed a broken bottle into his belly. They just managed to pull him through at the hospital. But what I felt most strongly was the brutality in the relationships between boys and girls. Everybody was talking about emancipation. But I'm inclined to believe that never before have boys treated girls as brutally as today. Somehow the whole frustration of the guys comes out here. They want to have power and success and they can't get it elsewhere, so they get it from women.

I developed a real horror of most guys in these discos. Perhaps because I looked a little different from the other girls, I was continually being chatted up by these guys. The wolf whistles and this 'well, old girl, how about the two of us,' pissed me off more than the carryings-on of my kerb-crawling customers in Kurfürstenstrasse. In Berlin, at least, customers smiled when they beckoned you to come to their car. These tasty guys thought they didn't need to smile. I believe the majority of customers were friendlier and even more affectionate than these young superfuckers in the discos with their chicks. And these guys wanted to fuck without a kind word, without the least affection and, of course, without paying for it.

My horror of boys went so far that no one was allowed to touch me at all. I found all these necking rules they had really perverted. That a boy should automatically presume he had the right to start necking not later than the second time he'd taken a girl out. And the girls let them, even if they didn't in the least fancy necking with the guy. Simply because that was the rule. And because they were afraid the guy wouldn't go with them any more, and then the boys would put the word out that she was a frigid old bag.

I couldn't do it. I didn't want to do it. Even if I liked a boy very much and went with him, I always made it perfectly clear from the start: 'Don't ever try to lay me. Don't touch me. If there's something doing I'll tell you.' In the six months since I left Berlin I've never told anyone. As yet any friendship finished as soon as the boy tried to lay me.

Of course, in this connection there's still one more bill I have to pay on account of my past. Even if I imagined that going on the game never really had anything to do with me, that it was only an unavoidable accompaniment of heroin addiction, it now contributed towards determining my attitude to boys. The way guys frequently behaved only reinforced my impression that once again men wanted to exploit me.

I tried to tell the girls in my form something of my experiences with men. Without being able to tell them exactly what experiences with guys I'd had. But I never got through with my message. Although in my form I became some kind of agony column auntie and was made to listen to all their problems with boys and dish out advice, because they sussed that somehow I had more experience. However,

286

they never really took in what I was trying to say to them.

Most girls live only for these guys. They fully accepted the whole brutality of their relationship. If, for instance, a guy ditched his chick and went with another girl, they were never pissed off with the guy, but with his new girl friend. She was an old bag, a fucking whore and heaven knows what else. And the most brutal guys were the ones they thought the greatest.

I only comprehended this fully when our form went on a trip to the Palatinate. Very close to where we were staying was a discotheque. Most girls felt they had to go there on the first evening. When they came back they raved about tasty guys with the latest motorbikes. For them guys with the latest motorbikes were the greatest.

So I went to have a look at this disco and sussed rather quickly what went on there. Guys from the neighbourhood came there on their mopeds, motorbikes and in their cars to lay schoolgirls who were on an outing with their forms. So I tried to explain to the girls in my form that in this disco they would only be exploited by guys. But I didn't get over to them with my wisdom. An hour before the disco opened, these women were standing in front of the mirror, messing about with their make-up and pulling their hair into place. Afterwards they didn't move in order not to spoil their hairdo.

And in front of the mirror they took off their whole self. Now they were only a mask of themselves, which was meant to please the guys with the fancy motorbikes. I was really pissed off when I saw this. In a way it reminded me of myself. I, too, had made-up to hide my real face and dressed up to disguise myself, first to please the guys of the hash scene and then the ones of the H scene. I, too, had somehow given up my self in order to be just a fixer chick.

The whole form trip was about nothing but these grotty guys, although at home most girls had a steady boyfriend. On the first evening, Elke with whom I shared a room, wrote a letter to her boyfriend. On the second evening she went to the disco and came back all depressed. She told me she'd been snogging with a guy. I think she only did it because she wanted to prove to the other girls that one of these guys was interested in her. She had a terribly bad conscience on account of her steady boyfriend and even started to cry. But she imagined she'd fallen in love with the motorbike guy. Of course her steady boyfriend didn't have a motorbike yet. Next evening she came back totally shattered and blubbing. Her guy had asked another girl in our class: 'Here, does this chick screw, or what gives with her?'

There was another girl, Rosi, she had a much worse experience. A teacher caught her with a guy in his car as the two were busy screwing. Rosi was so pissed, she could hardly walk. The guy had bought her one rum-and-coke after the other.

Rosi had been a virgin and now she was totally wrecked. The other girls called a meeting in order to discuss what was to be done with Rosi. Not that they were in any way outraged about the guy who had made Rosi drunk and then more or less raped her. They actually demanded that Rosi ought to be sent home. I was the only girl who spoke against it. They were terribly pissed off, those girls, because the disco was declared out of bounds. All they were concerned about was their own snogging and screwing.

Somehow it shattered me that there was no feeling of solidarity among the girls. That, at any rate, friendship ended when it was a question of guys. In a way it wasn't different from H which, again and again, spoiled the friendship between Babsi, Stella and me.

Although I wasn't really directly involved, this made me feel hopeless and depressed. During the last two days of this form visit I had a bad relapse. I was drunk from morning to night.

Still, in the meantime, I was determined to come to terms with the world as it was. I no longer thought about clearing out. It was plain to me that clearing out was once again a flight into drugs. And, again and again, I pointed out to myself that this hadn't done me any good whatsoever. I thought there must be some sort of compromise. Not to adapt myself totally to this lousy society and yet to come to terms with it. I was lucky to find a boyfriend who calmed me down a lot. I was able to talk to him. And yet he always seemed to know what mattered. He could dream, but he also had a practical solution for everything. He, too, found many things pretty lousy. But he thought if only you could achieve something, you might one day buy yourself free, as it were, from this society. He planned to become a business-man first and make plenty of money, and afterwards buy a log cabin in the Canadian forests and live there. For him Canada was the great dream, like for Detlef.

He was a grammar school boy and really got me into learning. I realised that even a secondary modern could still give me something as long as I worked for myself, and not just in order to pass this ludicrous useless secondary modern final exam. I read and read. Rather indiscriminately. Goethe's *Werther*, and the *Werther* by GDR writer Plenzdorf, Hermann Hesse and, above all, Erich Fromm. Erich Fromm's *The Art of Loving* came to be my Bible. I learnt whole pages by heart. Simply by finding myself compelled to read them over and over again. I also copied out passages from the book and put them up over my bed. This clever guy really knows what it's all about. If you were to keep to what he writes, life would be meaningful because you simply control it. Trouble is, it's so hard to live by these rules because the others don't know them. I'd like to talk to Erich Fromm about how he manages to live in this world according to his principles. At any rate, I realised that the way reality is, what he says is not necessarily always helpful in confronting it.

Be that as it may, this book ought to be the most impor-tant prescribed reading in school. So I thought. But in our class I didn't even dare talk about it because probably the others would have got at me again. Sometimes I took the book to school with me. Once I was reading it during class because I thought I might find the answer to a question which had come up during the lesson. Seeing this, the teacher looked at the title and immediately took the book away from me. After the lesson, when I asked if I could have it back, he said: 'So, the young lady reads pornography in class. The book is confiscated for the time being.' That's what he said, really. The name Fromm meant nothing to him, or else it reminded him of Fromm's*. And the title *The Art of Loving* naturally signalled pornography to him. After all, what else can love mean for these frustrated guys? He simply thought this old drug addict of a tart wants to corrupt the children in this class with pornography.

Next day he brought the book back and said the book was all right. Nevertheless, would I not bring it to school again because the title was so misleading.

There were things which got me down, worse than this basically trivial story about the Fromm book. I got into trouble with our headmaster. He was another totally frustrated and insecure guy. He didn't have a shred of authority, although he was the headmaster. He tried to compensate for it by drilling and yelling. In the mornings when he taught us, we had to start with a song and afterwards do exercises. To wake us up, as he said. He only gave good marks to those who spouted back what he had churned out to us in the first place.

He took us for music, too. One day he wanted to do us a favour by talking about the type of music in which we were so very interested. All the time he kept talking about 'the jazz music today.' I really didn't know what he meant. I thought perhaps he means pop music, and so I said: 'What do you mean by jazz music of today? Pop and rock are something totally music of today.' I really didn't know what he meant. I thought tone. Certainly I was putting in my oar without first considering what I was driving at with my talking. At any rate, this head-master immediately blew his top. He yelled like a lunatic and sent me out of the class.

In the door I tried to straighten things out and said: 'I think we must have misunderstood one another.' He called me back. But I couldn't have gone back for the life of me and

*The German brand name of a sheath.

spent the hour outside. At least I controlled myself sufficiently not to go straight home.

During the next lesson I had to go to the headmaster's office. As soon as I went in I saw the folder in his hand. As I stood before him, it was clear to me that this was once again my file from Berlin. He was leafing through the folder and pretending to be reading it. Then he said I wasn't in Berlin now. Besides, I was only a guest at his school. Under the circumstances he could expel me any time. So he would advise me to behave like a guest.

Afterwards, I didn't half do my nut. I didn't want to go back to school at all. As things stood, I was inclined to cave in mentally when coming face to face with much less important incidents. I could not bring myself to confront this. I could not bring myself to believe that this idiot cannot influence you in the least. If all he can find to fight you with is this file, then he is really even weaker than you.

At any rate, after this incident I kept my big mouth shut. Before it, influenced by my boyfriend, I had resolved to try for a good secondary modern final exam and then for a place at a comprehensive. Although I knew that it was terribly complicated for a secondary modern pupil to continue at school. However, after the incident with the headmaster, school, as far as I was concerned, had had it. I was certain I couldn't do it. Those psychological aptitude tests, that special permission from the school inspector, and whatever else you needed if you didn't want to remain a secondary modern pupil. And I knew that my Berlin file would already have preceded me wherever I went.

I had my very sensible boyfriend, and gradually I also made contact with the young people in the village whom, in their way, I liked very much. They were very different from me. But in any case they were generally more likeable than the kids from the small town. There was a real community spirit among the village youngsters. They even had their own little club. There were no stud-type guys among them. Somehow, everything was very proper in an old-fashioned way, even if, at times, the boys had too much to drink. And most of them accepted me, although I was so different.

For a time I thought I might become like them or like my boyfriend. But it didn't last long. I broke up with my boyfriend when he wanted to go to bed with me. I simply couldn't imagine sleeping with anyone except Detlef. That meant I still loved Detlef. I thought of him a great deal, although I did not want to think of him. Sometimes I wrote him letters which I intended sending to his former customer, Rolf, with whom he had last lived. But I had enough sense not to post the letters.

Then I heard that he was in the nick again. Stella, too, was in the nick.

I thought a great deal about Detlef and Stella, and in the neighbourhood there were youngsters to whom I felt more strongly drawn than to the young people of my own age from the village. I found it easier to talk to these youngsters, to natter to them more freely about my problems. They accepted me, and I didn't have to be afraid that they might find out about my past. They saw the world as I did. I didn't have to pretend or adapt myself. With them I was on the same wavelength emotionally. And yet, to begin with, I struggled against establishing too close a contact with them. They were all experimenting with drugs.

My mother, my aunt and I, we all thought that now I lived in a corner of Germany where there were no drugs. At any rate, definitely no hard drugs. Whenever the papers reported anything about drugs, they always referred only to Berlin, or sometimes to Frankfurt. I, too, thought: here you are, the only fixer for miles around.

But I knew better after one of my first shopping expeditions with my aunt. Early in 1978 we went shopping to Norderstedt, a sort of dormitory town near Hamburg. As always during these car journeys in my new surroundings, I observed guys who looked somewhat freaked out. I considered: do they shoot, do they smoke or are they just students? In Norderstedt we went into a snackbar for a quick bite. At a table sat a few wogs. Suddenly two of them got up and sat at another table. I don't know why, but immediately

292

I had a feeling that there was something going on with H. Somehow I knew how wogs behave when it's to do with H. I urged my aunt to leave the place without telling her anything about my suspicions.

A hundred metres further on, outside a jeans shop, we ran into the H scene of Norderstedt. Of course, I knew at once that there were fixers hanging about. I imagined that they were all looking at me. That they, too, had immediately recognised me as a fixer chick. I really did my nut. It was panic stations for me. I grabbed my aunt by the arm and told her I must get away from here at once. She also sussed something and said: 'But why, you haven't anything to do with it any more.' I said: 'Don't talk about it. I still can't face it.'

That was at a time when I no longer thought about clearing out. When I really thought I would never again have anything to do with heroin. It shocked me that they should have recognised me. At home I immediately got out of my clothes and wiped the make-up from my face. I never wore my stiletto-heeled boots again. From that day I tried to look like the girls in my class.

But in the club I associated more frequently with people who smoked hash and went on trips. Occasionally I would smoke a joint and occasionally I would dodge it. But I got into a really great crowd. Most of the people in this crowd were apprentices. They came from the surrounding villages. All of them were really together. They weren't totally apathetic like most of the people at the secondary modern. They really thought about things. I really enjoyed talking to them. Above all, though, there was in this group none of this brutality. All aggressions stayed outside. It was totally peaceful.

Once I asked quite stupidly why all this couldn't be done without turning on. And they said that was really a daft question. How could one switch off from the whole shit of one's day?

They were all terribly frustrated in their jobs, with the exception of one guy. He was in the union and an apprentices' shop steward in his workplace. For him there was meaning in what he did during the day. He looked after the interests of the young people in his factory and in this he found satisfaction. He was of the opinion that it might be possible to change society. Often he didn't need a joint to turn on, and only had a few mouthfuls of red wine.

The others saw absolutely no meaning in what they were doing. They constantly talked about chucking their apprenticeships. The only trouble was they didn't know what to do afterwards. They came from their work full of frustration and aggression. And when we sat together, one of them would start talking about their foreman, and that, and then another would say: 'Can't you stop going on about work, man?' Then a joint went round, and only after that they'd properly knocked off work.

I was actually better off than them. At times I even quite liked school. On the other hand, I was in the same boat as them. I wasn't quite sure either what good all this learning and the stress at school were, since I had realised that I wouldn't be able to go to the grammar school, nor would I be able to do my university entrance exam. And it had also struck me that as an ex-drug addict, however good my final results might be, I wouldn't find any job I really fancied.

In fact, I did get quite a decent final report. But no apprenticeship. Only a temporary job, under some law to get unemployed young people off the streets. I haven't had a shot for almost a year. But I know, of course, that it takes a few years before one is really off H. At the moment there are no great problems.

At night when we sit together with our group, drinking red wine, and the joint has gone round a few times, all these daily problems are gone. We talk about books we have read. We are into black magic and parapsychology and Buddhism. We're simply looking for people who are on a good trip so that we can learn from them. Because we have been on a rather grotty trip ourselves.

A girl in our group is a student nurse and she started bringing tabs to the crowd. For a time I turned on with valium again. I won't touch trips because I'm scared I might get the horrors. The others mostly quite enjoy LSD.

In our little town there's no scene for hard drugs. As a rule anyone taking hard drugs goes to Hamburg. There isn't a local dealer who sells H. So I'm not as easily tempted as in Berlin, Hamburg, or even Norderstedt.

If you want to get H, you can score without difficulties. There are guys with connections. Sometimes dealers drop in who have a proper trayful of drugs. If you ask one of these guys whether he has something to turn on with, he'll say: what do you want? Valium, valeron, shit, trips, coke or H?

In our group they all believe they've got the drug business under control. At least several things are different from three or four years ago in Gropiusstadt.

Our group here achieves a different kind of freedom with drugs. We don't need a Sound to intoxicate ourselves with unbearably loud music. For the people in this group it would be the end to play at being free under the advertising glitter of the Kurfurstendamm. All of us hate the city. We are totally on a nature trip. At week-ends we travel by car all over Schleswig-Holstein, and then go off on foot until we have found a totally all right place. Often we go on to the moors, to places where no other person ever goes.

But the greatest thing is our chalk pit. A huge hole right in the middle of the landscape. Almost a kilometre long and nearly a hundred metres deep. The sides are steep. It is very warm down there. No wind. Plants grow down below which we have never seen anywhere else. Incredibly clear streams flow through this crazy valley. Waterfalls come out of the walls. The water colours the white walls rust-red. White lumps are strewn everywhere, looking like the bones of primitive animals, and perhaps they are mammoth bones. At weekends the huge digger and the conveyor belts, which make such a nerve-racking din during the week, look as though they have been idle for centuries. The lime has long since turned them white.

We always imagine that we will buy the chalk pit once they stop working it. We want to build log cabins down there, make a huge garden, keep animals and have everything we need to live. The only way out of the pit would be for us to blow it up.

We shouldn't want to come up ever again, anyway.

Epilogue

Today Christiane F. still lives with her relatives in a small town north of Hamburg. She has not touched heroin since she was forced to leave Berlin in November 1977. Moreover, she has now broken away from the group who were using soft drugs and taking LSD and has been completely off drugs ever since.

Her relatives have played a significant part, for in them she has found a reliable substitute family who give her the support and supervision she still needs. 'Any fixer wanting to kick,' Christiane says today, 'requires constant support, something to lean on at all times.'

In her — so far successful — attempts to lead a drug-free life, Christiane has had no support from either public or private institutions. On the contrary. After she had completed the temporary job the local authorities found for her, she was keen to go back to school in order to get her *Abitur*. However, despite intensive efforts and pleas, no school was prepared to give a chance to a girl with Christiane's past. Today she is an apprentice bookseller.

Heroin is now available in her small town, and encounters with dealers and fixers are unavoidable. And even today heroin is, for Christiane, still a temptation she must actively resist. But, unlike in Berlin, her life with her relatives, her work and her new circle of friends are things she would not like to lose through a relapse. As she says, 'For me to relapse, my living conditions would have to get much worse.'

Since their release from prison, Christiane's friends,

Detlef and Stella, have been living in therapeutic communes. Stella hopes to continue her school education. Detlef, together with other ex-fixers, helps to decorate flats; as yet he has not decided on what he wants to do.

Although the positive course of their development gives reason for hope, it is by no means certain that in future Christiane, Detlef and Stella will be capable of existing without drugs.

Kai Hermann and Horst Rieck
Spring 1980

GO ASK ALICE
by ANONYMOUS

Alice is fifteen, white, middle-class. She diets. She dates. She gets decent grades. She thinks someday she'd like to get married and raise a family.

On July 9, Alice is turned on to acid. She digs it. Acid makes the world a better place. So do all the other ups. They open up the world of sex. They make Alice feel free. Sometimes Alice worries about taking drugs. She thinks maybe she shouldn't. But, she figures life is more bearable with drugs than without.

Alice's parents don't know what's happening. They notice changes. They have no idea she's on drugs. They cannot help her.

The difference between Alice and a lot of other kids on drugs is that Alice kept a diary.

0 552 09332 7 £1.00

JAY'S JOURNAL
Edited by BEATRICE SPARKS

The horrifying revelation of a sinister network of evil worshippers who claimed the life of a child!

Jay was an intelligent, high-spirited schoolboy – an enthusiastic participant in science fairs, school plays, dance contests, essay competitions – a lively young boy with a bright future in law or medicine . . . .

But on January 22nd, Jay placed a pistol against his right temple and pulled the trigger . . . for he had become a confused teenager, sucked into a powerful underground society – a terro-struck boy struggling with dark forces beyond his control!

JAY'S JOURNAL
the tragic story of a schoolboy . . . . a warning to all
parents!

SBN: 0 552 11603 3   Price: £1.25

I'M DANCING AS FAST AS I CAN
by BARBARA GORDON

'As chilling as One Flew Over The Cuckoo's Nest' –
Woman's World
    The intimate account of a woman who found the courage
    to mend her own shattered life

Barbara Gordon, a TV producer at the height of her career,
had just been nominated for her third Emmy Award. But
little did she know that, on the night of the awards ceremony
she would be confined in a mental institution . . . .

I'M DANCING AS FAST AS I CAN is Barbara's own story
of the harrowing events that drove her to commit herself to
a hospital as a mental patient – of the psychiatrist who
failed her, of her agonizing 'cold turkey' withdrawal from
tranquilizers – and of the lover who, when she needed him
most, became not her ally but her enemy.

'Makes horrifying reading' – Evening News

'An unnerving book, an autobiography that reads compell-
ingly like a novel' – Oxford Mail

'Gripping, provocative reading' – Time Out

'There's a warning for us all in this book' – Company
Magazine

SBN: 0 553 17729 X   Price: £1.50

THE RIGHT STUFF
by TOM WOLFE

THE MEN HAD IT! America's heroes . . . the first flyguys in space . . . battling the Russians for control of the heavens! Putting their lives on the line day after day!

THE WOMEN HAD IT! While Mr. Wonderful was aloft, it truly lacerated one's heart that the Hero's Wife, down on the ground, had to perform with the whole world watching . . . The TV Press Conference! 'What is in your heart? Do you feel with him while he's in orbit?'

It's a quality beyond macho. Beyond bravery. Cool courage! It's men like Chuck Yeager, fastest man on earth; Pete Conrad who laughed himself out of the running; Gus Grissom who almost lost it when his capsule sank . . . And John Glenn, the only space traveler whose apple-pie image wasn't a lie.

'Tom Wolfe at his best' – THE NEW YORK TIMES

SBN: 0 553 13828 6   Price: £1.50

PASSAGES
by GAIL SHEEHY

An amazing roadmap to the predictable crises of adult life:

The Trying 20's – The safety of the home left behind, we begin trying on life's uniforms and possible partners in search of the perfect fit.

The Catch 30's – Illusions shaken, it's time to make, break or deepen life commitments.

The Forlorn 40's – Dangerous years when dreams demand reassessment and sexual panic is common but when the greatest opportunity for self-discovery awaits.

The Refreshed 50's – Best of life for those who let go old roles and find a renewal of purpose.

0 552 10466 3   95p

A SELECTED LIST OF AUTOBIOGRAPHIES AND BIOGRAPHIES
PUBLISHED BY CORGI BOOKS

While every effort is made to keep prices low, it is sometimes necessary to increase prices at short notice. Corgi Books reserve the right to show new retail prices on covers which may differ from those previously advertised in the text or elsewhere.

The prices shown below were correct at the time of going to press.

☐ 10723 9	NO TIME FOR ROMANCE	*Lucilla Andrews*	85p
☐ 09332 7	GO ASK ALICE	*Anonymous*	£1.00
☐ 17002 3	MONTGOMERY CLIFT	*Patricia Bosworth*	£1.25
☐ 11676 9	OUR KATE	*Catherine Cookson*	£1.50
☐ 10063 3	JUDY GARLAND	*Anne Edwards*	75p
☐ 11363 5	NICE ONE, CYRIL	*Cyril Fletcher*	£1.25
☐ 10582 1	ROSA	*Michael Harrison*	85p
☐ 10555 4	TISHA	*Anne Hobbs & Robert Specht*	85p
☐ 11301 8	SOPHIA: LIVING AND LOVING	*A.E. Hotchner*	£1.50
☐ 11015 9	KING OF THE GYPSIES	*Peter Maas*	85p
☐ 10645 3	EVITA: THE WOMAN WITH THE WHIP	*Mary Main*	£1.25
☐ 10907 X	HOVEL IN THE HILLS	*Elizabeth West*	95p

ORDER FORM

All these books are available at your book shop or newsagent, or can be ordered direct from the publisher. Just tick the titles you want and fill in the form below.

CORGI BOOKS, Cash Sales Department, P.O. Box 11, Falmouth, Cornwall.

Please send cheque or postal order, no currency.

Please allow cost of book(s) plus the following for postage and packing:

U.K. Customers—Allow 40p for the first book, 18p for the second book and 13p for each additional book ordered, to a maximum charge of £1.49.

B.F.P.O. and Eire—Allow 40p for the first book, 18p for the second book plus 13p per copy for the next 3 books, thereafter 7p per book.

Overseas Customers—Allow 60p for the first book and 18p per copy for each additional book.

NAME (block letters) ....

ADDRESS ....

....